Hidden Depths

An Archaeological Exploration of Surrey's Past

Roger Hunt

with

David Graham, Giles Pattison and Rob Poulton

Surrey Archaeological Society

Published 2002 by
Surrey Archaeological Society
Castle Arch
Guildford
Surrey GU1 3SX
Registered Charity No. 272098

[www.surreyarchaeology.org.uk]

ISBN 0 9541460 1 8

Produced by Surrey County Archaeological Unit and Archetype Publications Ltd
for Surrey Archaeological Society

Printed and bound in Great Britain by Henry Ling Limited, at the Dorset Press,
Dorchester, DT1 1HD

Distributed by Millstream Press 01483 202270
millstreampress@aol.com

contents

preface

The Surrey Archaeological Society encourages as many people as possible to appreciate the archaeology and history of the county and *Hidden Depths* is a major contribution towards this end. The idea of the book arose during discussions between David Graham, then Joint-Secretary of the Society, and David Bird, Principal Archaeologist with Surrey County Council. It was subsequently decided that, with support from the County Council, the Society would publish an attractive book which was both popular and academically sound. Roger Hunt, who is a professional author with a deep interest in archaeology, was asked to prepare the text. Sourcing the illustrations and the work of designing the book was carried out by Rob Poulton and Giles Pattison of the Surrey County Archaeological Unit, who also provided much of the information. Additional help was provided by specialists within the Society and the County Council.

Sponsorship for the publication of *Hidden Depths* has been provided by the University of Surrey and this has meant that the cover price could be kept at an attractive level. The Society is very grateful for this support and is indebted to the Vice-Chancellor for providing the foreword. Contributions to the work of the Society by students taking archaeology on the part-time combined studies degree course at the University are greatly appreciated.

I feel sure that publication of *Hidden Depths* will generate increased interest in the archaeology and history of Surrey. The Society is ready to cater for this through its specialist groups which, for example, study the development of villages, local history, industrial archaeology, as well as organising the Young Archaeologists' Club and a Community Archaeology scheme which is run jointly with the County Council. These activities are supported by the Society's publications, lectures, symposia and excavations, and by its library and research facilities.

Professor Alan Crocker, DSc, CEng, FSA
President
Surrey Archaeological Society

foreword

I am delighted to be invited to contribute the foreword to this fascinating book. For those who have enjoyed, as I have, the opportunity to live in the beautiful countryside of this county, this work gives a superb guided tour through the archaeology and history behind the places we see today.

The University of Surrey is keenly aware of its own history, particularly this year as we celebrate our 35th anniversary of university status. We look back on the important events that brought us to Guildford, to those who led the way, and who contributed so much to the University attaining the world class status it enjoys today. Being able to look back at the many generations that went before us and the legacy they left provides us with a strong sense of place and of belonging within our own history.

For many years through its courses, the University of Surrey has made a contribution to archaeological study. More recently this has become part of a structured part-time combined studies degree, with students who undertake it participating in the work of the Surrey Archaeological Society. University staff, too, have made personal contributions to the work of the Society, notably current Society President, Professor Alan Crocker, and the late Dr Tony Clark.

Over the years, countless archaeologists have worked on unearthing Surrey's past. Much has been learnt about the history of the county, but hopefully, more too will continue to be revealed of our heritage, to help us to understand more the development of the rich and varied society of which we are part. This book will enable the reader to appreciate our knowledge of this area to date.

The University of Surrey is committed to playing a key role in the local community and in developing and maintaining strong links at every level. We are particularly proud of our association with the Surrey Archaeological Society and we hope that our co-operation and excellent relationships continue to flourish in the years to come.

Professor Patrick J Dowling, CBE, DL, FREng, FRS
Vice-Chancellor & Chief Executive
University of Surrey

1 RECONSTRUCTING THE PAST

Church Approach, Thorpe, retains the tranquil feeling of a former era with many periods contributing to the overall effect. The earliest part of the church is 12th century while the south transept (gable end on left) is dated 1488, the tower is 16th century and the lych gate 19th century. The house on the right is 19th century. The quiet evolution seen in the village contrasts sharply with the surrounding landscape which has been ravaged by 20th century developments that have, however, produced a wealth of archaeological information.

Caught up in the bustle of its towns or quietly enjoying its countryside it is easy to forget that beneath our feet Surrey has hidden depths — secrets that have been locked away, often for thousands of years, until by chance or design they are unearthed.

There are, of course, visible and living signs of the past in the many historic buildings that still survive and in the pattern of the landscape. Tantalising clues to the establishment of communities come from place-names, while maps reveal a host of information

The construction of the M25 across the Thames at Runnymede Bridge, Egham revealed a major archaeological site. This view of excavations in progress is looking north-east towards the River Thames. In the foreground Neolithic occupation has been exposed while further back the Late Bronze Age dark earth is being investigated.

about settlement patterns and the routes taken by our ancestors.

Little if anything of Surrey remains untouched by man. The surface has been turned over by the plough, roads and houses have been built, quarrying has been undertaken and gravel has been extracted but, even though this colonisation and evolution has resulted in a great deal being lost, these processes often directly lead to the past being revealed as well.

Sometimes discoveries grab the headlines and archaeologists are seen as history detectives standing over their prize in a muddy field, but archaeology is an activity involving far more than digging for artefacts; it embraces all physical evidence of the past both above and below ground. Whether it is a Victorian house or Roman pot, study and scientific analysis are required to provide context and meaning.

All contribute to the jigsaw of history but sometimes a single discovery is so important that it significantly alters the whole perspective of our understanding because it represents a missing link.

For example, when, in 1976, the work to take the M25 across the Thames at Runnymede began, a local archaeologist picked up a few sherds of pottery that had been disturbed. As a consequence of the excavations that followed the site is now recognised as one of the most important in Britain, a hitherto unsuspected Late Bronze Age trading community, located on an island in the Thames.

Other 'missing links' remain to be discovered, such as a contemporary settlement near one of the numerous early Saxon cemeteries in the county.

Archaeologists must also make use of documents to interpret the past, but these are only available for the later periods, and, even then, have many gaps. Medieval records, for instance, cannot give us the precise statistical information about health, diet, height and longevity which the study of bones excavated from cemeteries can provide.

Human beings can be distinguished from other animals by

various characteristics, such as the ability to walk upright, the possession of a relatively large and complex brain, and the ability to speak.

For an archaeologist though, the most important aspect of human behaviour is the ability to create and use tools to alter, and adapt to, the environment in which we live. Through this single capability our ancestors have left evidence of their lives strewn across the landscape. It was stone tools which, in the 19th century, provided the key to the realisation that the prehistoric period began long before the date of 4004 BC calculated by biblical scholars for the creation of the world.

DIVIDING THE PAST

The past may be divided into periods in many ways, depending upon the main focus of interest: geology, climate, politics, economics or some other facet of study.

In this book, the terms for periods generally used are those most commonly employed by archaeologists. While they are convenient labels around which a narrative can be constructed they are far from 'watertight' compartments, so it is important to remember that continuity between periods is more common than rapid change.

Encompassed by the prehistoric period is the time from the first human presence in Britain down to the arrival of the Romans in AD 43. Since the 19th century this has been subdivided, according to the dominant material used for making tools and weapons, into the Stone, Bronze and Iron Ages.

The Stone Age is further subdivided into three periods. The Palaeolithic (Old Stone Age), begins about 450,000 BC with the first recorded appearance of humans in Britain, at Boxgrove in West Sussex, and ends with the retreat of the north European glaciers around 10,000 years ago. It covers much the same span as the last Ice Age.

Early humans may be broadly divided into two groups: firstly warm-adapted, tall, long-legged individuals of *Homo heidelbergensis* type, as at Boxgrove; secondly cold-adapted, short, stocky individuals of Neanderthal type. Anatomically modern humans, like us, appeared in Europe around 40,000 years ago, just prior to the disappearance of the Neanderthals. All pursued hunting and scavenging subsistence strategies.

The Mesolithic (Middle Stone Age) covers the period from around 8000 to 4000 BC and is generally characterised as one in which human groups practised a nomadic hunter-gatherer lifestyle in a landscape dominated firstly by low tundra vegetation, then birch and pine woodland and finally by broad-leafed deciduous woodland. This sequence reflected climatic warming which resulted in a rise in sea level that separated Britain from the rest of Europe around 8,000 years ago.

Traditionally, the Neolithic (New Stone Age) is regarded as the period during which farming was first introduced to Britain along with new types of polished stone tools, pottery vessels and the construction of communal monuments of earth, wood and stone. The earliest agricultural economy was probably a mix of pastoralism alongside small-scale horticulture, supplemented by hunting and gathering.

The earlier part of the Bronze Age is best seen as the culmination of Late Neolithic practices. There is still little evidence for domestic settlement but burials beneath earthen mounds (round barrows) are an important new development. From about 1500 BC flat-grave cremation cemeteries appear and there is increasing evidence for open domestic settlements and the laying out of field systems. Towards the end of the period the construction of defended

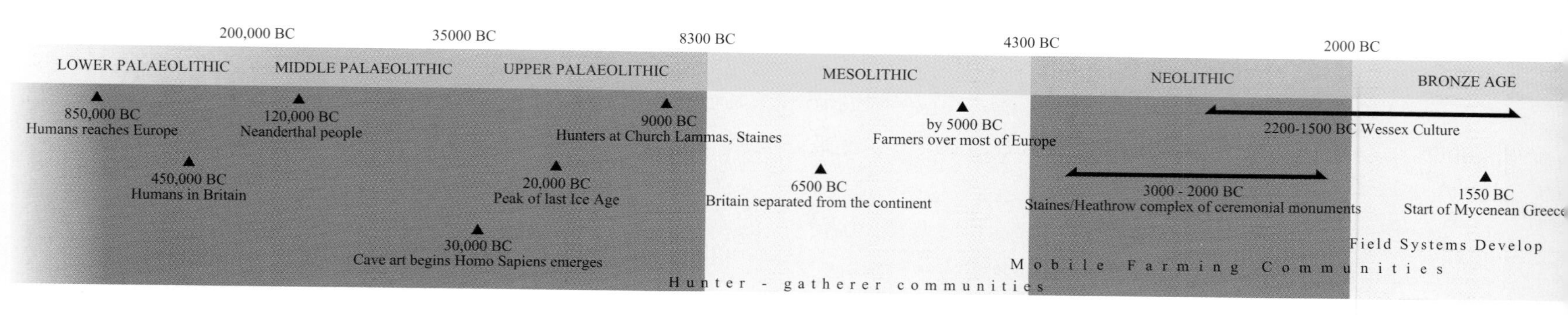

Chronological table of periods and main events.

HOW OLD IS IT?

Shown an object, the archaeologist is immediately assailed by the question 'how old is it?' An answer is swiftly followed by a further question 'how do you know?'

Usually, the answer to the first question will take a form such as '13th century' or 'later Iron Age', and can be given because of a technique called typological analysis. The general principle is that the methods of manufacture and the precise forms of objects change with time — this can be readily seen by looking at the evolution of the motor car.

Careful study of groups of objects has enabled archaeologists to construct typologies (sequences) which can be used to establish the relative date of a newly found artefact. The three bronze axes (right) show that the earliest were of similar form to the stone axes which preceded them. Gradually the appearance of the objects changed as it was realised that improved methods of hafting were possible. The most commonly used typology is for pottery, the style and form of which changed rapidly through time, but which was widely used, easily broken, and normally survives very well.

To be of practical use, typologies have to be linked to an exact chronology. In broad terms, from the Roman Conquest onwards this can be done by tying them to events that are documented, or to objects, such as coins, which themselves have precise dates.

Earlier periods, and sometimes later ones, now rely very heavily on scientific dating methods. The most frequently used is radiocarbon dating, which can be applied to materials, such as wood or bone, with an organic content. Large pieces of wood can also be dated through dendrochronology (tree-ring dating).

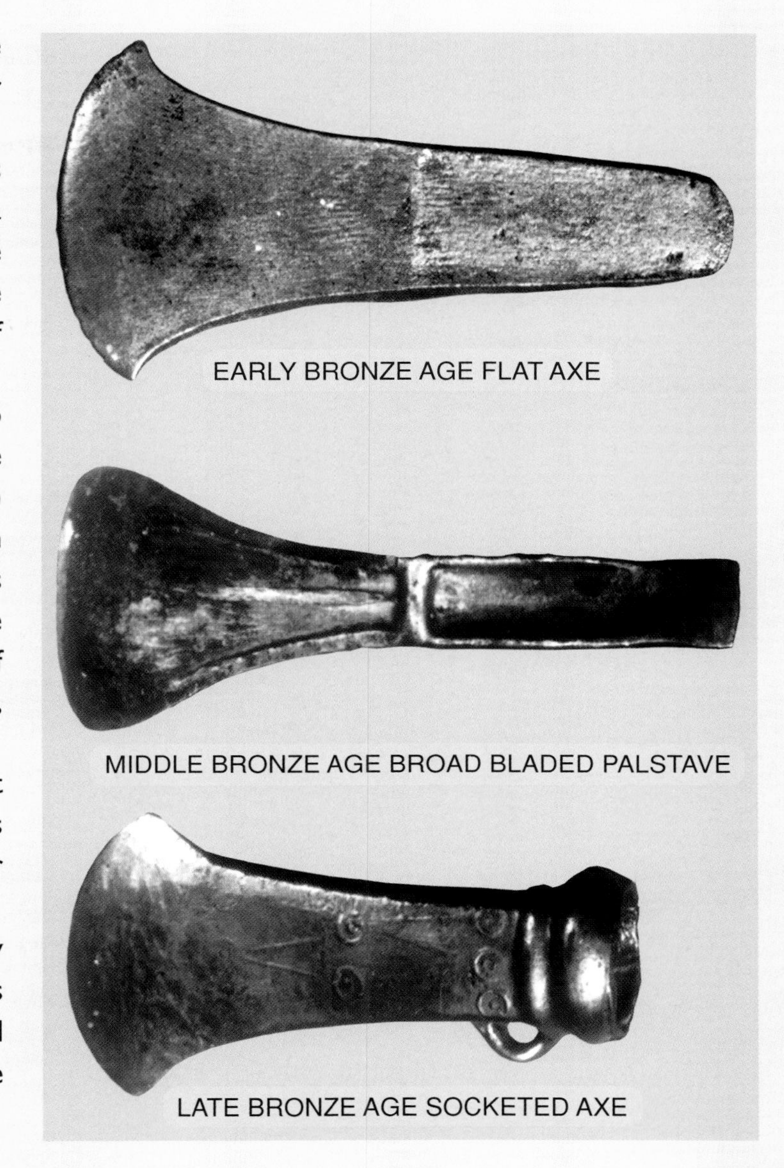
EARLY BRONZE AGE FLAT AXE

MIDDLE BRONZE AGE BROAD BLADED PALSTAVE

LATE BRONZE AGE SOCKETED AXE

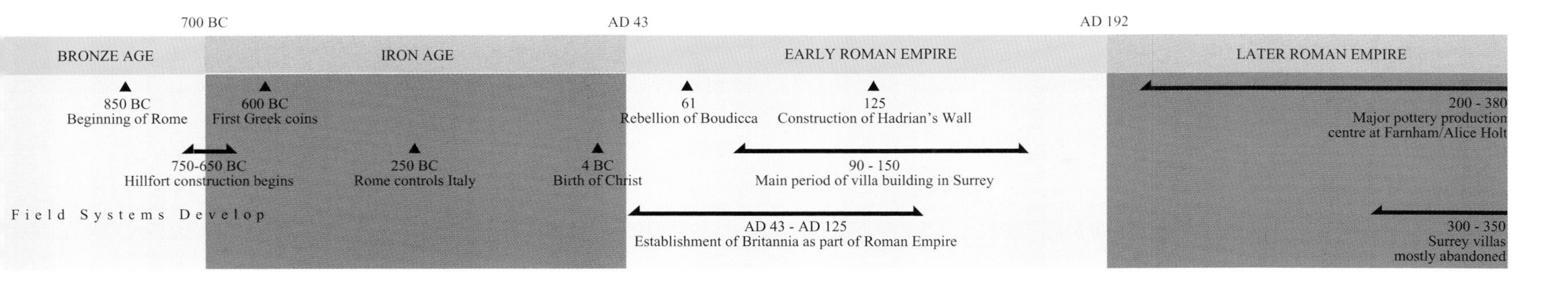

settlements began.

This trend is taken a stage further in the Iron Age from around 700 BC with the construction of hillforts. The vast majority of the population is likely to have lived in small mixed-farming settlements of various types. In the early part of the period long-established exchange networks with the Continent broke down, while in the later phase they were renewed.

Contact with Rome was of particular importance in paving the way for the Claudian conquest in AD 43. Britain became part of the Roman Empire and the new roads, towns and villas established at this time form a large part of the archaeological evidence. Nevertheless, many small Iron Age farms continued in use into the Roman period, and it would seem that new Roman temples frequently occupied already sanctified sites.

In the later Roman period both towns and villas began to decline, and then came to an abrupt end in the century between AD 400 and 500. Saxon invaders grasped political control of the country and a number of their cemeteries have been found in Surrey.

The six centuries down to the Norman Conquest in 1066 are called the Saxon period, but the term conceals enormous changes, with the petty kingdoms and self-sufficient communities of the early part eventually being replaced by a unified England, in which towns and trade were well developed.

Although the Saxons had been converted to Christianity in the 7th century, it is the medieval period which has left the greatest legacy of remains, in parish churches still standing and in the ruins of former religious houses. At the same time the forerunners of most of

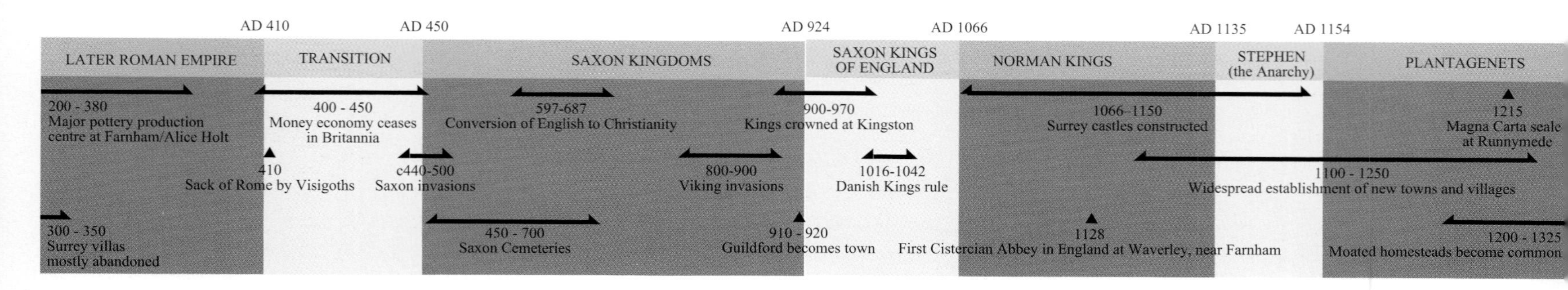

our towns and villages developed and each community organised the farming of the land around it. Initially, the Normans had needed castles to control the conquered land but the moated homestead, which had no serious defensive capability, was more characteristic of the long period of internal peace that followed.

The modern era is generally perceived as commencing in the early 16th century, when Henry VIII put an end to the monasteries and built new palaces in Surrey. These were important developments but the broad pattern of settlement and landscape continued with little alteration.

It was largely from the 18th century onwards that enclosure of the common fields began to change the appearance of the countryside. Even more radical change was to follow the Industrial Revolution with, from the mid-19th century, the coming of the railway resulting in great enlargement of many towns and villages, especially with people commuting to London.

THE FORMATION OF A LANDSCAPE

People have lived in Surrey for about 450,000 years — an almost unimaginable timescale. Picture it as the twelve hours of a clock face and life since the Industrial Revolution represents just seconds of time. Throughout this long period where and how they lived has been moulded and tempered by their local environment, so it is necessary to understand the character of the Surrey landscape to appreciate the developments which later chapters describe.

Travel the nearly 48km (30 miles) from Surrey's northernmost boundary to its southern edge and one will probably have crossed

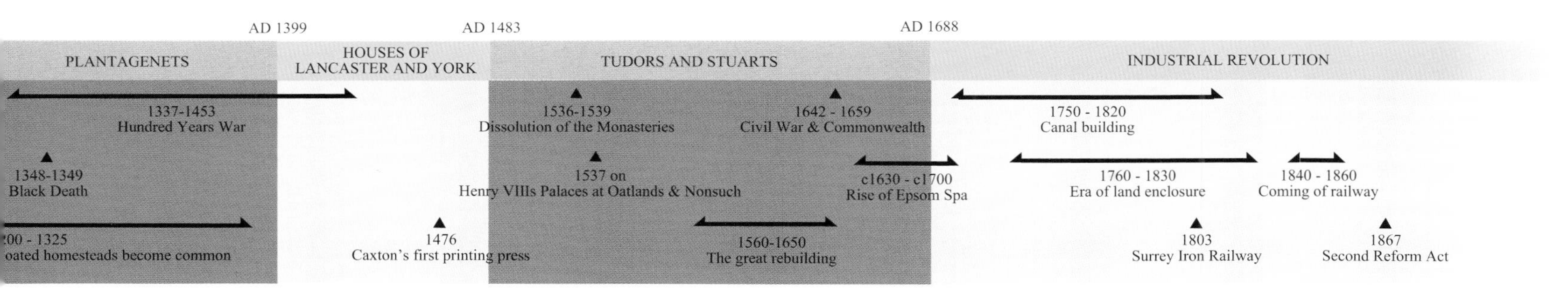

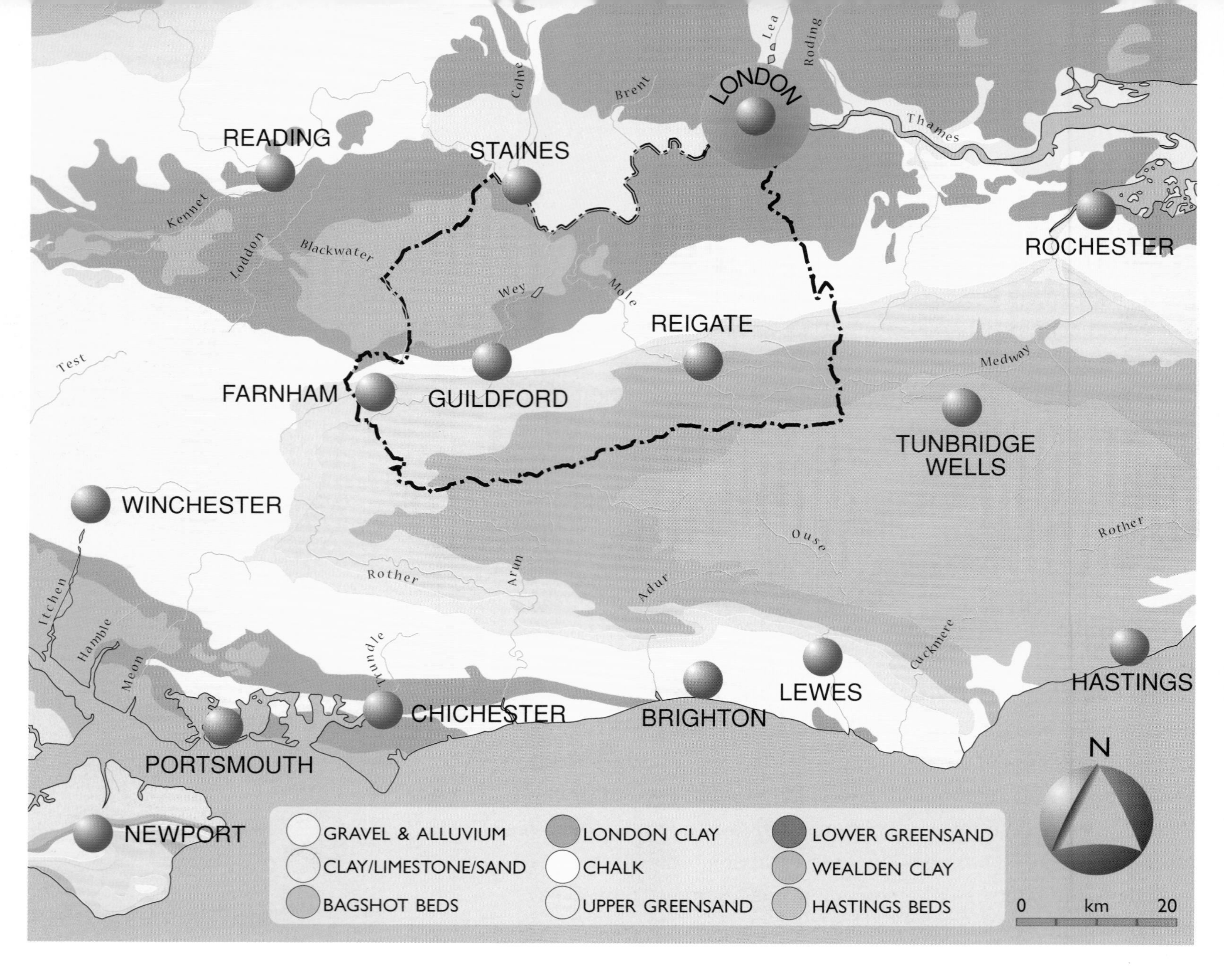

Geology of south-east England. The map shows only the principal strata, and a number of deposits, mentioned in the text, have been omitted in the interests of clarity. These include: gravels and alluvium in the smaller river valleys; Clay-with-Flints over much of the Chalk in Surrey; the narrow bands of Reading and Thanet Beds between the Chalk and London Clay; and the narrow band of Gault Clay between the Upper and Lower Greensand. The terms used in the key to the map are those most applicable to the local area.

at least eight soil and rock types. Go the 64km (40 miles) west to east and the picture is very different. All the ridges run in this direction and, with the exception of the river crossings where gravel and alluvium predominate, one need tread only chalk, clay or greensand.

It is this geological structure that is the very essence of the county, affecting its people, its industry and providing a rich diversity of landscape. It is a county of contrasts — constantly surprising terrain where, in just a few miles, one is rewarded by fantastic variety.

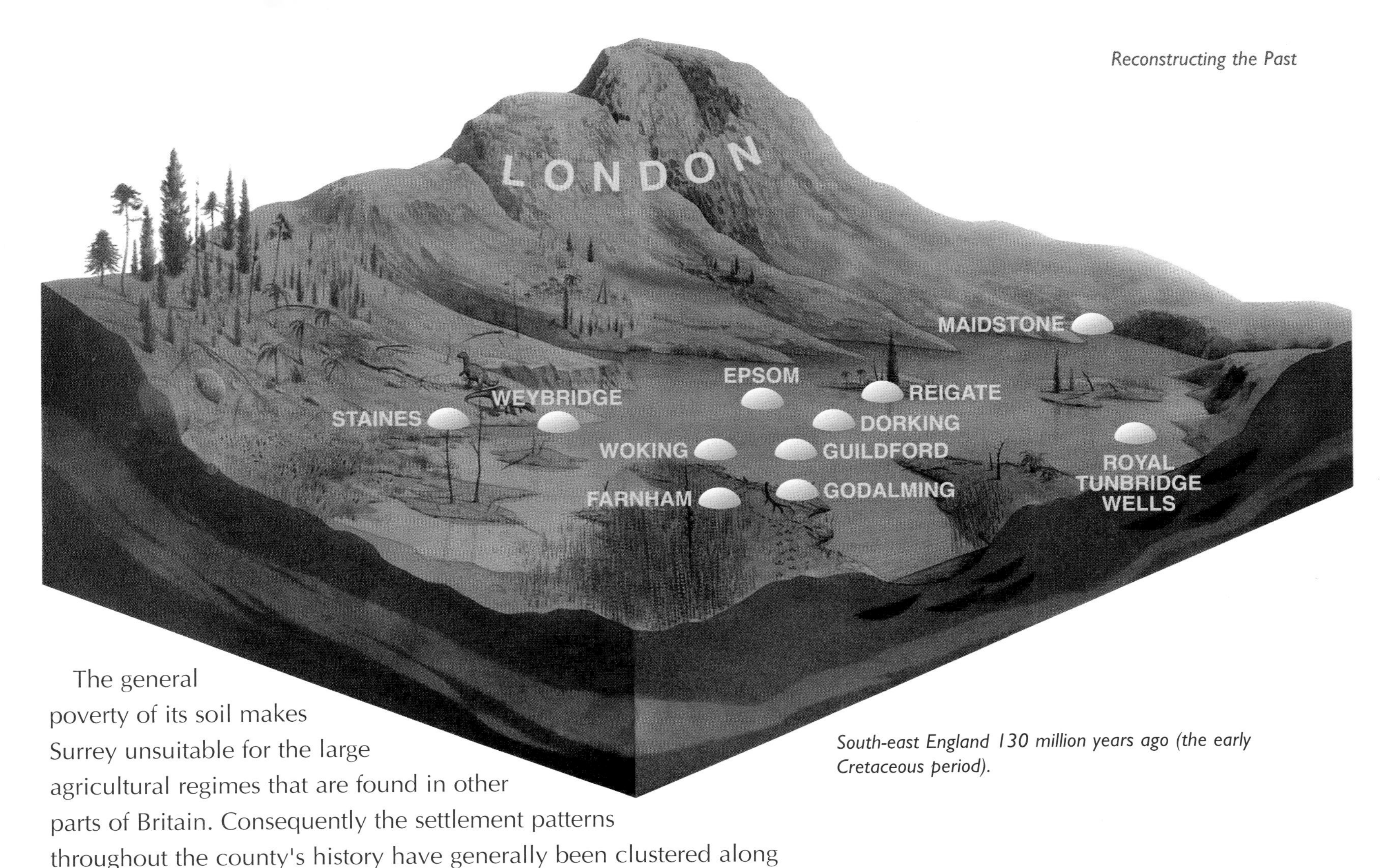

South-east England 130 million years ago (the early Cretaceous period).

The general poverty of its soil makes Surrey unsuitable for the large agricultural regimes that are found in other parts of Britain. Consequently the settlement patterns throughout the county's history have generally been clustered along the fertile spring lines or on the Thames floodplain and gravel terraces of rivers.

At the same time, because Surrey's geology runs in bands across the county, the varying features and advantages of these different habitats have been exploited by communities which have travelled north and south.

The landscape of the area we have come to call Surrey evolved over millions of years, as rocks and the remains of plant and animal material underwent chemical and physical changes and were crushed, folded and moved by the great forces of nature.

Straddling Surrey, Sussex and Kent the clay forming the great oval of the Weald was originally laid down around 130 million years ago when the area was very different.

Baryonyx was the top predator in the warm and swampy southern England of around 130 million years ago. Baryonyx is also known as the 'Surrey Dinosaur' from the discovery of the most complete skeleton known, in a brickpit near Ockley.

Where London is today, steep-sided mountains existed from which rivers flowed south to a sea that extended to what is now continental Europe. Tropical forests stood on the foothills and crocodiles hunted in and around the rivers, lakes and marshes.

Fossils of freshwater snails and small shellfish are now commonly found in the clay. The most graphic illustration of prehistoric times is given by the discovery of a 6m (20ft) long fish-eating dinosaur — *Baryonyx walkeri* — at Ockley lying in the Weald close to the edge of what was once the floodplain.

During the vast expanse of time when the sea covered much of England and the southern area formed the open water of a continental shelf, the rocks and sediment that collectively make up the Lower Greensand were deposited. They were followed by layers which successively formed the Gault Clay and then the Upper Greensand. Finally the remains of living organisms settled on top and very gradually consolidated to form a cap of chalk.

Some 25 million years ago the Wealden area was pushed upwards creating a dome-shaped formation. Over time, wind and water eroded the chalk, greensands and clay from the centre of the dome. What was left formed a lip surrounding the generally poorly drained low-lying clay of what is now called the Weald.

Containing thin beds of sandstone, limestone and ironstone, the only major variation in the geology of the Weald is around Lingfield and to the south. Here, extending to the sea, the Hastings Beds form the oldest rock outcrop in south-east England and produce high ground which is both well drained and wooded.

The Anglo-Saxon Chronicle of 893 describes the Weald as a forest. At that time, it was a huge tract of woodland which, made up predominantly of hazel and oak, spread through the three southern counties to form the greatest wood of Saxon England, a remnant of the 'wild wood' which once covered the whole country.

Hugging the Weald, the lip of freely-drained light acid soil of the Lower Greensand forms a range of hills including Gibbet Hill and Leith Hill, which is not only Surrey's but south-east England's highest point.

The range of chalk making up the North Downs is probably one of the most noticeable geological features of Surrey and is, in a way, its backbone. With steep escarpments on the south side, the dip slope descends gradually northwards towards the London Basin. Having always acted as a natural barrier across the county it is obvious even today that the main routes cross the chalk at the easiest points, such as where the rivers Mole and Wey cut through at Dorking and Guildford.

Chalk gives rise to thin soils on which sheep were extensively grazed in Roman and medieval times. Unlike the South Downs, which are relatively pure chalk, much of the North Downs, especially at the eastern end of the county, are covered by deposits of Clay-with-Flints and so offer a relatively poor habitat.

Clay also exists to the north of the Downs in the form of the dark brown or greyish London Clay, which weathers on exposure to a yellow colour. Stretching from the west towards London in an ever-widening band it represents good tree-growing land but is of little use for agriculture and so is still an area of commons. Some of this clay was employed in pottery and tile making especially on the spring line of the Reading Beds.

Leith Hill is the highest point in Surrey at 294m (965ft) and the tower was built in 1766 to provide a viewpoint across the Weald to the south.

These beds stretch right across the county and contain the fine-grained Thanet Sand, the widest belt of which is found near Croydon. It is along this band that water comes to the surface in springs, having seeped through the porous chalk.

The importance of water in the pattern of settlement should never be underestimated and the rivers snake across Surrey like plant roots as they carve their way through the soil types, casting around them their own localised environment of alluvial deposits and gravel.

Historically, the Thames formed the county's northernmost boundary and beside it are the terrace gravels which settlers found both dry underfoot and, because they give rise to light well-drained soils, good for agriculture.

To a lesser extent, gravels are also associated with other rivers and parts of the Blackwater and Wey valleys have also produced evidence for early settlement to compare with that from the valley of the Thames.

There has probably been a pond where the River Hogsmill rises at Ewell since early prehistory. It seems always to have attracted visitors and settlers, though the circus around 1900 may have been one of the more unusual arrivals.

To the north-west of the county the Bagshot, Bracklesham and Barton Beds form very poor sandy and loamy acid soil. Early exploitation by man gave rise to heathland, a fact reflected in the Domesday Book by the sparse settlements and low population density for what is a comparatively large area of the county.

Such areas graphically illustrate the way that the landscape of Surrey is the joint product of man and natural forces. Agricultural regimes have caused soil erosion, quarrying and gravel extraction have remodelled large areas, while the foundation of London and the coming of railways, canals and roads radically affected the local environment and have had a major influence on settlement patterns.

HISTORY REWOUND

Place Farm, Bletchingley. The Georgian fanlight doorway is oddly off centre to the bricked-in arch over what was the entrance to the inner courtyard of a Tudor double-courtyard house. It was built for the Duke of Buckingham, executed for treason in 1521, and Henry VIII's former wife, Anne of Cleves, later stayed there. Excavations have shown that the site was occupied from at least the Bronze Age.

In today's high-tech age it is easy to imagine the people of the past as simple-minded savages, but it is clear that these men and women had culture and style. They sought out beautiful things and exerted their energy, not just on the all-important job of survival, but also on improving their lifestyle through innovation and invention.

Although in terms of the modern world we may not immediately recognise it as such, a sophisticated society emerged relatively early with substantial groups of people coming together with common aims. They built, they traded, they worshipped, they farmed, they fought — all things we do today.

The following chapters expand on these themes, exploring them separately so that it is possible to understand the evolution of specific aspects of Surrey's past.

Rewind through the years and there is Georgian elegance, medieval expansion, Saxon toil, Roman organisation, the dynamic expanding society of the Iron Age, the craftsmanship of the Bronze Age, the farmers of the Neolithic and the hunter-gatherers of the Mesolithic and Palaeolithic periods. Villages grow into towns, timber, water and the local geology are exploited and churches, castles and great houses are built; but central to it all are the people who have made Surrey.

There is something strangely humbling about discovering the past, seeing and touching an object that has lain hidden for hundreds or maybe thousands of years. Suddenly there is an affinity with the people who lived in that time and a realisation that someday in the future it may be our present lives that someone is seeking to interpret.

2

HEARTH & HOME

Governed by regulations aimed at ensuring that it is a healthy and safe place in which to live, a house built today is a sophisticated structure both in terms of its design and the diversity of materials employed in its construction. We expect, among other things, running water, light and power, heating and ventilation.

The fact that a house gives shelter and protection from the elements is all but taken for granted yet, in the past, this would have been its chief purpose. People have always needed shelter from the cold and wet and no doubt, in earlier times, protection from wild animals too but, for the archaeologist, there is surprisingly little evidence of the dwellings of early people.

Church Lammas, Staines. An artist's impression of the temporary camp made by hunters in the bleak tundra landscape of 11,000 years ago.

With Surrey having an abundance of timber, this was the obvious construction material. However, by its nature, timber is ephemeral and over time the earliest structures have been swept away or have rotted, leaving little firm evidence of how people lived in the earliest times. Since evidence of dwellings is rare and fragile the archaeologist also depends on the accumulated artefacts of past ages to point to settlement, though occasionally this can be misleading. A high concentration of Mesolithic struck flint, for example, may simply indicate a site where flints were worked.

TENTS AND HUTS

One can look at just a small area of Surrey and find a heavy concentration of settlement evidence. The floodplain and associated terraces of the Thames and Colne rivers to the north-east of the county, for example, represent an area of great archaeological potential.

These beautifully worked long flint blades, found at Church Lammas, Staines, were made around 9000 BC.

A number of important prehistoric settlements and field systems have been sampled by excavation around this area. These include the causewayed camp at Yeoveney, near Staines, the Neolithic and Late Bronze Age riverside settlements at Runnymede Bridge, settlements and field systems of the 2nd and 1st century BC, landscapes at Thorpe Lea Nurseries and Petters Sports Field, near Egham, as well as a Neolithic and Iron Age settlement at Mixnams Farm, Thorpe. In addition, St Ann's Hill, near Chertsey, which occupies a prominent position overlooking the Thames Valley, was chosen as the site for an Iron Age fort.

Despite such evidence, we frequently have to adopt parallels from other counties to enable us to paint a better picture of what life may have been like in early times. Yet, this evidence can sometimes be misleading since local materials and conditions must have been important factors in dictating how people built their homes.

It is assumed that as the nomadic hunter-gatherers of Upper Palaeolithic and Mesolithic times roamed the land now called Surrey, the small family groups built flimsy temporary structures formed from animal skins and branches. Perhaps, even though they had neither horse nor wheel, they might have carried some form of tent and draped it over a simple framework of locally-cut poles.

The photo shows how the archaeological excavation at Church Lammas, Staines, was surrounded on all sides by rapidly-approaching mineral extraction. This rare Late Upper Palaeolithic camp was found only just in time.

More substantial structures developed when people began to settle and clear the woodland during the Neolithic period and erected shelters for both their family and animals. Homesteads began to develop and there is evidence from some parts of Britain for both round and rectangular buildings of wood and stone.

While considerable manpower must have been required to build the Neolithic monuments that have been found in the Stanwell/Heathrow area, the settlements of the monument builders have been difficult to identify.

The best evidence comes from Runnymede Bridge, Egham, where a considerable variety of evidence for a Thames-side settlement has been found, including axe-hewn oak piles. Interestingly, the activity centres on stake-built rectangular structures surrounded by midden deposits. Neolithic buildings are rarely found, and these are the

A Bronze Age bowl made from maple wood found at Wey Manor Farm, Addlestone. This is an extremely rare survival of a wooden domestic item which must have been very common at the time.

only certain examples from Surrey.

At Lower Mill Farm, Stanwell, the earliest dateable material present in significant quantities belonged to the period around 2200–1800 BC, the Late Neolithic and Early Bronze Age. The principal area examined seems likely to have been a small farmstead, and the evidence included midden deposits, pits, a post-hole and a possible enclosure ditch, but there were no obvious house plans.

A possible example of a Neolithic house was excavated at Weston Wood, Albury, on the Lower Greensand, where a shallow pit and traces of holes for stakes supporting an overhead structure were found along with a hearth. Unfortunately, it is not certain whether these are associated with the Neolithic pottery that was found or with the Bronze Age occupation that was also evident.

A plan of the Late Bronze Age occupation site excavated at Petters Sports Field, Egham.

The picture becomes somewhat clearer in the Bronze Age since archaeological investigation of Surrey sites has produced evidence of post-holes showing the location of huts. Other houses may have existed but merely rested on the ground leaving no telltale signs of their presence.

At Home Farm, Laleham, several Neolithic and Bronze Age settlements have been excavated revealing not only pits that contain pottery, animal bone, flint tools, and many 'pot boilers' but also the post-holes of the characteristic Bronze Age roundhouses.

Such discoveries are no longer as uncommon as they once were, but the excavation at this site of a middle

A hoard of Late Bronze Age scrap metal found during the excavation at Petters Sports Field, Egham. The hoard was in two small pits cut into the side of a ditch, and included parts of axes, spears, knives and many other objects.

Bronze Age post-built roundhouse that measured approximately 9m (29½ft) in diameter with a doorway facing to the south-east still remains a rarity in Surrey. A further example has recently been identified at Wey Manor Farm, Addlestone, set in a small enclosure.

In some ways the most interesting settlement was found at Egham. Driving along the M25, close to the Thames at Runnymede Bridge, few motorists would realise that the road bisects an important Late Bronze Age site. The former Petters Sports Field revealed evidence of multi-period settlement and at least six phases were identified, the earliest of which can be dated to Neolithic times while the latest is as recent as the post-medieval period.

The most significant activity occurred during the Late Bronze to

Early Iron Age and included the construction of a large ditch in which a hoard of bronze tools and weapons had been deliberately deposited, probably hidden by a bronzesmith.

Rings of post-holes indicated two complete hut circles and smaller parts of others, which could have been contemporary with the burial of the hoard. Definite reconstructions are difficult because of the irregularity of the post-hole spacing and the lack of standardisation of post-hole depths. Interestingly, all the posts appear to have been withdrawn, which implies that the huts were dismantled. The next identifiable phase of occupation did not occur until the Romano-British period.

In one complete hut circle archaeologists discovered some burnt daub and an area of burnt gravel that may indicate the remains of the hearth at the centre of the estimated 6–7m (20–23ft) diameter post-ring. The plan of the other complete hut excavated was roughly oval in shape, measuring some 8.5m (28ft) in diameter with a porched entrance and evidence that the hut had been partially rebuilt.

The beginning of the Iron Age saw farms and hamlets scattered across the Surrey landscape while hillforts stood at: Caesar's Camp, Farnham; Hillbury, Puttenham Common; St Ann's Hill, Chertsey; Hascombe; St George's Hill, Weybridge; Felday, Holmbury and Anstiebury near Dorking; War Coppice, Caterham and Dry Hill, Lingfield.

The purpose of these hillforts is still not fully understood. Presumably their overriding role was defensive, though some seem to have been sparsely occupied and perhaps served as stock enclosures or places of refuge in times of emergency. They may also have served as symbols of the power or prestige of a chief and his tribe.

A much greater weight of archaeological evidence is available than for previous periods but the buildings were still constructed using similar materials to those of earlier eras, so all the archaeologist generally finds are post-holes, a shallow gully, maybe a burnt area of ground, and fragments of pottery or bone.

Many Iron Age roundhouses, and even farms and hillforts, faced

THE IRON AGE HOUSE

While there was much individuality in construction, roundhouses appear to have dominated in the Iron and Bronze Ages and seem, usually, to have had a framework of stout wooden posts. The walls were formed with wattle and daub or by using planks butted edge on. In the soil around the outside a ring gully was often dug to provide eaves-drip drainage.

Larger roundhouses had an inner ring of upright posts surmounted by horizontal timbers and these, and the outer wall, supported rafters which met at the apex of a thatch-covered roof. At the centre of the floor, which was probably of beaten earth or chalk, was a hearth on which food was cooked. The smoke rose up into the roof and was dispersed through the thatch and, at the same time, it probably acted to cure hanging meat and, through the tarry deposit it left behind, helped to preserve the roof timbers. Contrary to popular belief there was no hole or chimney in the roof since this would have let in the rain and produced a forced draught through the house resulting in the use of considerable quantities of fuel. Baking was done in a simple oven built of clay but archaeologists can only speculate on the many features which leave no trace in the ground.

Reconstructions such as those at Butser Ancient Farm in Hampshire (above) can reveal much about such a way of life and, based on evidence discovered during excavations in various parts of Britain, the buildings present a fascinating insight into the work involved in building an Iron Age house.

The largest of the houses at Butser has a ground area of some 150sq m (1,600sq ft), considerably larger than the majority of modern homes. Over 200 trees were used in the construction, five tons of straw were employed to thatch the roof and ten tons of daub were plastered onto the walls.

Wattle panels (right) were formed with stout vertical members, around which were woven horizontal 'withies' in a basket-weave pattern. These were cut from willow-sticks, reeds, ash, chestnut, beech, oak, alder, birch or holly, although hazel was the most common.

Onto one or both sides of this base was applied daub. Clay, chopped straw, sand, lime and cow dung were common constituents, but flax stems, reeds and other vegetable fibres or animal hair were frequently added to bind the daub and to counteract shrinkage as the clay dried out. This technique continued to be used in medieval times as infill for timber-framed buildings and to create internal partitions.

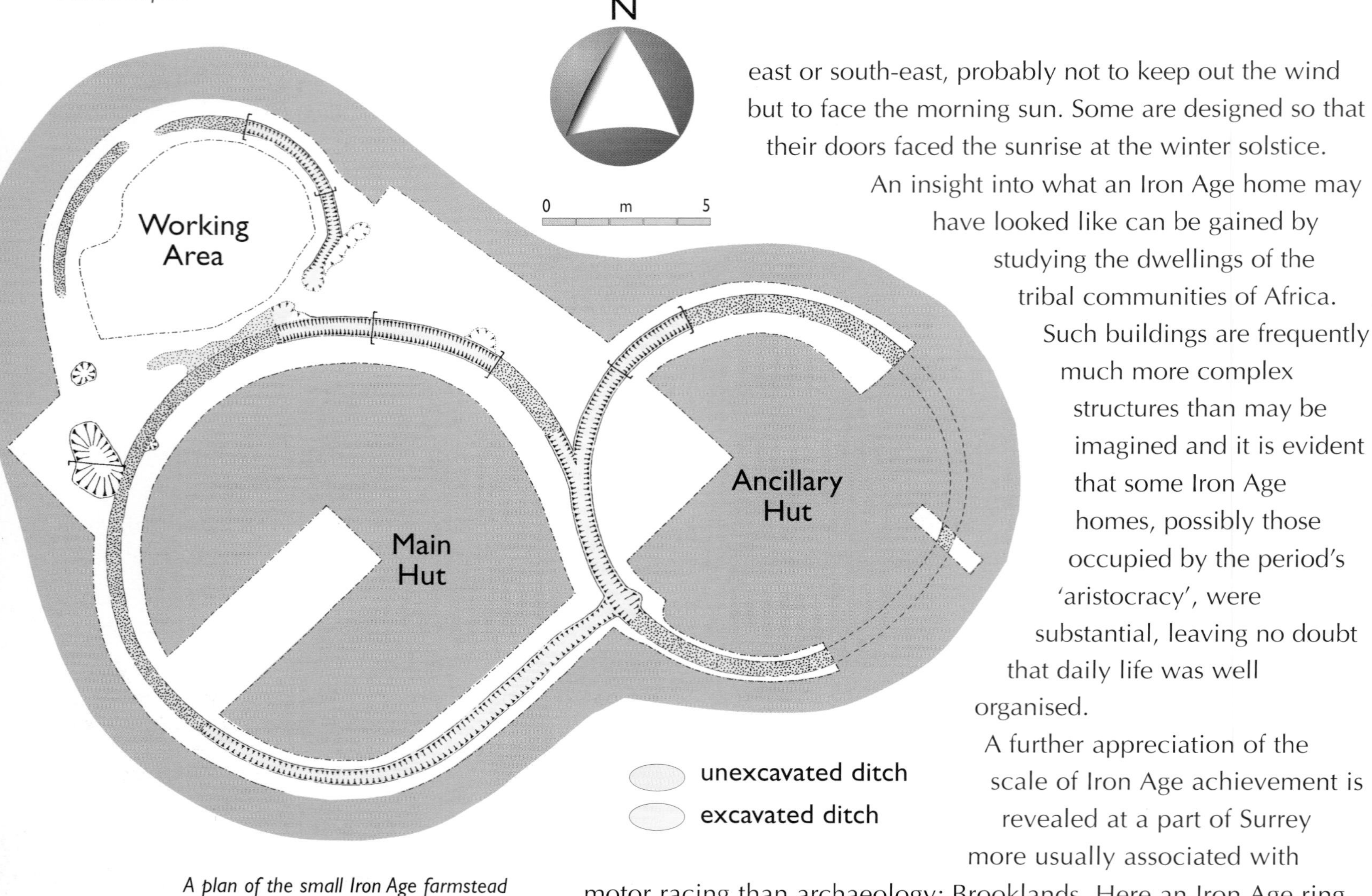

A plan of the small Iron Age farmstead excavated at Lower Mill Farm, Stanwell.

east or south-east, probably not to keep out the wind but to face the morning sun. Some are designed so that their doors faced the sunrise at the winter solstice.

An insight into what an Iron Age home may have looked like can be gained by studying the dwellings of the tribal communities of Africa. Such buildings are frequently much more complex structures than may be imagined and it is evident that some Iron Age homes, possibly those occupied by the period's 'aristocracy', were substantial, leaving no doubt that daily life was well organised.

A further appreciation of the scale of Iron Age achievement is revealed at a part of Surrey more usually associated with motor racing than archaeology: Brooklands. Here an Iron Age ring ditch measuring approximately 24m (79ft) in diameter, with an entrance towards the east, probably surrounded a single roundhouse.

At Lower Mill Farm, Stanwell, just north of Staines, eaves-drip trenches belonging to two roundhouses and an additional structure were recorded. The largest hut was probably the principal building of a small family settlement while the smaller hut was used for ancillary purposes. The third hut may have been of open-fronted construction.

No hint of post-holes was discovered and the posts may never have been embedded in the earth. Clear proof that this manner of construction was practised was found at Staines, where 1st century AD roundhouses were defined by their surviving floors and hearths. All evidence relating to their superstructure, including post-holes, was absent. Building in this way would have made it relatively easy to dismantle and remove virtually the entire settlement with the result that only a few fragments of burnt daub were left behind.

While little remained of the homes themselves, archaeologists gained some knowledge of the activities of the people who lived at the Lower Mill Farm site by examining scattered debris. This included: a fragment of a saddle quern for grinding corn; a fired clay slingshot for hunting; part of a loomweight, for weaving; the debris of meals including remains of sheep and cattle; bones from horses, presumably used for transport and then for food; and a few sherds of pottery.

The most important excavated Iron Age settlement in Surrey is probably that at Tongham Nurseries. The archaeological work at Tongham began as a result of the intended construction of new roads in 1993 and proceeded after the excavation of a large number of archaeological evaluation trenches had identified five areas of Iron Age occupation.

The resulting major excavation revealed that substantial enclosure ditches bounded the main Iron Age settlement areas. Within these lay the remains of at least eighteen roundhouses, including two that had been rebuilt, as well as smaller ditches, pits and post-holes. Large water holes were also discovered within or close to the enclosures along with two square four-posted structures, possibly used as granaries.

In the water holes archaeologists found a 2nd century BC bronze brooch, several largely complete

One of the roundhouses under excavation at Tongham. The circular wall trench has been exposed, and on the far side the large post-holes of the entrance porch are being revealed. The four post-holes in the middle would have supported a granary. This was built after the roundhouse was demolished.

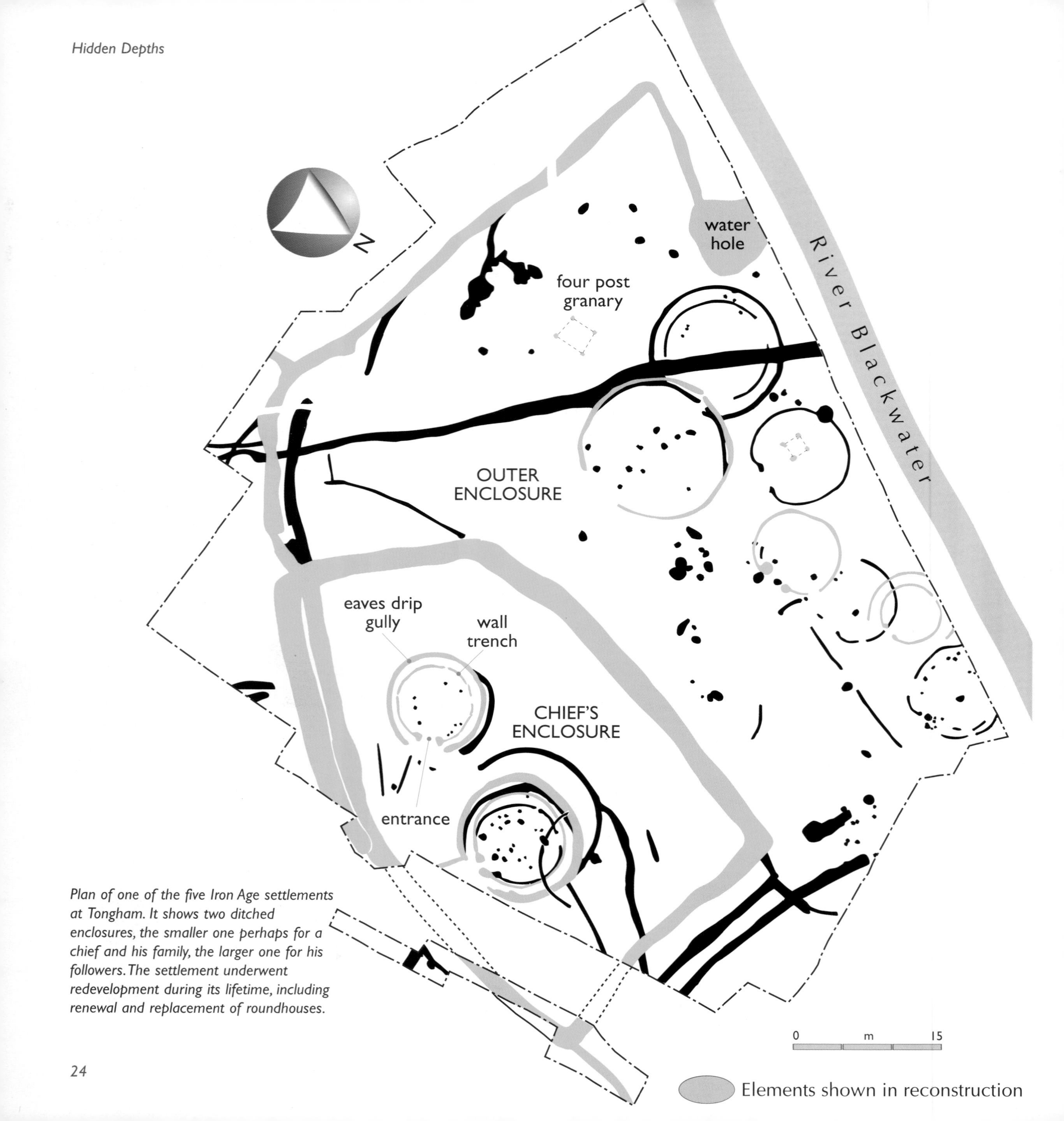

Plan of one of the five Iron Age settlements at Tongham. It shows two ditched enclosures, the smaller one perhaps for a chief and his family, the larger one for his followers. The settlement underwent redevelopment during its lifetime, including renewal and replacement of roundhouses.

Artist's impression of the settlement at Tongham shown in the plan. The viewpoint is from near the bottom looking towards the top of the plan.

pottery vessels, complete loomweights, part of a quern stone, well-preserved animal bones, and pieces of preserved wood including stakes and planks. The most substantial of these was identified as a log ladder, in which the steps had been created by cutting notches into an oak log. A very rare find, such ladders are still in use in some parts of the world.

Many questions arise from these discoveries such as whether the main enclosures were occupied concurrently by different groups, or whether one settlement replaced another once buildings began to deteriorate and land resources became exhausted.

A roundhouse at Staines. A quarter of the clay floor and part of the central hearth were exposed in the excavation. The house, despite its Iron Age appearance, was not built until AD 90, well after the Roman town was established.

NATIVES AND NEWCOMERS

At first sight contemporary information on how people lived in Roman times appears to be much more plentiful than for any earlier period. However, this evidence is a mere veneer that masks all that has been lost over the passage of time.

Little has been left to reveal the settlements or 'native' buildings in which the majority of ordinary people lived. Inevitably, as we look back through the mists of time,

Reconstruction of the Roman villa at Ashtead.

our view is clouded by images of sophisticated villas, bustling towns and straight roads. In reality, these were far from the norm and most of the buildings of the countryside were probably of the same appearance and ephemeral materials as those of the Iron Age.

Evidence such as rubbish pits and boundary ditches found in recent archaeological rescue excavations indicates that there were ordinary farmsteads at Thorpe Lea Nurseries near Egham, and at Brooklands near Weybridge. A long-term excavation at South Farm, Lightwater, has revealed an isolated rural settlement with some local ironworking.

None of Surrey's settlements or towns, with the possible exception of Staines, seems to have been sophisticated enough for any degree of formal planning, nor is there much evidence for defences, while the villas themselves appear to have been smaller and less pretentious than those seen in other counties.

Surrey has some seventeen villa sites scattered across the county, although others may be waiting to be found. They were not only places for living in, built by successful Roman Britons, but were the centre of working estates. While most of these estates appear to have concentrated on farming, others may have been associated with industries such as pottery production and the making of tiles.

Known villa sites include Titsey, Bletchingley, Walton Heath, Walton on the Hill, Ashtead Common, Chatley Farm near Cobham, Abinger, Broad Street near Worplesdon, Compton, Farnham,

THE ROMAN VILLA

Since villas were usually constructed on stone and flint foundations it is generally impossible to know whether they were built entirely of stone since materials were invariably robbed for other buildings at a later stage.

While stone was used for the walls of bath blocks, where there was a risk of fire, it seems likely that, in Surrey, most villas were probably of a timber box-frame construction built on a dwarf wall, with lath and plaster probably employed for infilling. Ordinarily, in this country, the Romans did not build complete buildings out of brick but instead used it in specialist ways such as for levelling courses in flint walls or to support heated floors. The low-pitched roofs were covered with large clay tiles and, at some sites, window glass has been found.

Little evidence for internal decoration survives but plaster bearing coloured patterns has been excavated and some floors were of mosaic. The colour painting (left) shows the fine mosaic found at Walton on the Hill in the 18th century. Other floors were tiled, finished in *opus signinum*, a kind of pink cement; or made of stone flags or small bricks laid in herringbone fashion.

Bath-houses were a key element in the Roman villa. An excavation at Compton in 1914 showed a typical arrangement (below). A furnace (A), in which timber was burnt, heated an adjacent bath (B), next to which there was a hot room or *caldarium* (C). Next door was a warm room or *tepidarium* (D) while a cold room or *frigidarium* (E) completed the range. A separate dressing room or *apodyterium* might also be provided.

Both hot and warm rooms, and sometimes living rooms, had hypocausts which were floors raised on stacks of tiles or *pilae* (as the detail of the Compton hot room (far right) shows), below which the heat could circulate. Within the walls, there were sometimes heating flues constructed from hollow box tiles.

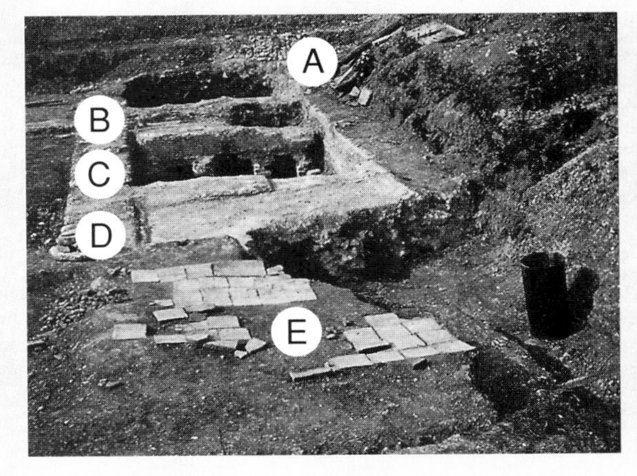

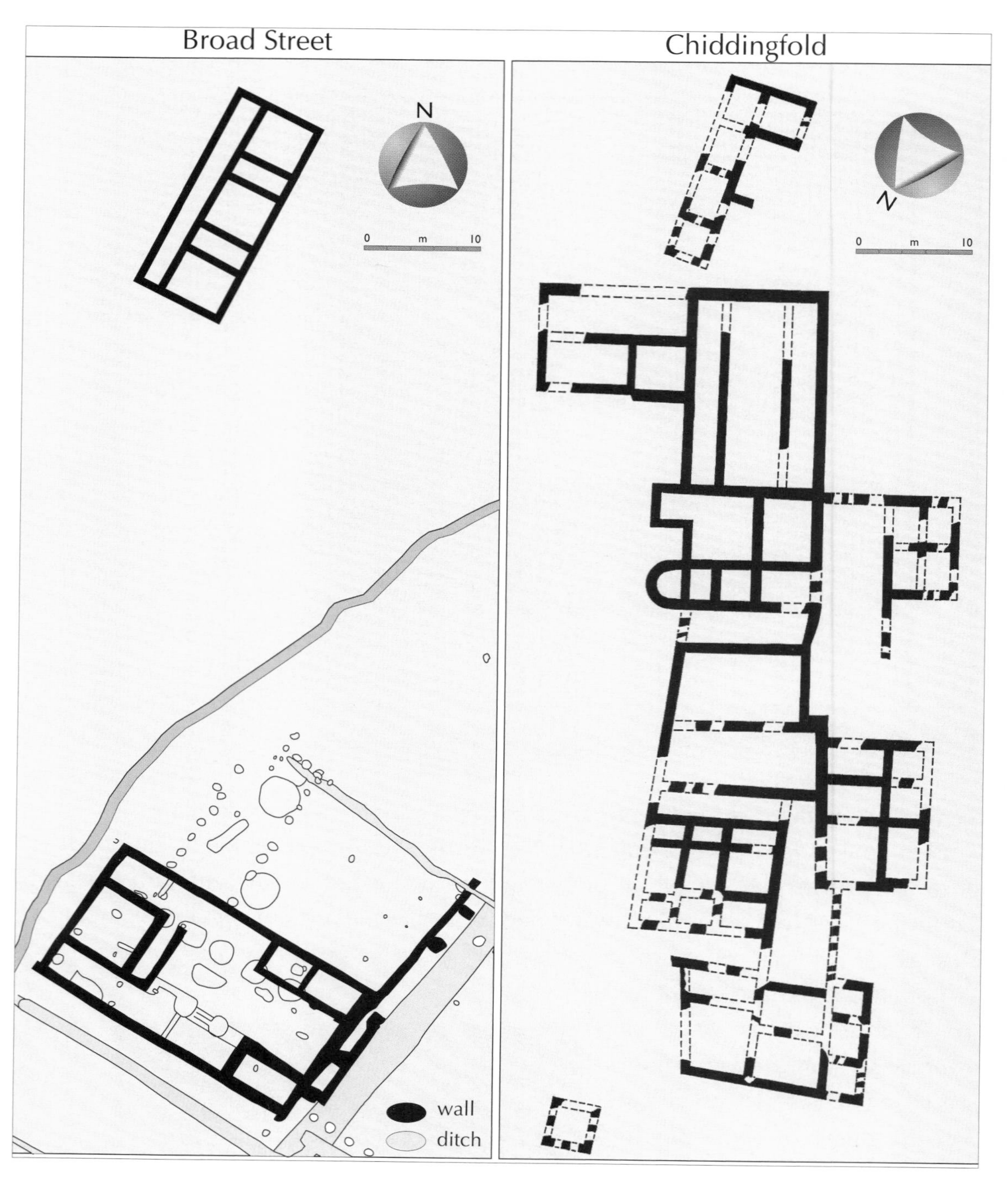

Comparative plans of the Roman villas at Broad Street (Worplesdon) and Chiddingfold. The buildings at Broad Street appear to be quite separate, but the ground between them has not been excavated. In reality, they may well be part of a large complex like that at Chiddingfold.

Chiddingfold, and Rapsley near Ewhurst.

It is difficult to be sure exactly how the buildings were used, especially since much archaeology undertaken in the 19th and early 20th centuries lacked the standards and understanding of

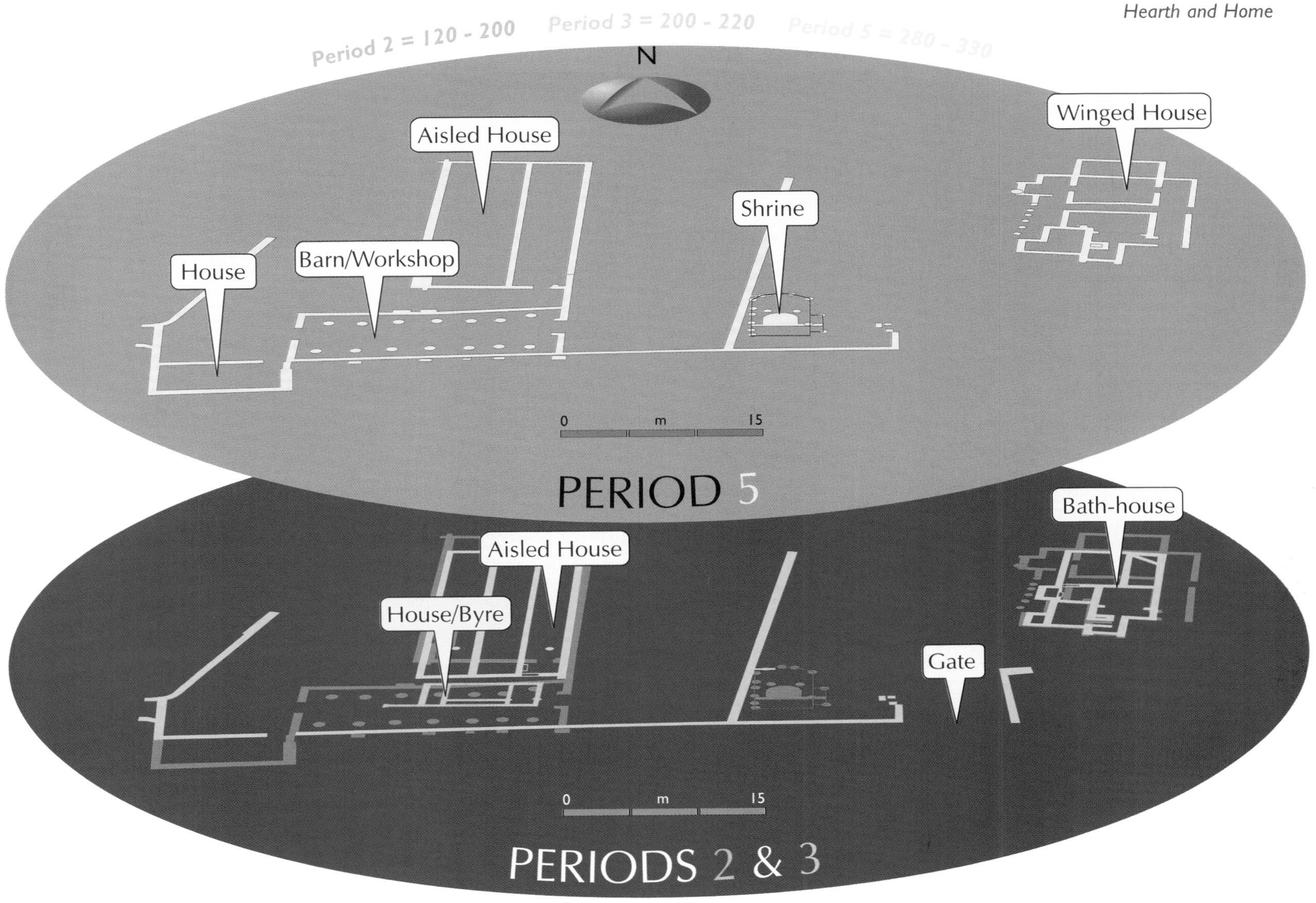

Block plans showing the evolution of the Roman villa complex found at Rapsley, near Ewhurst.

today and unfortunately resulted in the loss of vital evidence.

As new techniques develop, further examination is sometimes carried out, as at Titsey. The site was dug in the 1860s but has recently been the subject of a geophysical survey which suggests the presence of a second villa.

It is likely that most of Surrey's villas were occupied for at least a couple of hundred years and, just as with a house today, walls were knocked down, additions were made and the use of individual rooms changed.

Some Surrey villas had a large central hall while others had several rooms leading off one or more corridors between two projecting wings. The Walton Heath villa was one of the most luxurious with a superb mosaic floor but, unfortunately, little remains, since the site was first noted in the 1770s. Since then, it has been destroyed, largely by the crude efforts to investigate it of a number of well-meaning antiquarians.

The most complete insight into the development of a Roman villa can be gained at Rapsley, which was carefully excavated in the 1960s using modern archaeological techniques. Occupation began around AD 80, but it was not until about AD 200 (period 3) that the essentials of the main complex were constructed, with an aisled building and a separate bath-house. The aisled building collapsed and was rebuilt, apparently without aisles, about 4m (13ft) to the north. A new aisled building was constructed at right-angles to it and the bath block was converted into a small house with new rooms that included a mosaic floor at the northern end. These buildings were modified around AD 280–330 (period 5), before fire destroyed part of the complex and brought an end to occupation.

Reconstruction of a large Saxon hall found at Cowdery's Down, Hampshire.

A NEW DIRECTION

While what we know of the Roman period probably shows a distorted picture of settlement, delving into the lives of Surrey's Saxon people is even more frustrating. Though stone had replaced timber as the preferred construction material for churches by this time, there was probably nothing that could properly be called a house built of stone when William I defeated King Harold at the Battle of Hastings in 1066.

Some clues to where the people of

A conjectural reconstruction of the layout of the Saxon settlement discovered at Hurst Park, Molesey, showing a number of separate fenced enclosures, each for a large family group. Only the smaller huts were found in excavation and they were similar to the example from Shepperton (below), with a floor below ground level. The evidence for shallow features, such as the fences and foundations of the hall houses, may have been destroyed before excavation began.

Saxon Surrey lived might be given by the location of their cemeteries, a number of which have been found and excavated. The picture is, however, confused with many important Saxon sites suffering in the same way as those of the Roman period from damage caused by 19th century antiquarian excavation.

The work done in other counties paints a picture of the typical village or farmstead. Two types of buildings are present: rectangular timber-framed halls measuring some 10m by 6m (33ft by 19½ft) that probably served a communal role, and smaller roughly rectangular buildings with large flat-bottomed pits dug into the ground and with post-holes at either end to support the roof structure. These often have indications of specialist use, particularly for weaving.

In Surrey, single examples of sunken-featured buildings have been found at a few sites including Ham, Farnham and Shepperton County School, dating from the 5th and 6th centuries. A more substantial group has been excavated at Hurst Park, Molesey. Here eight 6th century buildings seem likely to be contemporary, but almost no other elements of the settlement were identified, which suggests that

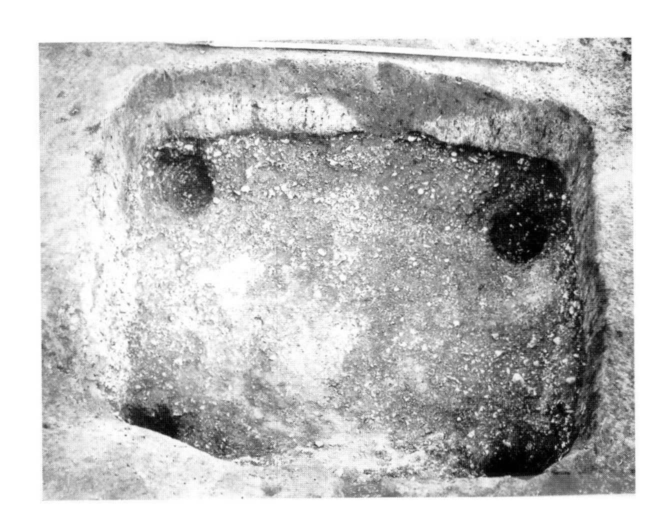

shallower features were destroyed before excavation began. The wide spacing suggests that occupation was well organised, and it seems likely that each of the sunken huts formed part of a complex including one or more of the rectangular halls, for which no below-ground evidence survived.

Settlements of this type have been found in adjacent counties, but not, as yet, in Surrey itself. At Chalton, Hampshire, excavation has revealed a village high up on the chalk Downs. It includes both halls and sunken-featured buildings, with indications of enclosures around separate groups. Cowdery's Down, also in Hampshire, is particularly noteworthy for the well-preserved evidence of the constructional techniques used in the timber framing of the halls.

PRIVATE AND COMMUNAL

For several centuries following the Norman Conquest there is little archaeological evidence for the houses that must have stood in Surrey and, as in previous periods, what does survive or has been excavated does not reflect the way ordinary people lived.

Most buildings would have been of timber. Those of the medieval peasants were very insubstantial and were spartan in the extreme, often with just one room that may even have been shared with their animals. Such buildings were soon replaced when living standards rose and very little trace would have been left for the archaeologist. Buildings dating

Reconstruction of the Norman house discovered at Castle Acre, Norfolk, which is closely similar in plan to one found at Bletchingley Castle.

TIMBER SKELETONS

Timber, the traditional Surrey building material, quite literally forms the skeleton of many old houses. Great trees were felled and fashioned into beams which were then jointed together as box frames and secured by oak pegs. Resting on upright posts and reaching from one side of the building to the other were trusses. The space between each truss is called a bay and the number of bays utilised for the open hall gives an indication of the status of a building.

Oak was the traditional wood used in timber-framed buildings and although it was 'green', having had little time to season, it was durable and strong. The tools used to work it were simple: an axe and iron wedges to split it and an adze to trim and square it. To saw a length of timber it was positioned over a pit so that, with one man below and another above, they could pull the saw rhythmically between them.

Often the frames were laid out in the carpenter's yard and were scribed with carpenters' marks — a modified form of Roman numerals — to ensure that they could be reassembled correctly. A similar process is now sometimes used to enable buildings to be taken down and built again elsewhere. At Holloway Hill, Godalming, a fine 16th century house, which had been concealed behind a 19th century façade, stood in the way of a relief road. It was carefully dismantled, as the photograph shows, with all the timbers being marked for proposed reconstruction at the Weald and Downland Museum.

The picture also reveals how the spaces between the timbers were filled with wattle and daub, plastered with a lime render and then finished with a protective coating of limewash built up over time by regular application, a job often done by farm workers when the land could not be worked.

from between about 1175 and 1300 have been excavated at Brooklands, Weybridge, and, lightly constructed, they had earth-fast posts as their main structural element. The house itself included three rooms in line, but none could truly be called a hall, and there were several other buildings including a detached kitchen. These buildings were made for the lord of the manor, but their constructional techniques are probably not very different from those of peasant dwellings.

It is, however, the evidence for higher-status houses that dominates our view of the earlier medieval period. At the grandest level are the castles. It is known that the castles of Surrey often served as residences, and sometimes as staging posts on journeys, for royalty and nobility. The footings for what could be described as an early post-Conquest house survive within the earthworks of Bletchingley Castle and are a very rare example of this type of building.

More common is the tower keep, defensively strong but providing a good range of accommodation on several floors. The example at Guildford Castle, built by 1150, survives as a substantial ruin. Its walls are 4m (13ft) thick and have an angled plinth at the base, designed to deflect the force of battering rams.

By the 12th century the mainstream pattern for the development of the higher-status English house can be identified confidently, although it has earlier origins. A large hall or communal living room is combined with a smaller building which serves as the lord's private chamber. This arrangement has been found at Alsted, near Merstham where the chamber was probably at first-floor level with an undercroft below.

Larger medieval houses could then be formed from sets of chambers, grouped with a hall or halls, and combined with other

Reconstruction of part of the Royal Palace at Guildford Castle. The view shows the Great Hall in the foreground, and to the left and behind it is part of the King's Chambers. On the right is the Norman motte or mound thrown up soon after the Conquest, with the keep on top.

LITTLE PICKLE, BLETCHINGLEY

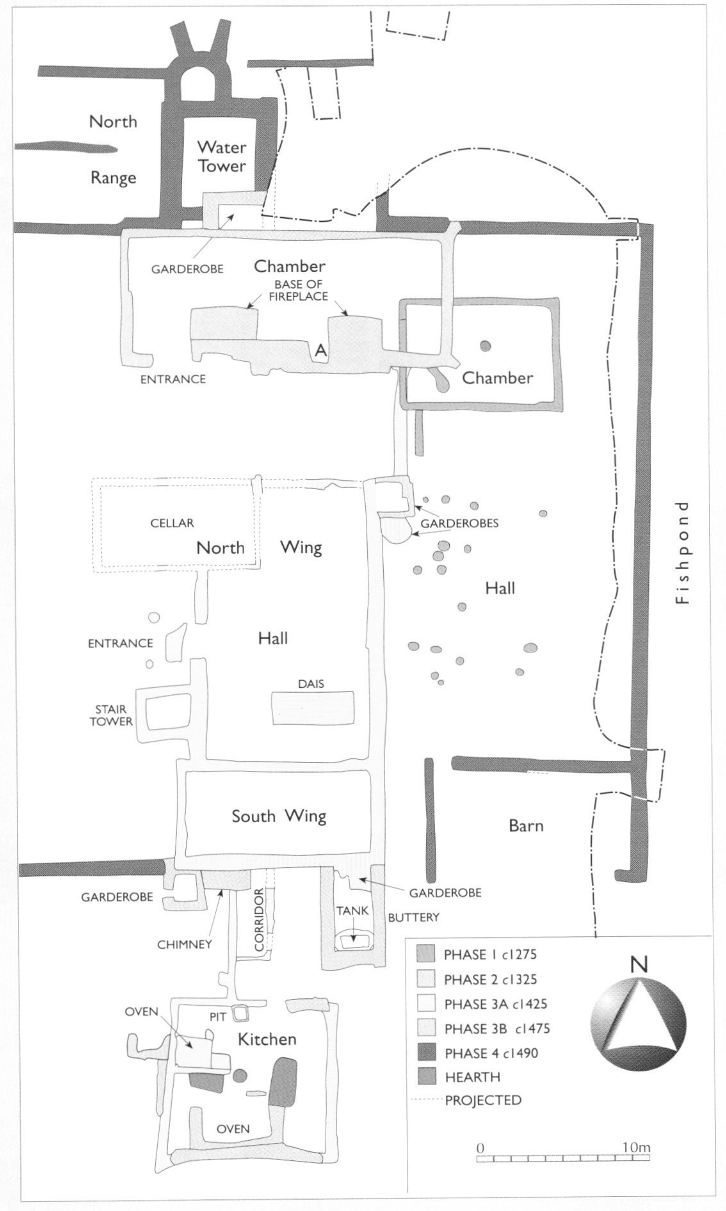

The lost manor of Hextalls at Little Pickle, Bletchingley, was discovered after planning permission had been granted in 1983 for a substantial extension to a long-established sandpit at North Park Farm. The archaeological investigation that followed revealed that, around 1275–1325, the building had been timber framed and roofed with tiles and was probably the hall-and-chamber residence of the keeper of the north and south deer parks in Bletchingley parish.

In the early 14th century the chamber was replaced with a larger and more sophisticated building. Probably of good quality ashlar, it is likely to have been a two-storey chamber block that had an external stairway to the first floor and, some time later, a garderobe was added to the north side of the building.

Around 1400, and possibly reflecting a change in the status of the occupants, the chamber was integrated into a range of buildings that included a new and substantial winged hall-house and a detached kitchen.

The next main development was carried out in about 1490 for Henry Hextall, one of the leading courtiers to the Duke of Buckingham. The site was transformed into a modest early Tudor country house when brick walls and ranges were added to the earlier buildings to create a privy court to the rear (east), and a front court equipped with a substantial gate house (to the west of the area shown on plan).

Hextall died in 1492 and the house was owned and tenanted by a variety of people before being demolished around 1550–9 when all salvageable materials were taken away.

Amongst the fragments found by archaeologists were a variety of moulded brick along with pieces of window cames which indicated some glazing in medieval times but much more extensive use of glass in the late 15th century. Fragments of water pipes point to water being supplied to all parts of the building, probably from a water tower.

In one large pit was the debris from what may have been an early 16th century feast. It included the drinking mugs shown right, which were imported from the Rhineland and the Netherlands in the years around 1500. It also included bones from a rich variety of birds and mammals, including both domestic and hunted species.

The timber-framed manor house at Walton-on-Thames was built around 1500, with a central open hall (now converted to two storeys), clasped by wings in which the first floor is jettied out.

buildings including kitchens, barns, stables and brewhouses, as at the 12th–14th century royal palace at Guildford.

In the larger towns merchants built first-floor chambers which often had stone undercrofts that could have served both as a store and shop. Examples of undercrofts survive or have been excavated in Guildford, Kingston and Reigate. The chamber above has, though, invariably been rebuilt at a later date.

From the start of the 14th century the functions of hall and chamber were combined in a single building: the hall house. Typically, such early medieval houses had a hall that was open to the roof while at one or both ends a first floor was inserted to provide two storeys. At the 'upper' parlour end of the hall, and perhaps on a dais, stood a table for the owner while at the 'lower' end doors led to the service rooms. Between these rooms and the hall, with the front and back door at either end, was a cross passage. The later phase at Little Pickle, Bletchingley, provides a good excavated example.

ROYAL PALACES

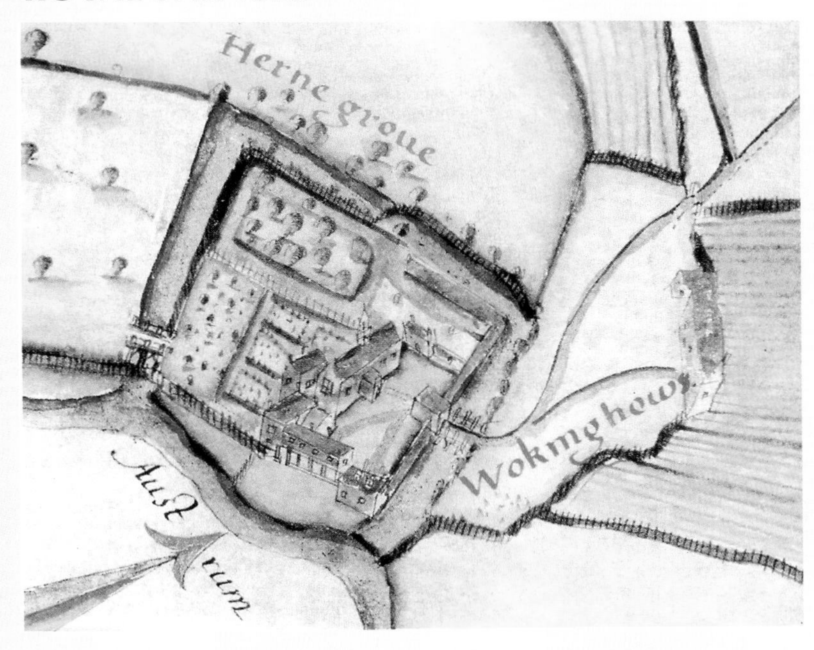

For many centuries Surrey was the playground of royalty and great hunting parties set out across its countryside. To sustain what were, at that time, major expeditions away from London, both hunting lodges and palaces were built.

Royal palaces once stood at Oatlands (Weybridge), Nonsuch (Ewell), and Woking, while Bletchingley Place was home to Anne of Cleves and Sutton Place and Loseley (near Guildford) were among the houses to receive visits from royalty.

Defoe, in 1724, described what is now Old Woking as 'a country market town' but 'so out of the way that 'tis very little heard of in England'. It was, however, a royal manor from Norman times and, on a loop of the River Wey to the east of the village, willows now stand sentinel over the remains of what was once a favourite palace of the Tudor monarchs.

It was described in a survey at the time of Edward II as 'a capital messuage surrounded by moats'. Two chapels are listed, lodging rooms for the knights, treasurers and other great officers, a moat and a drawbridge. Some of these features can be seen in a plan prepared by John Norden in 1607 (above left). The site was favoured by Henry VII and Henry VIII and most of the buildings belong to their time. A bridge and gatehouse are directly in front of the great hall. Southwards is a square building, perhaps a watergate, and next to this a long gallery with a cloister below, facing the river.

It is said that Henry VIII chose the site for Nonsuch Palace, near Ewell, when he stopped for refreshment on the way back from hunting on Banstead Downs. For the local inhabitants it was an unfortunate visit since the king ordered that the village of Cuddington, including the manor house and the church, be razed to make way for the building.

On 22 April 1538, Henry began building Nonsuch Palace to celebrate the birth of his son and heir, Edward, and it was planned to outshine all other buildings in Europe. Indeed its name is taken from the French *nonpareil*, meaning without peer or parallel.

By November 1545, £24,536 had been spent on the palace. The splendour of this work is well illustrated in the late 16th century painting of its main front (right).

Despite all this it was demolished less than 150 years later and the site was lost until 1959, when major archaeological excavations revealed its plan.

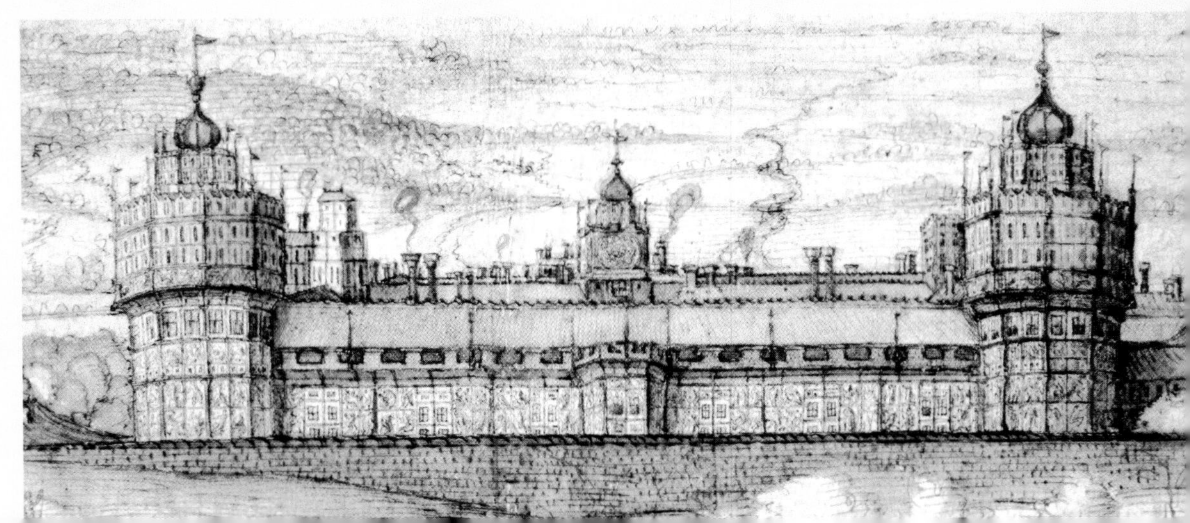

An open hearth generally made of pitched stones or tiles set on edge would have heated the hall. The smoke drifted up and blackened the rafters above, finding its way out between the tiles of the roof or through holes at the end of the ridge. Later these halls were often converted to two storeys, but the telltale signs of the open hall can still be found in the sooted roof timbers. The new windows inserted as part of such a conversion can be clearly seen in the Old Manor House at Walton-on-Thames. Ventilation came from unglazed windows with wooden shutters. The kitchen was generally detached as a safeguard against fire.

Around 1500, houses began to appear with one bay of the hall ceiled over and soon afterwards the smoke bay was introduced which also contained both the front door lobby and staircase.

Smoke bays and smoke hoods, basically timber-framed chimneys, continued to be built until about 1620, but houses with brick chimneys began to appear in the last quarter of the 16th century. An interesting example at Trout's Farm, Ockley, dated 1581, has the accommodation on two floors with a central brick chimney stack, but, oddly still retained an entry through a screens passage in the manner appropriate to the medieval hall house. From about 1600 the ground-floor accommodation was increased at the back of the house with an 'outshot' formed by extending the roof to ground-floor ceiling level.

Initially brick or stone houses were built to exactly the same plan as existing timber-framed houses. The single-ended hall became the simple two-up-two-down cottage. Larger versions were given a chimney at each end and sometimes an entrance hall containing the stairs.

Double-pile houses, with one room behind the other, made their appearance by the middle of the 17th century and most had a central entrance hall with two rooms on either side. The front rooms were usually the reception rooms with working rooms behind, but larger houses often had a basement to accommodate the kitchen while, in farmhouses, the front door might open into the kitchen.

FROM LOSELEY TO LUTYENS

Timber began to be abandoned in favour of brick and stone in the first half of the 17th century. After the Roman period the art of brick making had been lost in Britain but it was revived in the late Middle Ages and perfected in Tudor times. By the middle of the 17th century, bricks were as cheap as timber and were frequently made on site using local clay. Clay tiles began to be manufactured rather earlier than bricks and began to replace thatch or wooden shingles on the roofs of buildings from about 1175 onwards.

Walk down any Surrey street and it is all too easy to take the buildings that stand at its margins for granted. Many

This view of the rear of Thorpe Farm, near Egham, shows the timber framing of the 17th century core of the building. This is hidden behind later remodelling on other elevations.

LOSELEY HOUSE

A medieval house once stood on the site of the present Loseley House which was constructed between 1562 and 1568 by Sir William More, one of Queen Elizabeth I's most trusted advisors and supporters in Surrey.

It is said that he built it so as to be able to entertain the Queen and she subsequently stayed on four occasions. A survey made soon after 1600 shows it as a half-H-shaped house with the open end closed by a wall and gatehouse. Said to be the best house of its date in the county, what remains today is the north wing which contained the main rooms including the Great Hall.

Much of the stone used to build the new house at Loseley came from one of Surrey's other great buildings, the Cistercian Abbey of Waverley which had fallen into disrepair after the Dissolution of the Monasteries.

The romantic image presented by Helen Allingham of a 19th century cottage (above left) conceals the very basic living conditions revealed by the photograph (above right) of the wife of a 'broom squire' in her cottage near Hindhead.

have undergone considerable changes as they have been adapted to suit the fashions and needs of the period and of those owning them.

Timber-framed buildings still stand in the county but, in Georgian times, considerable numbers were re-fronted in brick or were hidden behind a mask of tile-hanging while others have grown from humble compact dwellings to much larger and rambling homes.

At first their façade may seem to give little clue to a hidden past but the telltale signs of change can sometimes be seen in the fenestration: windows may be unevenly placed or be of different styles and patterns. Frequently the roofline changes and so too does the detailing of the brick courses and other embellishments.

Like those in all of England's counties the vernacular buildings of Surrey reflect local traditions and the availability of materials. Timber and clay, in the form of brick and tile, still predominate but stone must not be forgotten, for although localised and not of the best quality, it features in many of the villages and hamlets scattered across the landscape.

In recent times even the simple cottages of farm labourers have been gentrified and are seen as personifying the rural idyll. Painters like Helen Allingham and Myles Birket Foster epitomised this halcyon

ALBURY

It is easy to imagine that lost villages are something of the distant past yet, at Albury, the village originally stood close to the mansion of Albury Park, where today, all that is left is the Saxon church of St Peter and St Paul and a few scattered houses. The foundations of the former village lie under the grass of the parkland where sheep now graze. From 1780 the villagers were harassed into moving by the then owner of the estate who closed the roads through the park, enclosed the village green and annexed a corner of the churchyard to form part of his grounds. The majority of the villagers moved to Weston Street (right), a hamlet a mile to the west which has become the present village of Albury.

concept in their delightful watercolours of rustic Surrey cottages but, while such paintings can guide the historian, it is generally acknowledged that they represent a romanticised way of life that was the exception rather than the rule.

When the railway age came, the green lanes, fresh air and rolling landscape of Surrey attracted the wealthy businessmen of London who bought land and employed an architect to design their country house.

Most famous amongst the architects who gave us the 'Surrey style' is Sir Edwin Lutyens but there were others such as Nevill, Voysey, Falkner, Shaw and Baillie Scott. In their work they echoed the vernacular architecture of the countryside and, in a single generation, changed the county forever so that, for a brief moment in the early 20th century, Surrey led the world in domestic architecture.

Munstead Wood is generally acknowledged as one of the masterpieces of Sir Edwin Lutyens. It was built for Gertrude Jekyll, who created an enormously influential garden in the grounds.

3 FOOD & FARMING

Caught up in the hubbub of the supermarket checkout it is easy to take for granted that milk, bread, vegetables and all the other staples of life are available by the basket load whenever they are required.

The seasons pass virtually unnoticed with tomatoes, strawberries and a host of other foods on the shelves all year round. Exotic dishes from every corner of the world are there to excite the taste buds and ready-prepared meals are packaged for convenience. At home they can be kept in the freezer or refrigerator and cooked in the microwave to be ready in minutes.

Only a few generations ago the situation was very different. Shopping was an almost daily chore and the kitchen was a place of constant industry where ingredients had to be combined, the stove needed tending and food could not easily be kept fresh.

The reconstruction shows a woman using a Palaeolithic flint scraping tool.

In the countryside even those people not directly employed on the land lived in close harmony with its rhythm, so blackberrying and the harvest were all elements of the yearly cycle with produce like apples and potatoes carefully stored ready for winter.

A large flint axe found in a gravel terrace formed by the River Wey at Farnham. Modern experiments have confirmed how effective such tools were for butchering animal carcasses.

EARLY MAN

Long before humans planted their first crops or domesticated animals, the area we now know as Surrey was occupied intermittently and as the early inhabitants roamed the landscape they relied for their existence on foraging and their ability to hunt and trap wild animals. Flint handaxes, discovered in the gravel of the River Wey at Farnham, were used some 400,000 years ago for skinning and butchering the carcasses of animals such as elephant and rhinoceros.

A clue to the way in which meat might have been eaten was found amongst human remains from Boxgrove in West Sussex. Two teeth show signs of distinctive scratches to the enamel suggesting that teeth were used like a vice in which food or hides were gripped before being cut or sliced with a sharp flint edge.

Modern man came, perhaps in pursuit of reindeer herds, via the land bridge linking Britain with continental Europe during the last Ice Age — around 40,000 years ago.

Some of the earliest evidence of these people in Surrey was discovered close to Wraysbury Road at Staines. During gravel extraction beautiful long blades of flint were found in a meadow called Church Lammas where, in medieval times and later, cattle were turned out to graze at 'Lammastide' or Harvest Festival. These were typical of the tools used by Upper Palaeolithic hunters about 11,000 years ago.

Careful excavation followed, revealing the remains of a temporary camp where hunters may have spent a night or more out in the bleak, unyielding landscape of the end of the last Ice Age. As well as making flint and bone tools they had dismembered the carcasses of wild cattle, wild horse and reindeer. Such sites have very rarely been discovered in Britain outside the protective environment of caves and rock shelters.

Tundra conditions prevailed and as the ice sheet, which had reached as far south as Oxford, started its northward retreat, the frozen subsoil thawed and forests of birch and then pine and later hazel began to grow in its wake.

This was the birth of the landscape we know today and when, some

8,000 years ago, the sea engulfed low-lying land to link what is now the English Channel and the North Sea, Britain became the island it has remained ever since.

AFTER THE ICE AGE

The Mesolithic period saw small hunter-gatherer groups living off what they could find, exploiting seasonally-available sources of protein such as hazelnuts, berries and fruit along with wild cattle, deer, pig and perhaps the larger fish and fowl.

THE HUNTER'S TOOLKIT

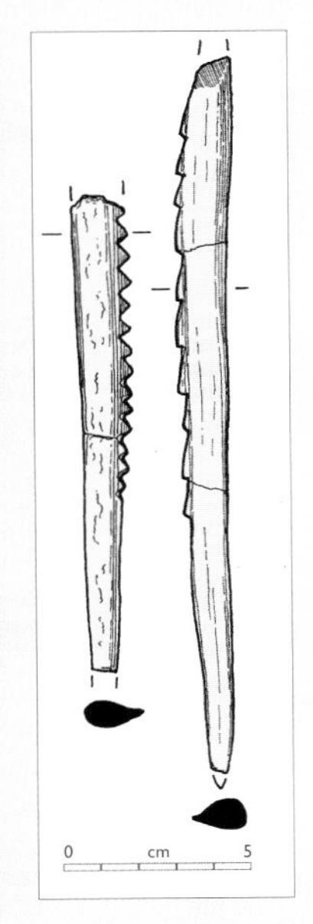

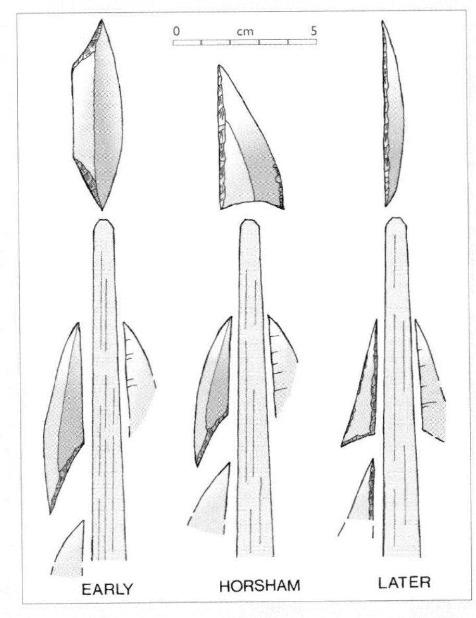

The hunter-gatherer lifestyle was tremendously successful, though it could support relatively few people in any one area at a time. Evidence of their presence in the form of their hunting equipment is revealed in barbed antler spearheads (above left), found in the Thames, and in flint microliths, which were used to barb wooden shafts (above centre), as well as flint tools. These implements have come from the North Downs, from the river gravels where the soil was light, usually well watered, well drained and easily worked and, most notably, from the greensand where concentrations of archaeological material imply some sort of semi-permanent occupation.

Hunting did not come to an end with the development of farming. The skeleton of an aurochs found in a pit at Harmondsworth still had six Early Bronze Age arrowheads embedded in it. The drawing (above right) shows a reconstruction of the hunt.

The popular view sees stone axes such as these as the tool with which Neolithic people waged war on the primeval forest. Fire, though, may have been a more effective weapon. This axe is from Abbey Meads, Chertsey.

At first the presence of these early people probably had little more effect on the environment than wild animals, although there is evidence to show that clearings were made in the woodland and that later Mesolithic people burnt areas to encourage grass and heathland.

To survive, the hunter-gatherers needed large areas of land so that when the food resources in one place became exhausted they could move on. They exploited the varying habitats provided by Surrey's geology and unwittingly they compacted the soil, snapping twigs underfoot, thus wearing into the landscape the north – south tracks that still dominate today.

Generally, like most of those who lived later, the Mesolithic people chose to live on the drier, warmer soils close to a spring, river or stream and they may have established semi-permanent camps from where they hunted further afield. The importance of a ready water supply is clearly illustrated at Ewell which, centred on its spring, is well represented archaeologically in every period from the Mesolithic onwards.

Neolithic stone objects, like this example from Abbey Meads, Chertsey, are described as pestles, but whether they were really used to grind grain or other foodstuffs is unknown.

As the number of hunter-gatherer groups grew, the way of life must have become increasing difficult to sustain because of the limited seasonal resources of the wild.

Whether by indigenous development or, as is widely believed, through the spread of farming practices from the Continent, people in the Neolithic period began to experiment with the cultivation of plants and started to herd and domesticate animals including cattle, sheep and pigs.

The need to look after crops and livestock meant that more static

THE NEOLITHIC DIET

Bones from midden deposits at Lower Mill Farm, Stanwell (showing as a dark soil in the photograph, right) revealed a diet of mainly beef, with some pork and, more rarely, mutton. Red deer and two fragments of beaver bone were also found along with a single aurochs bone that had been fashioned into a scoop (below right).

At Runnymede Bridge near Egham butchered remains included cattle and particularly pig, an animal much favoured for feasting purposes. Burnt food residues inside broken pottery vessels show that their contents had been fruit and malt, pork dripping, fish and honey-based products. Other seasonally gathered foods included hazelnuts, crab-apples and sloes, while a primitive variety of wheat called emmer, bread wheat and barley were grown and ground into flour using stone querns.

To boil meat a pit was dug, lined with clay and then filled with water. Stone 'pot boilers' were heated in a fire, plunged into the water and continually reheated and immersed until the meat was cooked. After the meat was consumed the bones were probably discarded for the dogs and, at a later stage, the larger bones were picked up and thrown in the river or a midden.

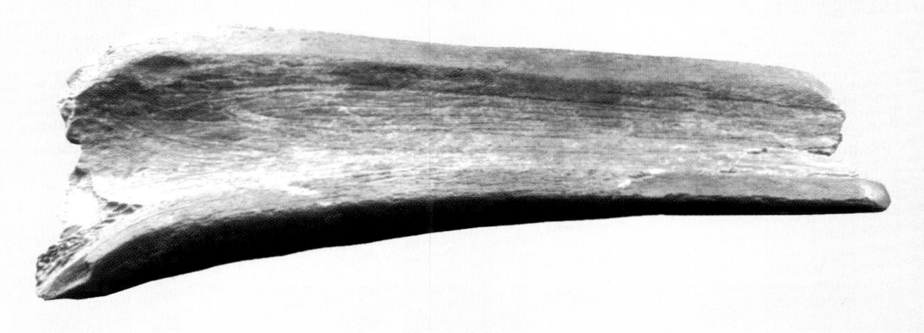

settlement occurred and, by means of stone axes and fire, greater areas of forest were cleared. Scrapers employed in cleaning hides, as well as sickles and saddle querns, provide evidence of this subsistence economy.

An ard, a plough made of wood and suitable only for use on light soil, was used for cultivation so the easily worked and well-drained soils of the Lower Greensand and the Thames Valley, with its associated gravel terraces, were ideal.

Wildfowl and mammals as well as edible plants, shellfish and fish would have been found in abundance in swamp, marsh and river areas, while concentrations of flint arrowheads found around Tilford, Crooksbury, Blackheath, Albury, Holmbury, Abinger and Limpsfield, suggest hunting grounds.

A plan showing cropmarks at Stanwell, overlaid on a 1999 aerial photograph. By then most of the archaeological features that produced the cropmarks had been destroyed by quarrying and road building. The Neolithic cursus is overlain by a Bronze Age field system.

During the Bronze Age, field systems were laid out on areas of lighter soil and land tenure was formalised, resulting in stability that led to farming settlements being long-lived. These developed in roughly the same areas as in the past but there was constant evolution and subtle shifts in the exact location of dwellings.

The best evidence of a Bronze Age field system in Surrey overlies and ignores the Neolithic *cursus* at Stanwell. The fields were laid out with droveways defined by double ditches provided to allow stock and carts to pass through the fields without damaging the areas of cereal cultivation.

A Late Bronze Age axe from Shepperton. A bronze tip was fitted to a larger wooden blade, which in turn was attached to the wooden haft. The bronze element has in the past been regarded as the whole axehead, but this find shows the true potential of an essential tool in clearing the land and building new settlements.

With less reliance placed on wild resources, the exploitation of more productive lands intensified as some marginal areas were abandoned as a result of the combined effects of soil exhaustion and a wetter climate.

Wheat and barley were grown and stock raising was undertaken on lush pasture land such as that in the lowland areas of the Thames valley where the landscape was largely treeless by the Late Bronze Age. Cattle were herded and sheep and goats probably grazed the chalk and heathland. Pork was popular for feasting and was either roasted or boiled in wood-lined troughs or large bronze cauldrons.

Dating from this period, a primitive variety of wheat called spelt was found at the site we now know as Runnymede Bridge which, by

HEATHLAND

Nearly all heathland has been created by people because, for it to survive, it must be cut, grazed or burnt to keep fresh tree growth at bay. In the Bronze Age and probably earlier, trees were increasingly cleared across much of western Surrey to make way for crops and stock. On Whitmoor Common at Worplesdon traces of early field systems exist which might have formed part of the Bronze Age landscape. Fragments of other field boundary systems have been observed near Woking on Smarts Heath and Horsell Common.

The soil in such places quickly became impoverished and the resulting heaths form a characteristic landscape of heather, gorse, bracken and grasses along with areas of bog and scrub woodland, as the photograph (below), looking towards the Bee Garden across Chobham Common, shows. This site, at Albury Bottom (strikingly revealed in an infra-red aerial photograph, above), is a rare example of an earthwork on the heath. It seems too elaborate to have been built as an enclosure for beehives, though bees were kept on the common. A more likely explanation is that it is a stock enclosure, used in the medieval period to help manage the large numbers of pigs which foraged there.

The heathland was an important resource through the ages providing not only grazing but also fuel and materials for more specialised pursuits. Most famous of these was the making of brooms by the 'broom squires', who peopled them in the 18th and 19th centuries — a time when heathland was far more extensive in Surrey than it is now.

St Ann's Hill, Chertsey rises abruptly from the valley below. In the Iron Age the hillfort at its summit would have dominated and controlled settlement in the region.

900 BC, had become a Thames-side trading settlement and must have been an important marketing centre for the arable economy.

The site is one of a number which indicate that major developments were taking place at the end of the Bronze Age including some, such as the establishment of hillforts, which are usually linked with the beginning of the Iron Age. By then, but possibly earlier, tribal elites exerted control over such things as the storage of grain and their territories were well defined.

The Iron Age agricultural economy was more complex and sophisticated than is normally assumed. The diagram shows how hillforts, such as St Ann's Hill, near Chertsey, were linked to local settlements, such as that at nearby Thorpe Lea Nurseries.

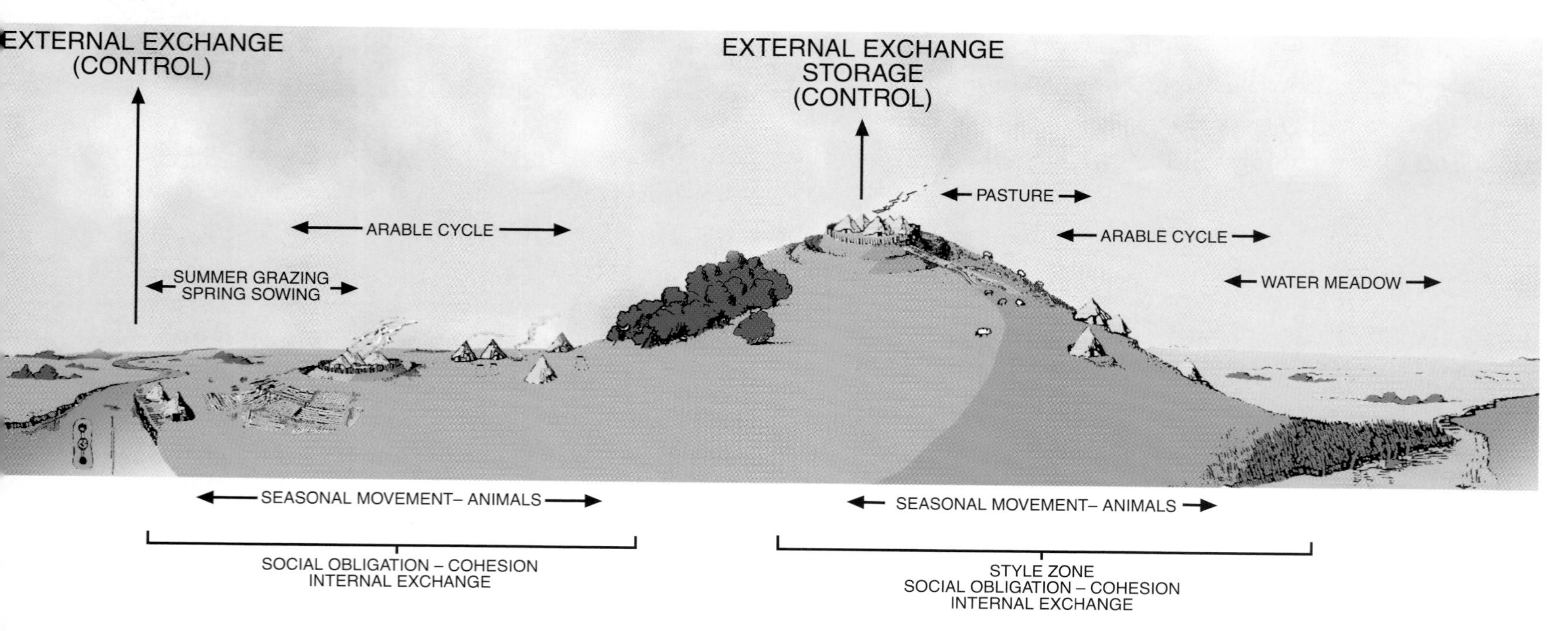

The particular functions that the landscape served were important. In the valleys, rivers allowed goods, animals and people to be transported easily. On the hills, forts were built to act as centres to which produce could be brought, where manufacture might take place and goods could be redistributed. In the surrounding landscape related farmstead and settlement sites were engaged not only in agriculture but possibly in other forms of production as well.

An Iron Age sickle from Kingston. Agricultural implements rarely survive for archaeologists to discover.

At various periods the forts had different functions that were also dependent on their location. On the greensand they served a role in controlling the movement of livestock as the varying landscape that reached southwards to the Weald was exploited. The Weald provided summer grazing, but there do not appear to have been any permanent settlements, so hut clusters and individual farmsteads were largely concentrated on the dip slope of the North Downs.

In contrast, the hillforts in the north may have served as centres for marketing and exchange at a time when the population was growing. The agricultural economy was also becoming increasingly sophisticated, and would have been supported by farming settlements on the river gravels where the soil was good.

In some places ditches were used to delineate field systems and one complete plot of about 100m by 60m (325ft by 195ft), was discovered by excavation at Runfold Farm near Badshot Lea. Aerial photography has revealed field systems, distributed fairly evenly across the Downs, which give evidence of cereal cultivation. Sheep formed an important part of the economy and grazed on the chalk pastures and also on the heathlands.

Both at Effingham and on Epsom Downs at Tadworth, banjo-shaped enclosures have been found. Belonging to the later Iron Age

This bronze bucket excavated at Weybridge is a rare import from the Alpine region of Italy. It is of early Iron Age date, and formed part of a wine-mixing set.

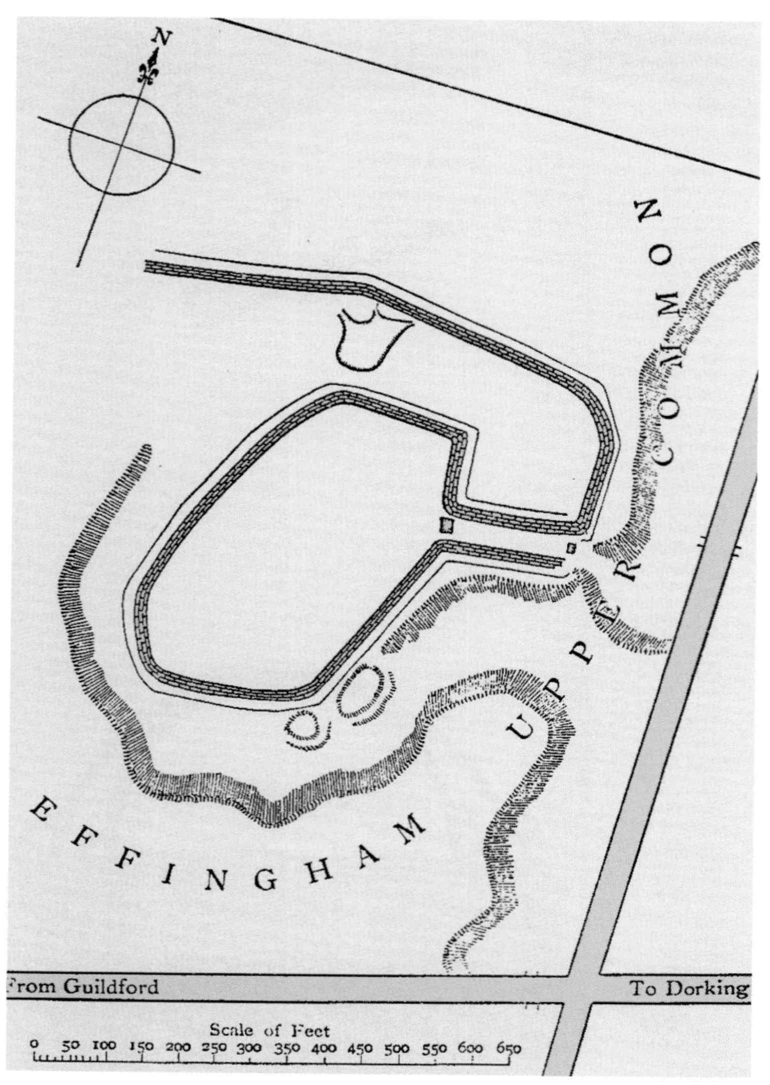

An Iron Age 'banjo' enclosure on Epsom Downs, near Tadworth. These 'banjo' enclosures were formerly thought to have been associated with stock control, but now examples excavated elsewhere have been found to contain houses. The drawing shows it still surviving as an earthwork in the 18th century, but it was destroyed in the early 19th century.

they are formed of banks and ditches and were probably once surrounded by a fence.

Livestock was important throughout the Iron Age and Roman periods, as bones discovered at Thorpe Lea Nurseries near Egham demonstrate. Here, the main source of meat appears to have been cattle, while sheep and goats were probably important for wool and possibly milk as well as for meat. Pigs provided meat, lard and perhaps leather.

Another site to have produced evidence for animal husbandry is Hawk's Hill, near Leatherhead, where the bones found include cattle, horse, sheep or goat and pig with small numbers of deer, fox and bird also present. Importantly, the evidence showed that animals had not been slaughtered annually so it is clear that storage of fodder was properly organised and stock could be overwintered for as long as was required.

At Weston Wood, Albury, evidence was found for the use of barley and wheat. Much later, material from a storage pit at Hascombe hillfort included wheat, barley and oats. Experiments have revealed that grain and other foodstuffs could be kept fresh in such storage pits because, once they are sealed with clay, the build-up of carbon dioxide inhibits bacterial growth. More commonly, as at Thorpe Lea Nurseries, there is evidence of 'four-posters' — granaries raised off the ground by four wooden posts to prevent rats and mice eating the grain. Querns appear to have been used extensively, implying that a good deal of corn was being ground in local settlements.

THE ROMAN PERIOD

With perhaps as many as five million people, the population of Roman Britain was high. Surrey's inhabitants are likely to have adapted their settlement pattern gradually to the framework of new

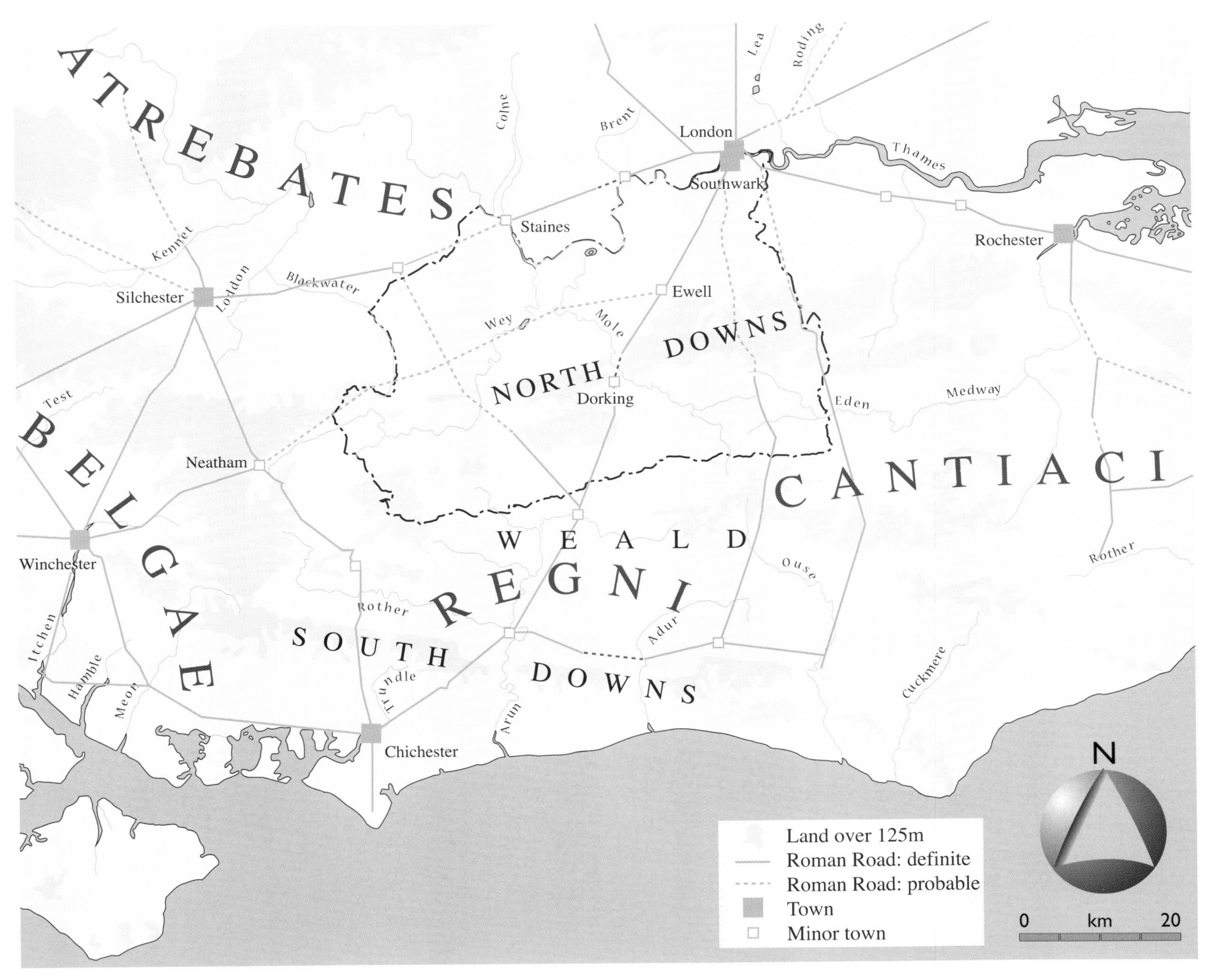

Roman roads helped to integrate the tribes of Iron Age Britain. They also helped the development of larger towns and settlements, in which trade was of considerable importance.

towns and roads, but it is clear that the bulk of the population lived in the countryside where the transition from the Iron Age was peaceful, with a continuity of individual farmsteads.

The Iron Age settlement at Thorpe Lea Nurseries continued to develop through Roman times. A new field system was established in the middle of the period with, as in other places, the fields laid out in a more regular pattern.

As part of a regional economy there was greater emphasis on trade, exchange and money, so there was more organised and deliberate exploitation of resources such as those of the London Clay and the Weald.

There can be little doubt that woodland management was a major occupation in these areas. Villas such as the one at Broad Street, near Guildford, were established in order to exploit the extensive woodland and pasture resources on the clay and on the heaths to the north. Chiddingfold villa may also have been the centre of a major forestry estate, based on the Weald.

ROMAN FOOD

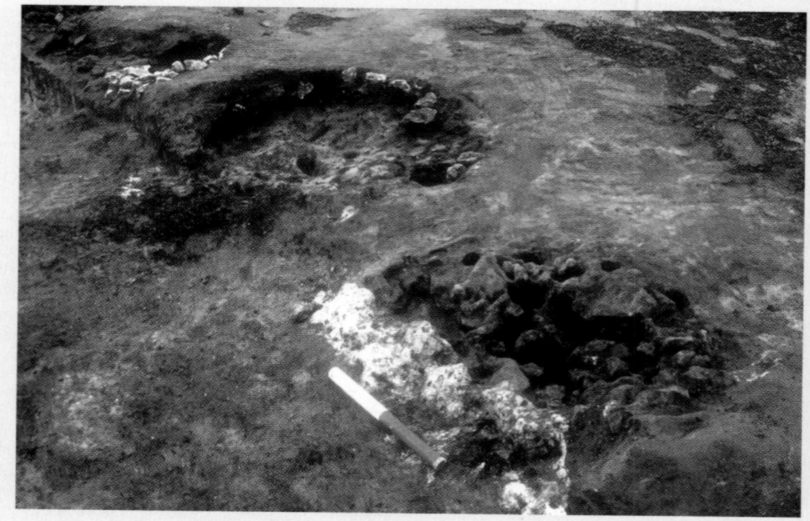

No doubt supplied from farms in Surrey and north Kent, Southwark, as a 'suburb' of London, served the needs of travellers. Seeds, bones and other remains found there present a fascinating insight into the diet of those who lived in and passed through the area.

There are indications of the presence of fig, grape, raspberry, blackberry, plum, cherry, damson, apple or pear, lentils, peas, the cabbage family, coriander, mustard, dill, millet and flax, oysters, mussels, cockles and limpets, mackerel, herring, smelt, eel, plaice or flounder, pike, dace, possibly roach, gudgeon and chub, cattle, sheep, pig, domestic fowl and small percentages of red deer, roe deer, hare, wild boar, badger and woodcock. Wine and fish sauce also brought a flavour of the Mediterranean to London.

Such variety may be exceptional, but discoveries elsewhere in Surrey also show a good range of foodstuffs as well as revealing hints of the well-organised agricultural economy which produced them. In Staines, footprints of cattle, discovered in the mud of a pond, showed that the animals were brought in and watered before being slaughtered for meat. At Ewell, the jaws of sheep indicate that the animals were aged between one and three years old and had therefore been over wintered. Their condition shows that there was a good standard of shepherding with selective culling.

Astonishingly, at Betchworth part of a loaf was found preserved in a ditch close to where ovens were used for baking bread, perhaps for ritual (above right).

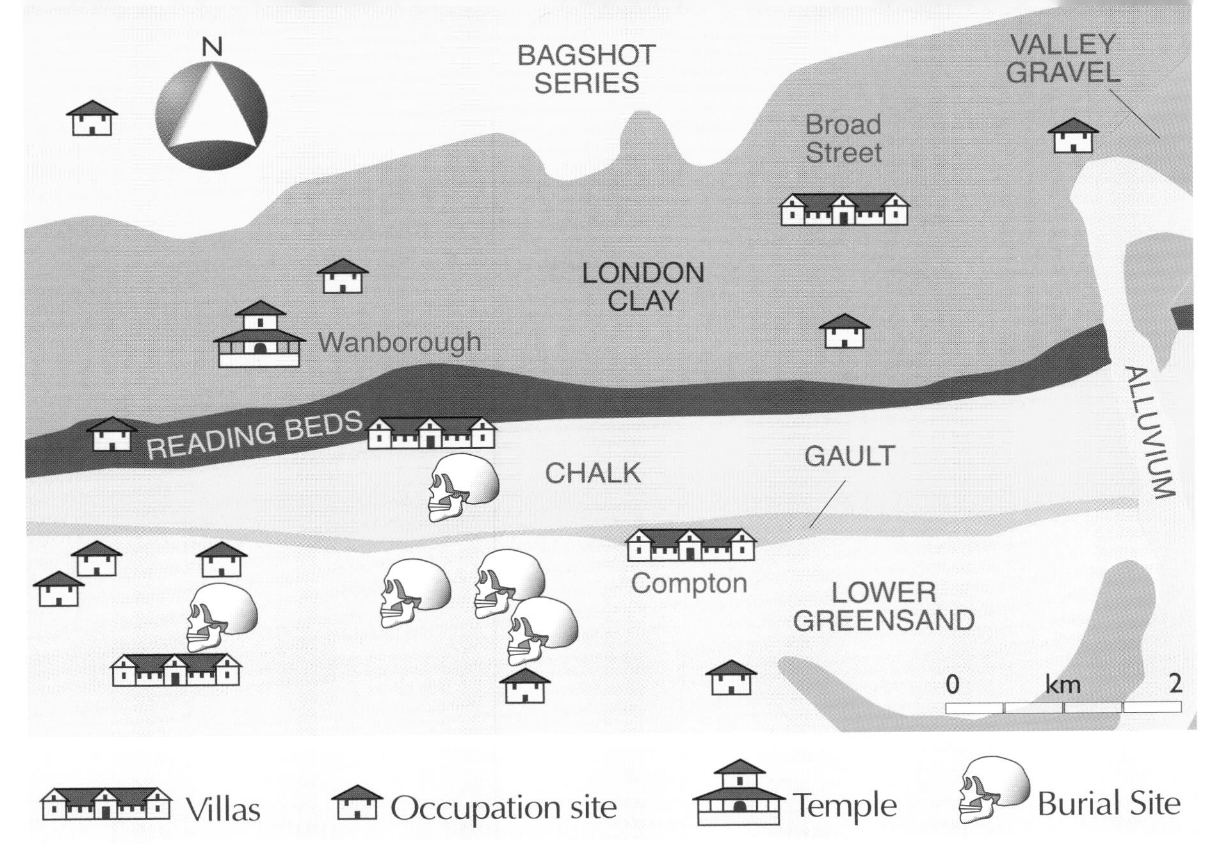

Roman sites west of Guildford. The heavy London Clay was little used for settlement before the Roman period. Villas, such as that at Broad Street, Worplesdon, were established in order to exploit the extensive woodland and pasture resources on the clay and on the Bagshot Heaths to the north. Meanwhile, on the other side of the Hog's Back, the villa at Compton had farmland to the south.

Most of the villa sites however were on the good and mixed soils and, like those in Kent and Sussex, lie around the edge of the Weald. It therefore seems that their siting was little influenced by their relationship with London.

The villa seems always to have had an economic basis as the centre of a substantial estate, but it also offered the comforts of a country house. A sophisticated lifestyle was, however, one of the attractions that the towns of Roman Britain offered, and the two effectively competed with each other. The absence of villas around Staines suggests that the local gentry preferred its more cosmopolitan attractions to those of the countryside, and used it as the base from which they controlled their land and estates.

THE SAXONS

Between AD 400 and 450 Britain lost regular contact with the rest of the Roman Empire and was no longer part of a money-using economy. Quite rapidly, marketing and trade ceased to be important activities, and those institutions most dependent on them, the towns

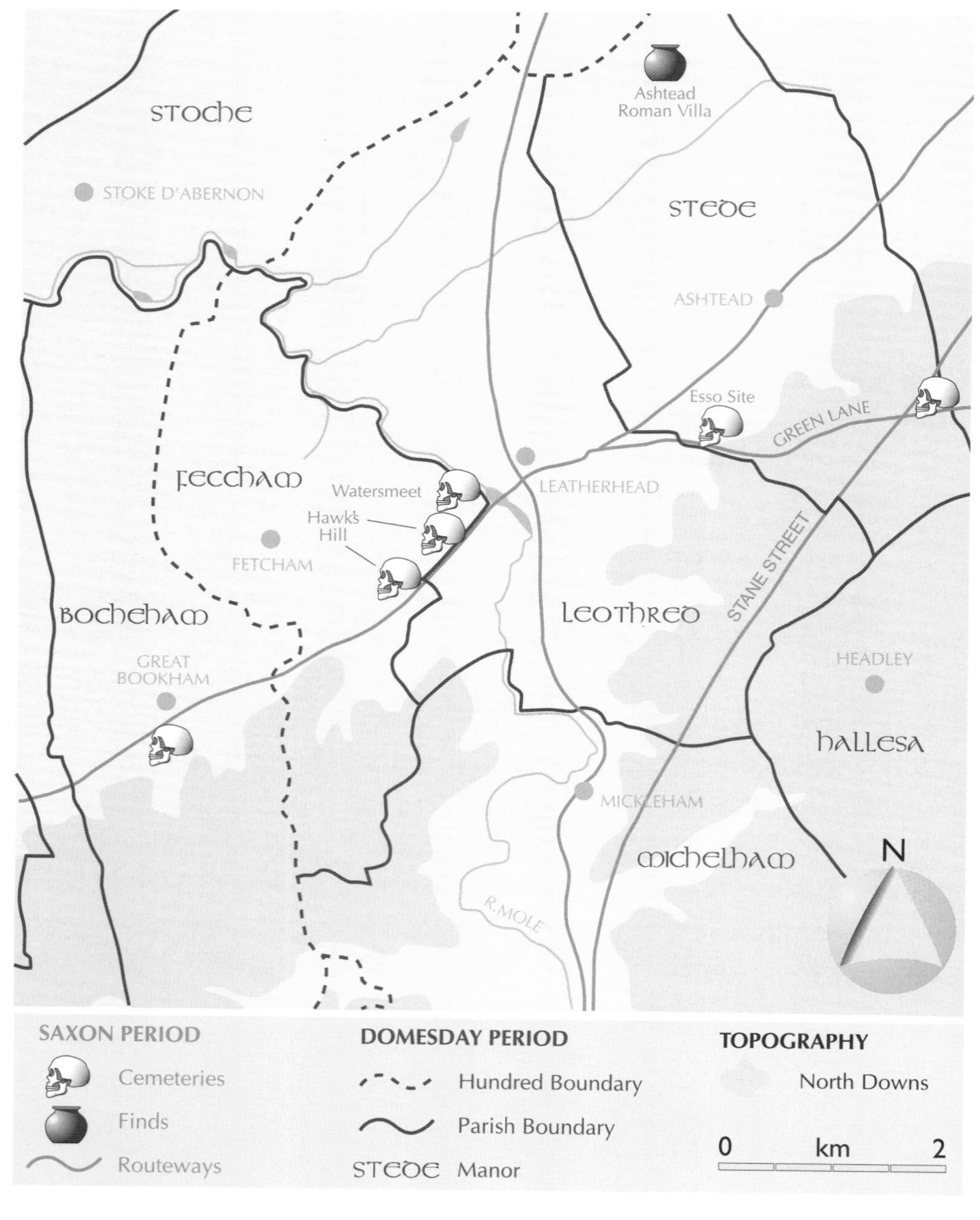

The manors in the Leatherhead area share a number of common features. Ashtead, Leatherhead, Fetcham and Bookham are all long and narrow, extending from the North Downs across the varied geology of its dip slope onto the London Clay. These patterns already existed by the early Saxon period, and suggest a deliberate subdivision so that each estate had a share of the varied resources supported by the differing geologies.

and villas, were abandoned.

Despite this, as the Roman influence waned, it is unlikely that Surrey was suddenly thrown into chaos. The overall settlement pattern probably remained much the same, with the varied resources of the county exploited in the traditional way, although the separate communities would have become more self-sufficient.

One strong indicator of this continuity can be found in an examination of the relationship between parish boundaries and the siting of early settlements and cemeteries. Many modern parishes have boundaries virtually identical to those of the manors described in the Domesday Book in 1086, and early Saxon cemeteries — such as that at Esso House at Ashtead — are regularly found on the boundaries to these estates. This shows that they already existed in the 6th century AD and it is quite possible that these farming units were first established in the Roman period.

The names of some of these manors suggest that sometimes they pooled their resources, with each holding having its own speciality. One confederacy of manors in north-east Surrey has Saxon names indicating that its units included a goat farm (Gatton), a horse enclosure (Merstham), an area specialising in bean cultivation (Banstead), and a market centre (Chipstead).

FISH AND EEL TRAPS

Gravel extraction at Ferry Lane, Shepperton revealed four rows of wooden stakes (below) that are interpreted as part of one or more late Roman or early Saxon V-shaped weirs designed to catch fish or eels. The 'V' probably pointed downstream and nets supported by large stakes or piles may have been used to make a larger trap. There might have been a structure from which a fisherman could tend his

baskets or nets at the eye of the 'V'. Rough weights were also found which could have been 'net sinkers' although they may have been attached to an eel basket or fish trap to hold it in place.

Similar techniques remained popular through the medieval period and are well illustrated in the 14th century Luttrell Psalter which shows a water-mill with fish traps in the mill stream (above).

The pace of change during the Saxon period was generally very slow, and it was not until the 10th century that major changes began to occur, creating the enduring medieval pattern. In 893 the Anglo-Saxon Chronicle describes the Weald as 'the great forest we call Andred' and the major use of the area in the earlier Saxon period was as swine pasture, amongst the trees. There were few, if any, permanent settlements within it, the herds being driven down from the parent settlements to the north each summer. In late Saxon times the 'daughter' camps become much more noticeable in records as settlements in their own right, as the old pasture was converted to arable. By the end of the 12th century much of the forest was cleared.

These processes were, at least in part, set in motion by the rapid growth of the late Saxon economy. Across the country increased trade was accompanied by the development of new commercial centres. In

Surrey the town of Guildford emerged, and was the location of a mint. Overall, though, Surrey was rather slow in developing larger settlements, being partly inhibited by its proximity to London. Another contributory factor was the poverty of the soil since there would have been insufficient agricultural produce to support a larger population.

THE MEDIEVAL PERIOD

At the time of the Domesday Book the population was still considerably more dispersed than might be imagined, with small hamlets and individual farms scattered across the county. Godalming provides a good example, with the Domesday record indicating at least two hamlets, and excavation having demonstrated the existence of a third. It was not until the 13th century that the present town emerged.

The Domesday Book of 1086 reveals much about late Saxon Surrey since, although it was a survey carried out by the Normans, it is an inventory reflecting England as it was when William I conquered and ended Harold's rule. In today's parlance it showed that Surrey was a 'going concern'. Each manor that it recorded was subject to the control of a lord, sometimes resident, but

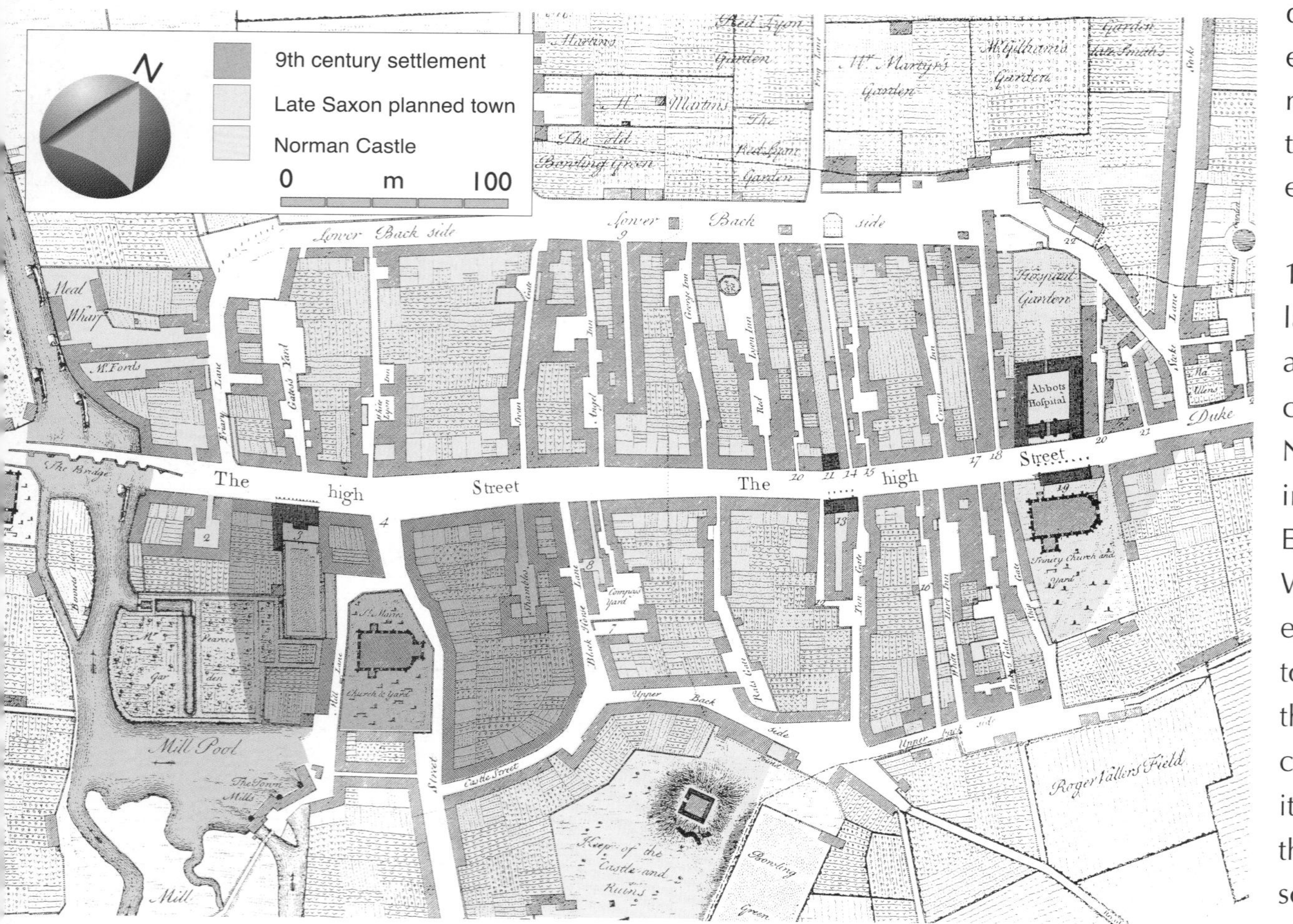

The main elements of the town plan of Guildford, as drawn in 1739, were unchanged from the medieval period. It was not much larger than the new town founded in the 10th century, although the ditch, which originally surrounded it, had been infilled, and was now used for roads, such as Lower Back Side (now North Street). The market was held in the High Street.

HUNTING

Hunted animals did not make a large contribution to the diet of commoners but hunting was probably important to the local economy. Many of the lower classes would have been involved either in the manufacture of hunting equipment and dress or employed directly in the hunt as beaters, gamekeepers or forest wardens.

Following the Norman Conquest the hunting of deer had been restricted to the king and his court so venison symbolised wealth and social standing and was a highly prized commodity. Partridge, woodcock and swan were also important and in the medieval period hawking was a popular pastime of the upper classes.

Royal control extended to large areas of land in which the prey was protected. Windsor Forest covered substantial portions of north-west Surrey as the extract from Norden's map, made in 1607, shows. Development of farms and clearance of woodland for agriculture proceeded much more slowly here than in areas like the Weald which were free of the restrictions of forest law.

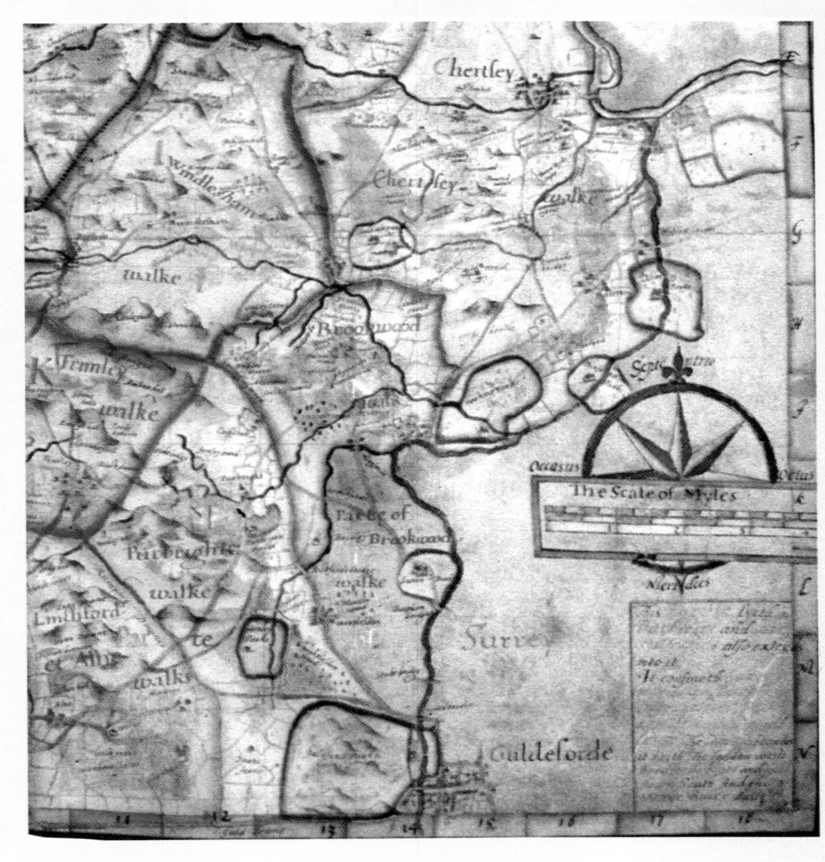

more often not. Whichever was the case his power was immense and remained so throughout the Middle Ages.

It was largely the desires of the lord of the manor that determined whether a town was established, as only his influence could obtain a grant from the king of the right to hold a market. Nearly all such grants in Surrey date from the 12th and 13th centuries. The ambitions of a lord were not always matched by a grasp of commercial reality. At Bletchingley the de Clares had obtained a grant of a market before 1262 and laid out a new town. Although it had some initial success the market had disappeared by 1325.

In general the development of towns in Surrey was quite limited, and probably the only settlements, other than Southwark, with anything approaching true urban

Facsimile of the Domesday Book entry for Ashtead. It reads: The Canons hold ASHTEAD from the Bishop of Bayeux. Thorgils held it from Earl Harold. Then it answered for 9 hides, now for 3 hides and 1 virgate. Land for ... In lordship 2 ploughs; 33 villagers and 11 smallholders with 14 ploughs. 9 slaves. From grazing. 7 pigs; meadow, 4 acres. Value before 1066, £10; later £6; now, £12.

A view of the High Street and market place area of the medieval town of Bletchingley.

status were Kingston, Croydon, Farnham, Guildford, Godalming and Reigate. This was no doubt largely due to the dominance and close proximity of London as a trading centre.

The towns were not the only places where growth was evident. Exactly the same period saw the widespread emergence of villages, supplementing and replacing the earlier more dispersed pattern of settlement.

These villages frequently included both a church and manor house and took two common forms. Either they were spread along a street or the side of a green as in the case of Chiddingfold or alternatively like Charlwood were a more random cluster of various dwellings either loosely spread out about an area of common pasture or clustered around a green.

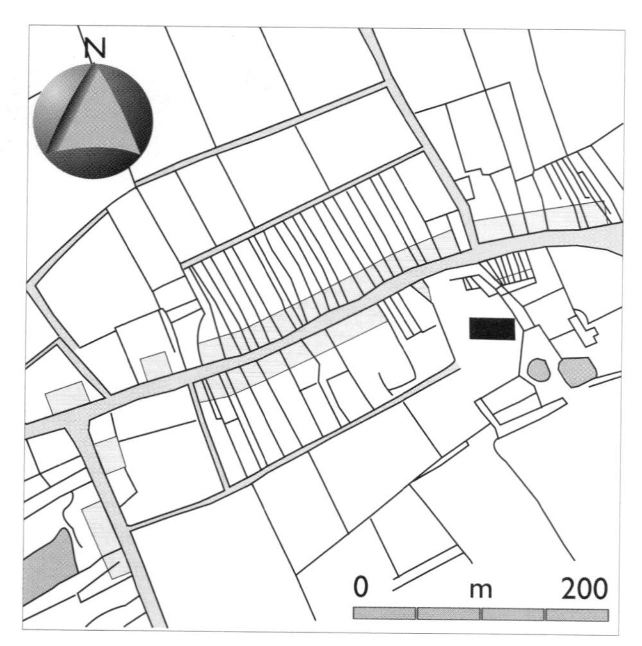

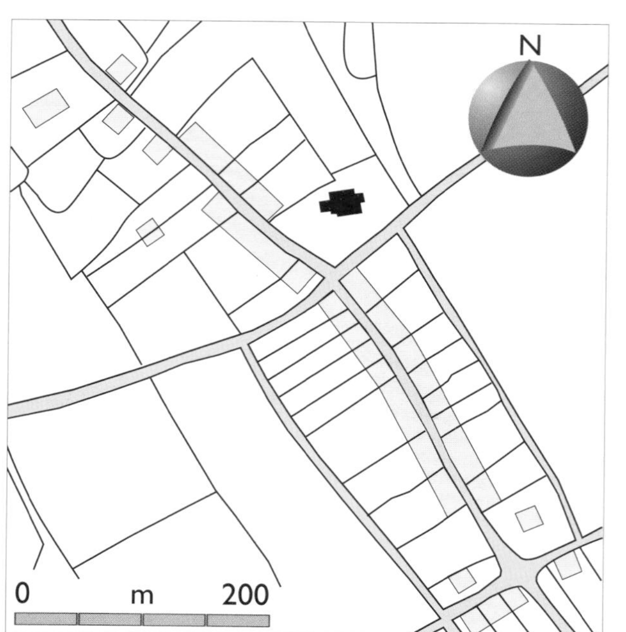

Egham (above) and Great Bookham (right) may be two of the villages founded on the Chertsey Abbey estate in the 12th century. The new village plans (based on early maps) were regularly arranged, with houses and their attached plots fronting onto one or two main streets, and the church set back from the road in its own large plot.

THE TITHE BARN

Some barns such as the one at Wanborough, which was built by the monks of Waverley Abbey, stored the community's tithes. This was a tax of one-tenth of annual produce of land or labour levied to support the church and clergy and was generally paid in kind.

Barns were much more than just places of storage; the design and layout was geared to the processes associated with the harvest and the processing of crops. On either side were large doors through which wagons piled high with sheaves of corn entered and left at harvest time.

In the winter, the sheaves were flailed on the floor in the space between the doors. When the grain was winnowed, both sets of doors were flung open and, as the farm hands tossed the grain in the air using a wooden shovel or a scoop-shaped basket, the through draught helped to separate the grain from the dust and chaff.

At the periphery a back lane formed the boundary of 'tofts', the plots of land behind the dwellings. These allowed individuals to cultivate herbs and vegetables as well as to keep poultry and perhaps a pig or cow.

It is hard to see a great deal of evidence of deliberate planning in most such villages, and they could largely be the result of piecemeal development. Undoubtedly, though, some villages had planned origins. Chertsey Abbey owned huge tracts of land in north-west Surrey as well as scattered manors elsewhere in the county. In the 12th century the farming of some of these estates was reorganised so that it was based on people living in a village rather than in scattered farmsteads. The open fields which such arrangements imply can still be glimpsed behind later arrangements in the earliest large-scale maps, such as those of John Rocque in the 18th century.

Farming techniques varied considerably but one of the most widely recognised is what is commonly known as the three-field system. At their simplest, the three fields were arranged around the village and within them the villagers held strips. Each had a share of

Ploughing with oxen, as shown in the 14th century Luttrell Psalter.

strips spread across the fields to ensure that they had an equal proportion of good, bad and indifferent land and a fair division of each year's rotation. The simplest form of rotation might mean that the first field contained wheat and rye, the second barley and the third remained fallow.

The system is best suited to large areas of good agricultural land, as in the Midlands where it is best known, but was rarely present in its classic form in Surrey, with its more varied terrain and large extent of 'waste' — undeveloped heath and woodland. Large fields whose tenure was divided amongst numerous peasants are common, but fully organised rotation was not. Instead of the three-field rotation systems some villages had an infield which was continuously cultivated land close to the village and an outfield which was cropped on a shifting system.

In addition a meadow would provide hay for winter feed while the common pasture offered grazing for the animals that were vital for ploughing, meat and milk and also supplied the manure necessary for the fertility of the soil. Pigs were turned out into the wood and wasteland which also offered necessities such as wood to burn and timber to build with, berries for food and reeds for roofing. Sheep, goats, ducks and geese were also kept.

Failure of the harvest could bring not only economic hardship but also famine and epidemic. The threat of disease and death

TRAVELLERS' FARE

Close to Staines, excavation at a site dating from the 13th century led to the discovery of what may have been a stopping place for drovers taking cattle or sheep to market in the nearby town. Large quantities of cooking pots were found, perhaps because the site functioned as a medieval version of a 'fast food' outlet. Other vessels are lacking but this could be because of the use of 'camping equipment'. People may have carried a vessel for cooking but more readily transportable items such as skins or leather jugs, which are perishable and rarely found, would have made suitable containers for liquid refreshments. The dig revealed the plan of a building (right). Its unusual, almost square, shape and the absence of any associated structures, would be surprising features for a domestic settlement but quite appropriate for occasional communal use.

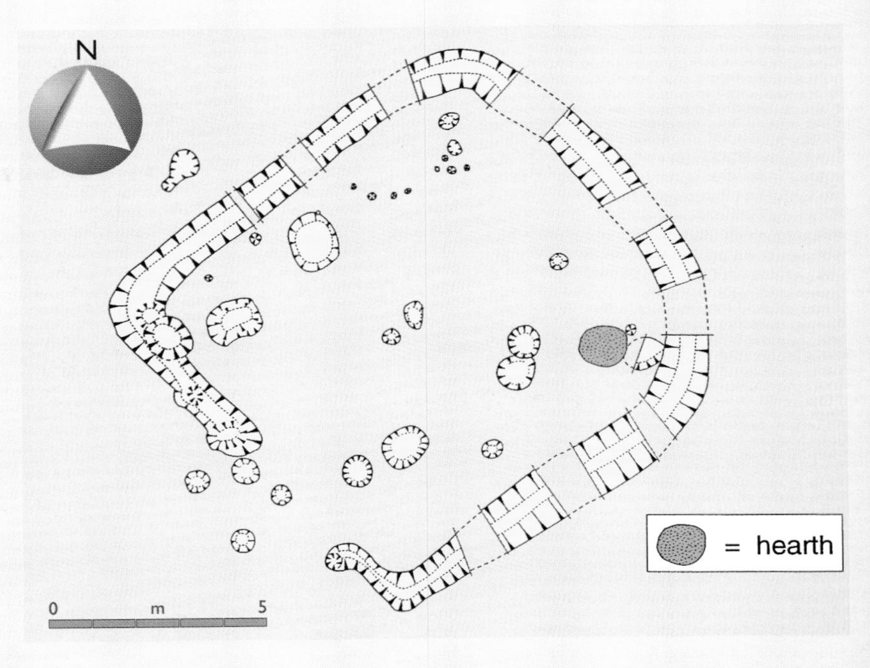

hung over Surrey throughout much of history, but nothing was as disastrous as the Black Death of 1348–50 when communities were shattered and farming methods changed as survivors shared the extra land and the feudal system began to collapse.

Large areas of open fields and commons were enclosed. Further enclosure occurred with the Dissolution of the Monasteries from 1530–40. The effect was to emphasise the sheer variety of the medieval Surrey landscape — its most interesting and characteristic feature.

In general the diet of the medieval peasants would have been largely dependent on local produce, and over much of England it is known to have

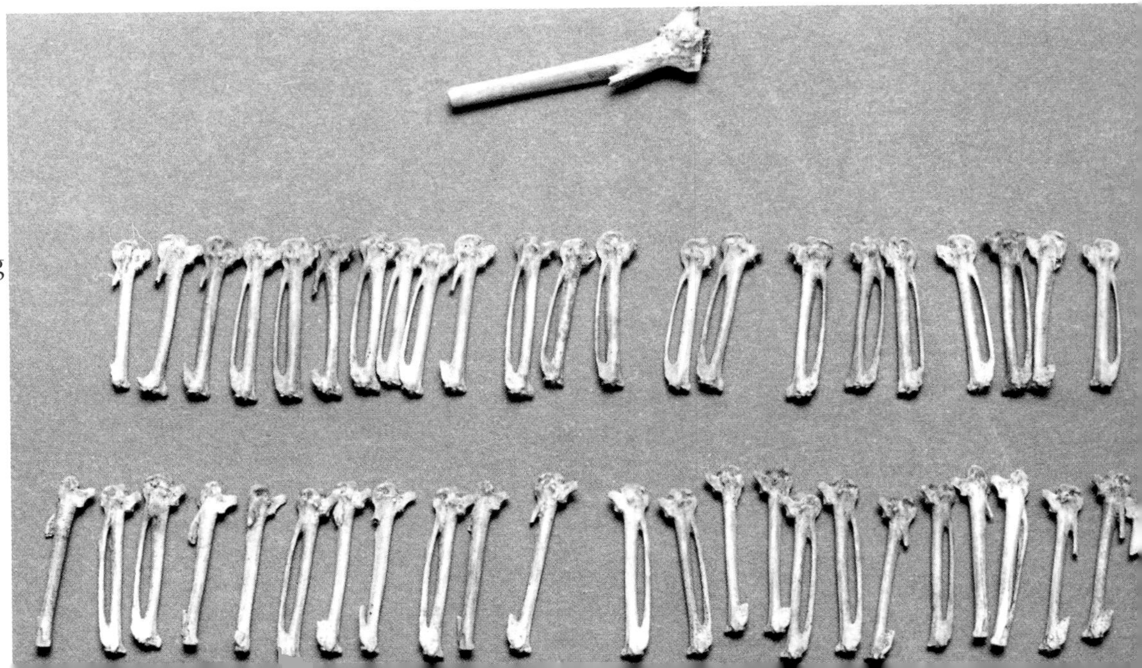

Some remains of Tudor feasting found at Little Pickle, Bletchingley. This is a small sample of the many carpometacarpals trimmed from the lower wings of birds. The main rows are of lapwing, woodcock and golden plover; while the single carpometacarpal above is of a heron, cut in trimming.

Hampton Court: the restored Tudor kitchen.

been based on grain and vegetables, with little meat or other protein. The Surrey peasants with their wide range of farming practices and an emphasis on pasturing of animals, may have been luckier. As yet, though, only in the towns and in the upper levels of society is a more varied diet proven by excavation. At Southwark bread, meat, fish and other foodstuffs, some of which were grown locally, were sold in its market and shops and in 1444 it was granted the right to hold a fair.

An examination of medieval rubbish pits in Southwark has shown some of the foods that were available. These include apples, plums, grapes, figs, blackberries, strawberries, elderberries, cabbage, carrots, black mustard, sorrel, peas, beans, barley, wheat, rye, oats, hazelnuts, pine nuts and opium poppies. Bones of cattle, sheep, goat, pig, rabbit, hare and domestic fowl were found along with oyster and mussel shells. The discovery of many bones of herring, smelt, eel, cod, plaice and dogfish confirm that fish formed an important part of the diet.

Until comparatively recently vast quantities of salt were required to preserve meat and fish throughout the winter. However, many manors and most religious houses possessed their own fish ponds, providing a superior supply for the more fortunate. These not only offered a reliable source of food but also provided for the numerous 'fish days' that were observed throughout the year and on which no flesh could be eaten.

Tudor times are synonymous with feasting, not only for the king and his great courtiers but even for minor gentry. At Little Pickle, Bletchingley, the remains of many birds, including lapwing, woodcock and golden plover have been found as evidence of a great feast, although it is uncertain who enjoyed it.

At Hampton Court, Henry VIII's household of some 1,200 people were fed from kitchens that had 50 rooms with 3,350 sq m (36,000 sq ft) of food production capacity.

The aristocratic Tudor diet was about 75 per cent meat and in one year the court ate more than 1,240 oxen, 8,200 sheep, 2,330 deer, 760 calves, 1,870 pigs and 53 wild boar. Some 300 barrels of ale and an almost equal quantity of wine were drunk in the same period.

THE EARLY MODERN PERIOD

The medieval pattern of fields and settlements largely endured until the start of agricultural improvements in the 17th century and the radical changes set in motion by the Industrial Revolution and the enclosure movements of the 18th and 19th centuries. New breeds of livestock, crops, farming practices and machines were then adopted and perfected.

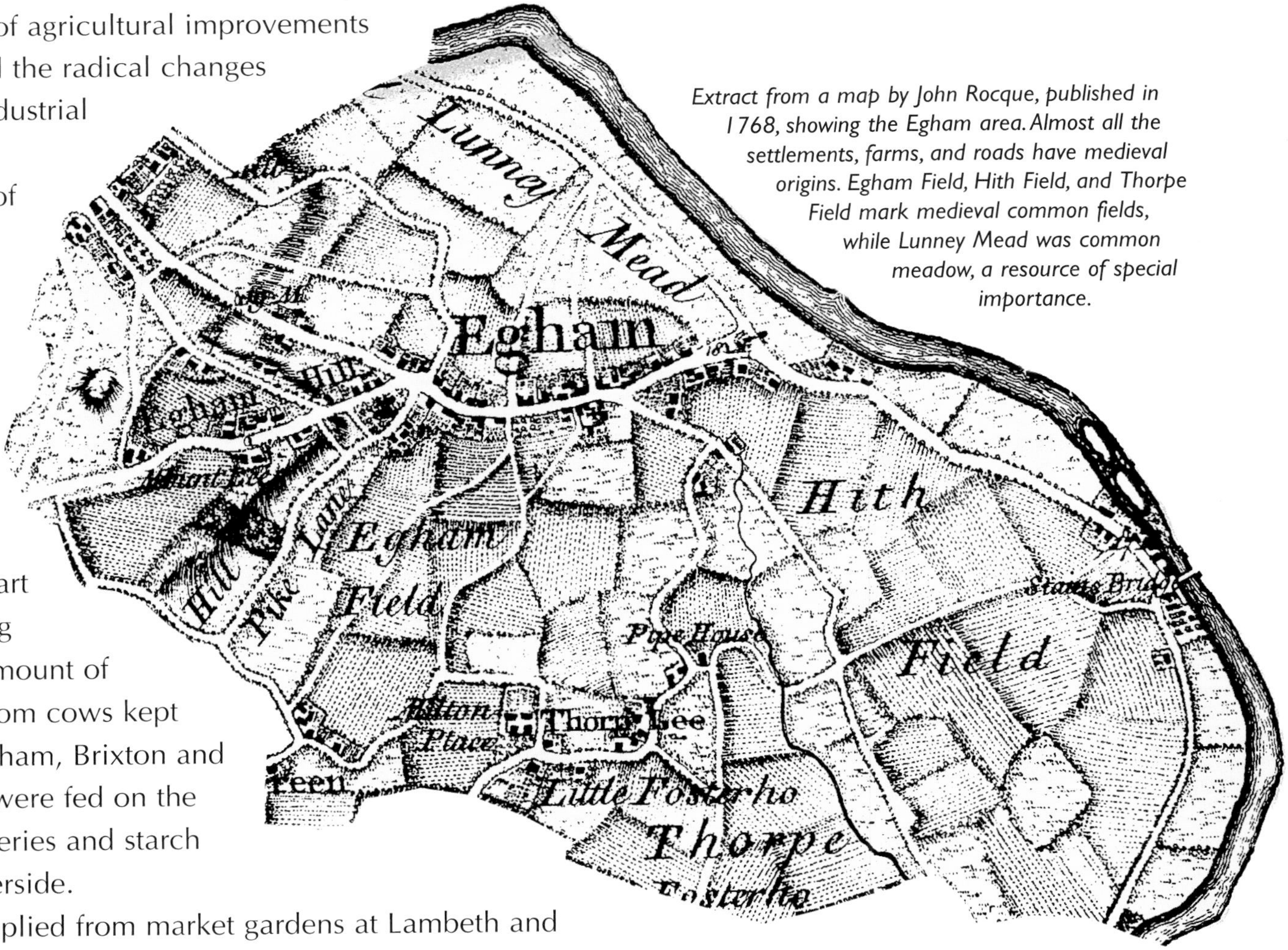

Extract from a map by John Rocque, published in 1768, showing the Egham area. Almost all the settlements, farms, and roads have medieval origins. Egham Field, Hith Field, and Thorpe Field mark medieval common fields, while Lunney Mead was common meadow, a resource of special importance.

By the early 18th century the northern part of Surrey was providing London with a huge amount of produce. Milk came from cows kept in places such as Peckham, Brixton and Camberwell and pigs were fed on the waste from corn distilleries and starch factories along the riverside.

Vegetables were supplied from market gardens at Lambeth and

Guildford's Corn Exchange of 1818 is a surprising and dramatic feature of the modern town.

Battersea where the soil was particularly fertile and the main crops were carrots, melons, lavender and asparagus sold in 'Battersea bundles'. Lavender was also produced in Mitcham where the cultivation of medicinal and aromatic herbs including peppermint was a major activity.

Nevertheless, as land was taken for building, the rural economy was slowly engulfed by an urban way of life which is starkly illustrated by the fact that while in 1851 agriculture had employed over a fifth of the population by 1901 this had dropped to less than a tenth.

A respite from this decline came with the First World War of 1914–18 when there was again huge demand for home-grown produce and the 'Dig for Victory' campaign of the Second World War 1939–45 saw allotments used for growing food.

Surrey has also played a large part in producing plants and flowers for pleasure, with some of the most influential and famous nurseries founded in an area centred on Woking but extending across the whole western area of the county. They introduced new species and distributed literally millions of plants not just throughout the British Isles but to the world at large.

Nowadays, with one machine capable of doing the work of countless farm workers, few people in Surrey work on the land although many have a close affinity with it. Reminders of the past are still present even in the centre of Guildford where, although the livestock market may no longer be held, the massive portico built in 1818 as the Corn Exchange still stands at Tunsgate.

4 RELIGION & RITUAL

Wedding festivities at Bermondsey, around 1570. What would survive from such events for archaeologists to find?

Visit any Surrey village or town and there is likely to be a church or some other focus of worship. One may hear the sound of bells drifting on the breeze, a bride and groom may be standing in a shower of confetti, mourners may be brushing away tears or a baby may be howling with the shock of baptism.

It is sobering to realise that all these sights and sounds are ephemeral, so the very fact of their having happened and the significance of their ritual may be lost to those wishing to understand our way of life in the distant future.

In the same way, when we wind back the clock of history, ritual,

SURREY'S HENGE

Surrey's closest rival to Stonehenge was a much smaller monument at Staines Road Farm, Shepperton, where, prior to gravel extraction, archaeologists found a ditch forming a circular enclosure (right).

Viewed from the centre, the entrance pointed directly to where the sun rises on Midsummer's Day and was 'guarded' by a human skeleton (below). This skeleton was of a 30–40 year old female who was buried in a tightly flexed (foetal) position. It seems that when her body was in an advanced state of decomposition parts of it were removed.

A second skeleton, the torso of a 25–30 year old, probably male, was also found, but one of the oddest discoveries was the deformed skull of a wolf and a lump of red ochre nearby. Similar finds have occurred at several other sites, giving credence to their involvement with ritual.

The ditch itself revealed objects deliberately placed as offerings, including flint arrowheads, antler picks and large parts of a Neolithic pot very similar to the Mortlake bowl, a complete pot recovered from the Thames.

Nobody can be certain of the exact purpose of henges but they could have had astronomical functions and were perhaps social and religious centres where sacrifices were made.

religion, and the loves, lives and deaths of everyday people, become the most difficult and challenging areas of the past to comprehend and interpret. Archaeologists may find burials, ritualistic sites, and the paraphernalia of worship, but what do they really mean?

In our modern world we know what causes thunder and lightning, rainbows, or an eclipse but, until recently, these were regarded as strange unexplained happenings that must have sent a cold shiver of fear through entire communities. They were seen as portents of famines, floods and other disasters; in short it was thought that the gods were angry!

As a consequence the gods were courted in the hope of ensuring good harvests and the general wellbeing of the population. Religion must, therefore, have permeated everyday life from the earliest of times. The evidence is diverse: there are the remains of monuments and shrines, and offerings to gods, as well as burial grounds and provision for the afterlife. The ritual of death varies from burying or burning bodies to leaving corpses so they are exposed to the elements or even casting them adrift in boats.

The gravel terraces above the floodplain of the Thames and Colne rivers were the scene of an important period of monumental construction in the Neolithic period. The cursus emphasises the importance of the link to the river which was a means of transport, a vital resource, and an object of worship.

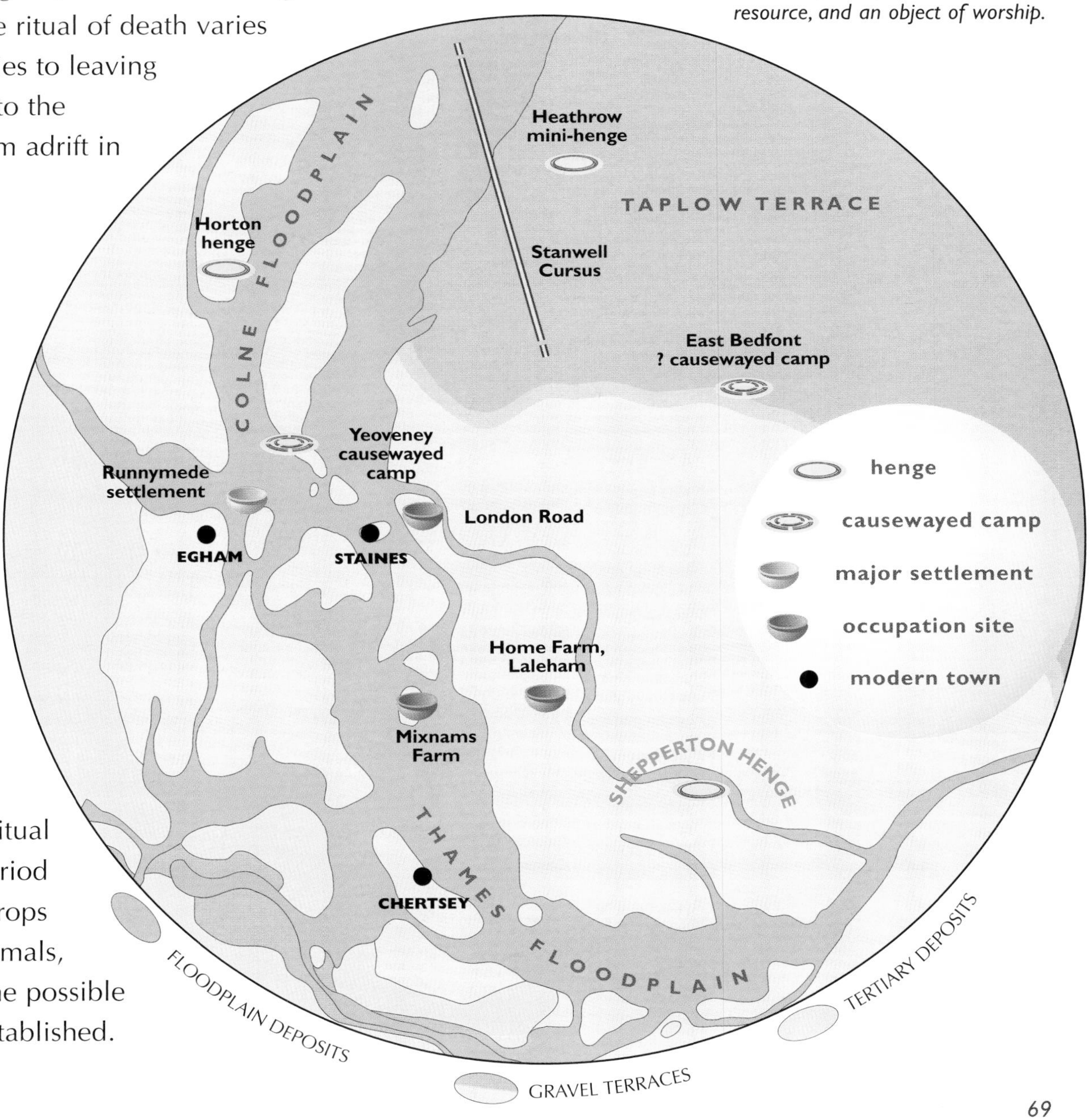

PREHISTORIC WORSHIP

For the Palaeolithic and Mesolithic periods the evidence in Surrey is scant but natural features, such as a particular tree or spring, are likely to have served as a focus for ritual and the gods to whom these early people paid homage were almost certainly those of the natural world.

The first real evidence of ritual comes from the Neolithic period when, with the planting of crops and the domestication of animals, permanent settlement became possible and territories were being established.

Reconstruction of a ceremony at a causewayed camp. The evidence from the similar site at Yeoveney Lodge, Staines, suggests that it was used for both ritual and domestic purposes.

Standing at the centre of Salisbury Plain in Wiltshire, Stonehenge is the most visible testament to the ingenuity of Late Neolithic and Early Bronze Age man but there are many other monuments that, although not so obvious, are just as mysterious.

Although Surrey has no stone circles, there are standing stones. Close to Pyrford Church is a sarsen block, incised with a cross, that was used as a boundary mark before the Norman Conquest but was probably originally a prehistoric standing stone, perhaps a relic of pagan worship transferred to Christian use.

Surrey's greatest Neolithic ritual finds have come from the north-west of the county where early settlers occupied the gravel terraces that had once been the floodplains of the rivers Colne and Thames. North-west of Staines, at Yeoveney Lodge, a causewayed camp was excavated in the early 1960s in advance of gravel extraction and produced both deliberately placed items and human remains. Originally constructed on a gravel spit but now to the north of the present course of the Thames, an enclosure had been formed by two roughly concentric ditches interrupted by solid causeways. Unsuitable for defence or for corralling cattle, and with little evidence of any permanent structures inside, causewayed camps are sometimes interpreted as being built on tribal boundaries, perhaps to act as neutral gathering places used at intervals to exchange goods or hold seasonal fairs.

Ritualistic uses are indicated by the fact that human remains are sometimes found spread across the enclosure. Rather gruesomely, the bodies from which they came were left in the open to be stripped of their flesh by wild animals and birds.

Whatever the original function of the enclosure at Yeoveney

Lodge, it is clear that building the 2.2ha (5½ acre) enclosure represented a considerable undertaking in terms of manpower and there is little doubt that it held a position of great local importance.

Within the ditches archaeologists found substantial amounts of earlier Neolithic pottery, flintwork and animal bone, while in the outer ditch lay part of a human forearm along with two skulls. One belonged to a female aged about 20 while the other was from a 25–30 year old male, who showed signs of healed head wounds, but had finally been killed by a further series of blows to the head.

Perhaps more than any other Neolithic discovery in Surrey, it is the Stanwell/Heathrow *cursus* that excites the imagination. At first interpreted from aerial photographs as a stretch of Roman road, it was some 21m (68ft) wide and extended north-north-west from Stanwell village for more than 4km (2½ miles).

The name *cursus* was coined by the 18th century antiquary William Stukeley, while recording an example at Stonehenge that he believed was intended for the celebration of funeral games and was similar in function to a Roman racetrack.

Rivalled in length only by a *cursus* in Dorset, which extends to more than 10km (6 miles), the long avenue of the Stanwell *cursus* was defined by two parallel ditches with an earthen bank between them.

Exposure of corpses, rather than burial, was widely practised in primitive societies. It was probably the rite for most people in Britain until the Christian era.

Excavation of one of the substantial ditches of the cursus at Stanwell.

The long barrow at Belas Knap, Gloucestershire, is one of the best preserved in the country. Sadly, Surrey's only known example, at Badshot Lea, was only recognised in the last stages of its destruction by gravel working.

It seems probable that the raised bank helped enhance the visibility of ceremonial processions along this route. Together with the other sites in the Thames Basin, it implies that the area had a very successful farming community and points to an organised hierarchical society with large numbers of people ready to work together.

The earthworks constructed by Neolithic people included burial mounds called long barrows and those buried within them were almost certainly 'special'. However, no human remains were found when the only known long barrow in Surrey was discovered at Badshot Lea near Farnham in 1936, probably because of damage by chalk quarrying. Two flat-bottomed parallel ditches were identified but the mound and much of the southern ditch had been destroyed before

The Bronze Age site at Church Lammas, Staines. The date of the site is proven by finds of pottery and flint, but there does not seem to have been regular domestic occupation. Like the Neolithic causewayed camp at nearby Yeoveney, the site is located right on the edge of a gravel 'island', with wet and marshy ground immediately beyond.

the barrow was recognised, while the excavated northern ditch contained a causeway towards its western end. From this evidence, the excavators estimated the original length of the barrow to have been around 43m (140ft).

Towards the end of the Neolithic period and in the Early Bronze Age, round barrows started to be used for burial and are found widely scattered across Surrey.

By the later Bronze Age cemeteries with cremated remains in pots were in use at places such as Oatlands Park, Weybridge, where the pots appear to originate from the Low Countries. Other cremated remains were simply buried in scoops in the ground.

It is rare to find Bronze Age ritual sites, yet at Church Lammas near Staines, close to the causewayed camp of Neolithic times, archaeologists discovered an unusual rectangular enclosure bounded by a ditch on three sides. Inside was a square ditched feature with an entrance in the middle of its eastern side while roughly in the middle of this was a large pit which may have contained a burial or was at the base of some sort of totem pole. Cremations were found within the outer enclosure. The site is unique and is, perhaps, the closest we have come to discovering a Bronze Age shrine.

Burial rites were not confined to humans. During the Bronze Age a horse received a ritual burial in a pit at Runnymede Bridge and from the Iron Age animal deposits and sacrifices together with ritual shafts and wells have been found.

In excavating the Iron Age settlements at Tongham Nurseries a waterhole was discovered and various items, that would not normally have been discarded, were present, including a log ladder and a number of perfectly usable loomweights suggesting that ritual deposition was being practised. Other material included the remains of a structure, which may suggest the finds relate to rites of commencement and termination, as often associated with building work.

A rare example of an Iron Age log ladder found preserved under water in this well at Tongham.

ROUND BARROWS

There are various types of round barrow, but most of those in Surrey are bowl barrows with a simple mound of earth surrounded by a ditch. They tend to survive best on heathland, because elsewhere over three millennia of settlement and farming have removed all remains above ground. Most are isolated but there are small nucleated groups including a triple mound on Crooksbury Common, Elstead, a quadruple one on West End Common at Chobham and dispersed groups such as the three barrows on Horsell Common near Woking (below).

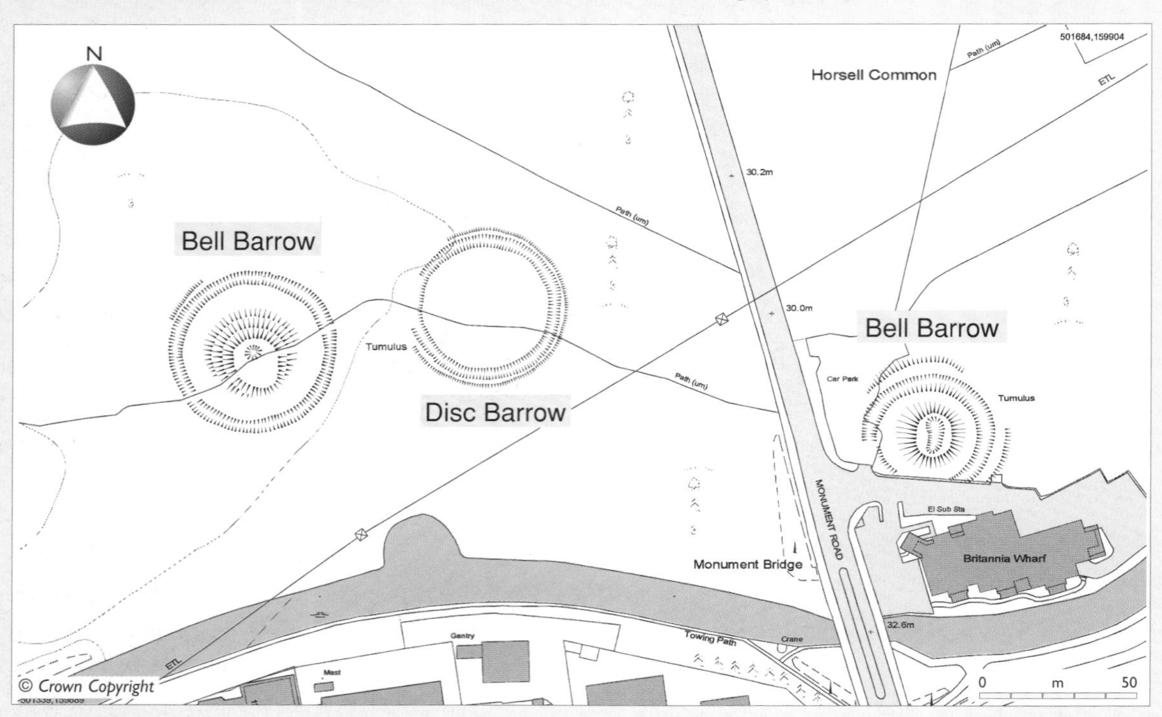

The Horsell examples are interesting since they are types more usually found in the vicinity of Stonehenge. Two are bell barrows (below right), the mounds each encircled by a level 'berm' or flat area between the mound and the enclosing ditch while the third is a disc barrow (below centre) with only a small 'tump' within the circular bank and ditch. Bell barrows covered the cremated remains of male tribal leaders while disc barrows were for high-status females.

Some barrows contain fairly complex structures and at Deerleap Wood, Wotton, the central turf core was partially covered by a stone capping and encased in a sand mound. At Gostrode Farm, Chiddingfold, a circular 'hearth' of stone was laid on the ground and a burial, accompanied by a pottery vessel and brass fragments, perhaps of a clasp or buckle, probably lay on the floor. In other barrows stone 'cists' enclosed pots containing cremated human bones, although this is often only a token relic, gathered from the funeral pyre . These cremation urns are also found on their own and show considerable variety, as the selection of Surrey examples illustrated (below left) shows. The largest of them is about 50cm (1½ft) high.

THE SACRED RIVER

Rivers not only served as territorial boundaries and highways but were venerated as sacred places. In Surrey none was more important than the Thames and the river, along with its former channels and tributaries, has been a rich source of finds including many items of great beauty and value that span a period from the Neolithic to the 10th century AD and perhaps beyond.

These include some of the most famous British prehistoric objects, including pieces of Iron Age parade ornament such as the Wandsworth shield boss, the Battersea shield and the Waterloo Bridge helmet (above), which has often been mistakenly associated with Viking warriors. Exceptional preservation also makes important more everyday items such as an Iron Age dagger, complete with its bronze-bound sheath, from the Thames at Mortlake (above right).

The process of gravel extraction has produced many such items from silted-up former channels of the Thames. In 1985, at Abbey Meads, near Chertsey, the only Iron Age shield in Europe made entirely of bronze was recovered by a drag line operator (above left). It was probably 'parade ground' armour, rather than for practical use on the battlefield. Other items found included a skull, a Neolithic polished stone axe and a 'pestle', the actual purpose of which is uncertain.

From the gravel of the Shepperton Ranges (left) came a spectacular Iron Age sword with bronze scabbard mounts (below) as well as a bronze bowl probably dating from Roman times. At the same site a Roman hoard of five pewter plates was brought up in the bucket of a mechanical excavator.

Viewed in isolation, the presence of these items could have various explanations such as accidental loss, battles at river crossings, and erosion from nearby settlements. Seen in context, there is little doubt that they had been deliberately placed in the river or marshland as offerings. At Shepperton Ranges the tight grouping of the finds made during gravel extraction seems to suggest that a particular place was venerated over a very long period of time.

A question that remains unanswered is whether items were offered on their own or were associated with rites of burial and were set adrift with a body, for the river has yielded many human skulls.

ROMAN AND CELTIC

Many of the Iron Age (Celtic) religious traditions continued after the conquest. For example at Ewell around ten Roman shafts were found to contain deposits laid down in an orderly manner. One had successive layers of large animal bones, distinctive Samian pottery ware, soil containing organic matter with fruit pips and stones, cock and hare bones, and the skeleton of a large dog. Others had similar items including human bone and iron nails and may have been seen as linking daily life to the underworld.

An unusual rectangular building found at Heathrow was associated with an Iron Age settlement and seems to be a shrine or temple. Its shape anticipates that of the Romano-Celtic temples which emerged soon after.

Iron Age people worshipped their gods at shrines, such as that revealed by excavations at Heathrow, but they also venerated sacred places in natural settings, like woods, glades, springs and streams.

The Romans normally tolerated the religions of the people they conquered and the Roman and native gods were worshipped

Artist's impression of the Romano-Celtic temple at Farley Heath.

alongside one another. As a result the distinctive Romano-Celtic temple developed. Surrey's three known sites at Titsey, Farley Heath and Wanborough all had temples of similar design and seem to have been relatively remote, standing on marginal land but close to a road.

Such sites may have developed a role as centres for fairs or markets and one can imagine festive open-air gatherings and processions taking place both on particular occasions and in times of trouble.

The square chamber or *cella* at the centre of the temple served as the sanctuary of the deity or deities and might have contained ritual objects and representations of the gods sacred to the site. Around this was a veranda while the building itself stood in a sacred enclosure or *temenos*.

The Romano-Celtic temple at Titsey appears to have been one of the shortest-lived temples of the time in Britain. Very similar in plan, but in use for much longer, the temple at Farley Heath was probably built soon after the Roman Conquest. Some way from any established settlement, it was reached via a spur road off Stane

*The site of the temple at Farley Heath is marked on the ground, and the visitor can appreciate it in something like its original, remote position. It was set within a substantial enclosure (*temenos*), providing plenty of room for pilgrims, or for visitors to the fairs that were probably held there.*

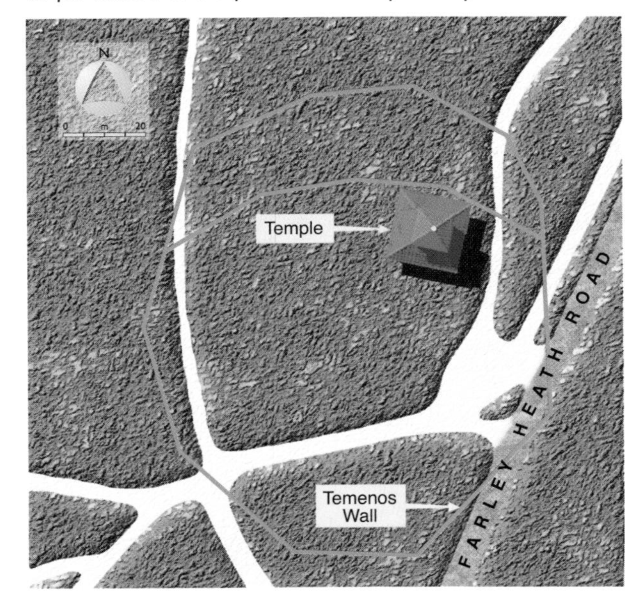

Bronze binding for a priest's sceptre, as drawn after its discovery in the 1840s at Farley Heath.

Street and stood in an elevated position so must have been visible to approaching worshippers across the heathland.

Farley Heath revealed many interesting finds including a priest's crown and a sceptre binding decorated with figures. These have been interpreted as depicting a number of Celtic deities, including one associated with the Roman Jupiter, and possibly indicating an association of the temple with ironworking. Small enamelled model stools from the site were probably used for ritual and the huge number of coins, brooches, beads and other objects discovered must have been offerings by worshippers.

Not all sites can be as easily explained as those where temples once stood. Discoveries in advance of sand extraction at Betchworth hint at religious activities and imply an amazing continuity of use from the early Neolithic period to the 1st century AD.

Excavations revealed many pieces of Grooved Ware — a type of Neolithic pottery that is frequently associated with ritual and prestigious sites — ovens, pits, a Late Bronze Age track, and small ditched enclosures of early Roman date. All this conjures up images of the past: festive gatherings in a sacred grove and the heady scent of bread drifting on the air as it was baked in the ovens.

From the eastern part of their Empire, the Romans brought cults such as those of Mithras and Isis. At Chiddingfold a bronze ibis figure was found hinting at the worship of Isis and at Southwark a flagon was discovered apparently from a temple to the same god.

Excavations at Rapsley villa, near Ewhurst, led to the discovery of

WANBOROUGH TEMPLES

So nearly wrecked by the vandalism of treasure seekers, the site at Wanborough not only yielded spectacular secrets — two temples and indications of religious activity dating from pre-Roman times until perhaps AD 350 — but ultimately also contributed to the reform of the law of Treasure Trove.

Looting had begun before the first major excavations could start in September 1985 but as the archaeologists worked on the sticky London Clay they discovered the flint foundations of a square 2nd century Romano-Celtic temple. The only evidence for the rest of the building came from rubble: flint, blocks of Lower and Upper Greensand and roof tiles. It seems that the walls were of flint with stone quoins and that the roof had been tiled.

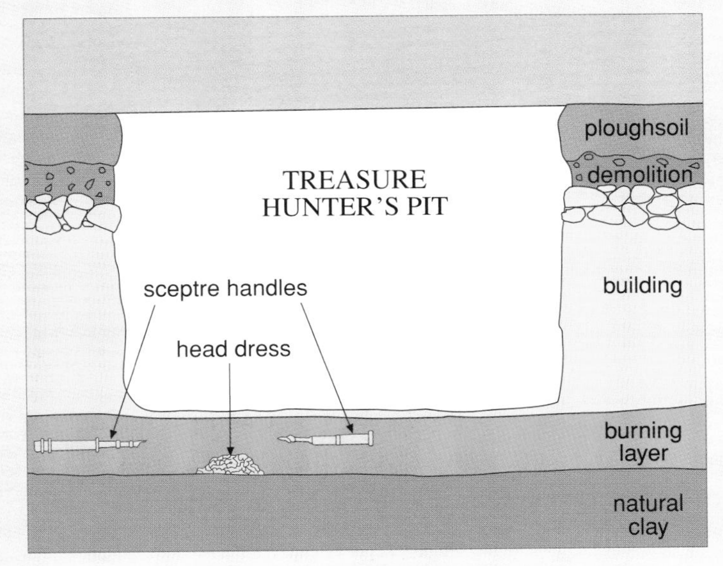

Meticulous work brought to light priestly regalia (right) including chain head-dresses and, amazingly, one complete sceptre along with fifteen other sceptre handles. The wooden staff of the sceptre was sheathed with a continuous bronze strip so that when first made it would have resembled a magnificent 'golden' rod. The layer from which these finds came had only just survived the damage by treasure hunters (left).

The chain head-dresses would probably have been attached to a leather skull-cap. Out of eight known British examples, five are from Surrey and four of those are from Wanborough. Unusually, three have a bronze disc at their top with a wheel mounted upon it, standing vertically. A Celtic sun symbol, the wheel was representative of a god who was equated with Jupiter, with specifically solar attributes.

Digging revealed what was thought to be the apse of another building nearby. More than twelve years were to pass until, in the summer of 1999, this area was fully excavated to reveal a second stone temple which had collapsed in the 1st century AD (right). Much of the earlier work was thus put into historical context and the regalia are now believed to have belonged to priests of the first temple.

This temple closely mirrored a circular temple found at Hayling Island near Chichester that dates from the early stages of Roman occupation and both temples stand in the tribal territory of the Atrebates.

Much of the massive hoard of gold, silver and bronze coins discovered at the Wanborough temple site was lost to treasure seekers, but those coins that were saved date from both Iron Age and Roman times and there is evidence from elsewhere to suggest that temples acted as banks.

ROMAN CEMETERIES

The cemeteries of Roman towns are generally found outside the settlement, alongside one of the major approach roads. South-east of Southwark, next to Watling Street, excavations have revealed a fascinating burial site of the 2nd and 3rd century AD. The reconstruction drawing shows (right) a small building, perhaps a temple, with a walled cemetery (11m by 9m; 36ft by 29½ft) next to it. At its centre the base of what may have been a monumental tomb was discovered. A second building is interpreted as a mausoleum, a very large above-ground tomb, and beyond this is another walled cemetery, also with evidence for a central feature. A number of burials were found both within the walls and outside them, the latter including three chalk-lined graves. There is no sign of intercutting burials and this suggests that there was continuity of ownership of private burial plots by wealthy families over several generations.

Inhumation was the most common rite, with some 25 examples. One of the five cremations was a *bustum*, a rectangular pit dug beneath the funeral pyre to aid burning, which was then used for burial of the cremated remains. With the human bone were the ingredients for a meal, including pine cones, dates, figs, almonds, a cereal, and chicken, as well as lamps and pottery vessels which may have been used for incense burning. A *bustum* has also been found at Staines, containing glass vessels and Samian pottery (far left), and a pair of enamelled brooches (left). Here too the cemetery lay outside the Roman town, along the main London to Silchester road.

a pot, thought to be linked with the worship of Cybele, as well as terracotta pine cones used in a number of Eastern religious ceremonies.

From this evidence it is clear that when Christianity became the dominant religion of the later Roman Empire it did not appear in a religious vacuum. Yet, in Surrey, the only Christian material to have been found is half a jet finger ring discovered at Bagshot, probably dating from the late Roman period.

While no Iron Age burials have been revealed in the county, the burial rite of cremation reappeared during the Romano-British transition and there were early Roman cemeteries at Charterhouse, Haslemere and Tilford, where cremation remains were found in urns. In the later Roman period bodies were buried and, at Beddington Church, both a stone and a lead sarcophagus survive.

Apart from these, outside of Southwark, there are frustratingly few burials or grave goods from the Roman period but an unusual insight into the way of life of that time is provided by a group of bone gaming counters found with a burial near Ewell. At a site at London Road, Staines, seventeen hobnails from a pair of boots lay around the feet of a Roman skeleton and a further unidentified iron object was found beneath the right fibula.

Part of a late Roman ring from Bagshot with the Christian rho-cross symbol.

Gaming counters (left) found with a Roman burial at Ewell. One reads: RIIMI V, which may mean 'I shall pay back 5 denarii'. The counters are shown (below) on a board constructed for an alignment game, such as Nine Men's Morris.

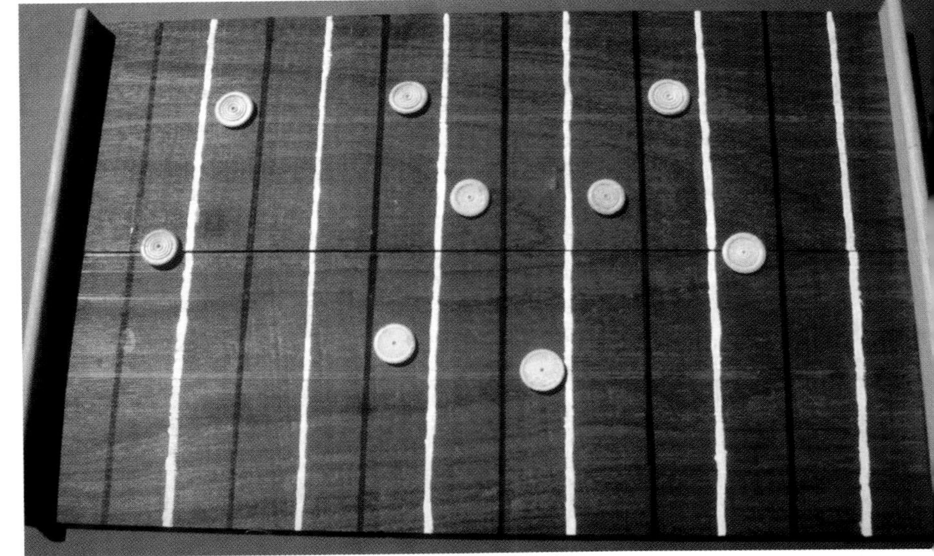

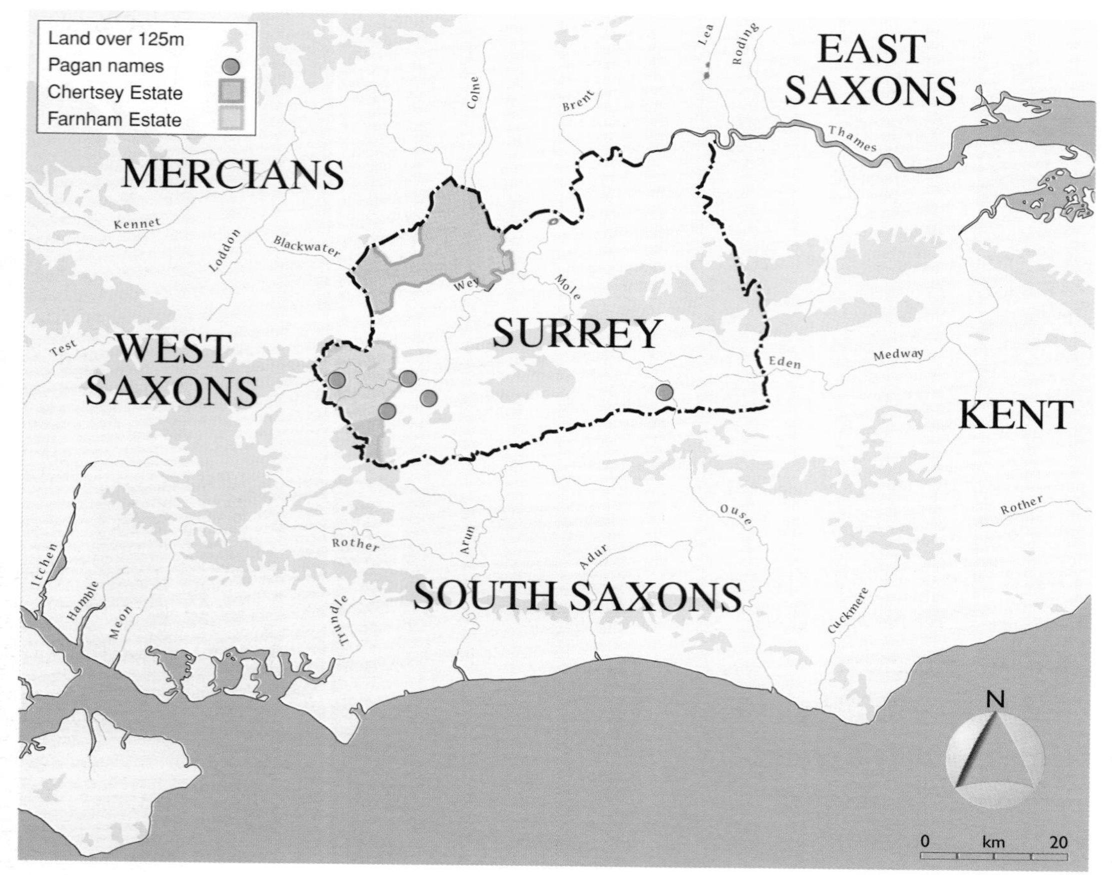

Saxon kingdoms around AD 700. Surrey began as an independent kingdom, but came under the control of Kent, then Mercia, and, in the 9th century, Wessex (the West Saxon kingdom). By this time the kingdoms were nominally Christian, but earlier religions still persisted, perhaps especially in south-west Surrey. The monastic estate at Farnham may have been granted around 685 with the intention of converting the remaining pagans.

THE ESTABLISHMENT OF CHRISTIANITY

The Saxons, Angles and Jutes who arrived in England from the early 5th century were pagan and tantalising evidence for their religion and sacred sites lies in place names. The pagan god Thunor is remembered in Thursley and at Thunderfield in Horley, while the Harow of Peper Harow is from Old English *hearg*, a temple. Another reference is Willey, near Farnham, derived from *weoh*, an idol or shrine, and *leah*, a clearing.

Both burial and cremation were practised and discoveries at Shepperton, made in the 19th century, may indicate that the rites were peculiar to individual communities. At one location a warrior burial and other inhumations were found while at another, cremations were discovered in elaborate and well-made urns.

In the later 6th and early 7th centuries barrows, similar to those of the Bronze Age, were raised over the burials of military leaders or men of high social status. At Beddington,

19th century water-colours showing a 5th century Saxon cremation urn (right) and a 6th century Saxon warrior burial (below) found at Shepperton.

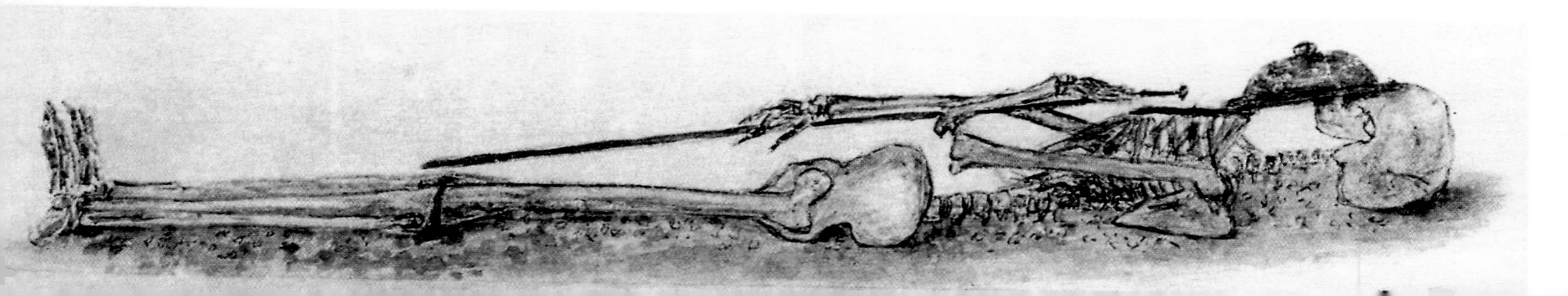

ASHTEAD CEMETERY

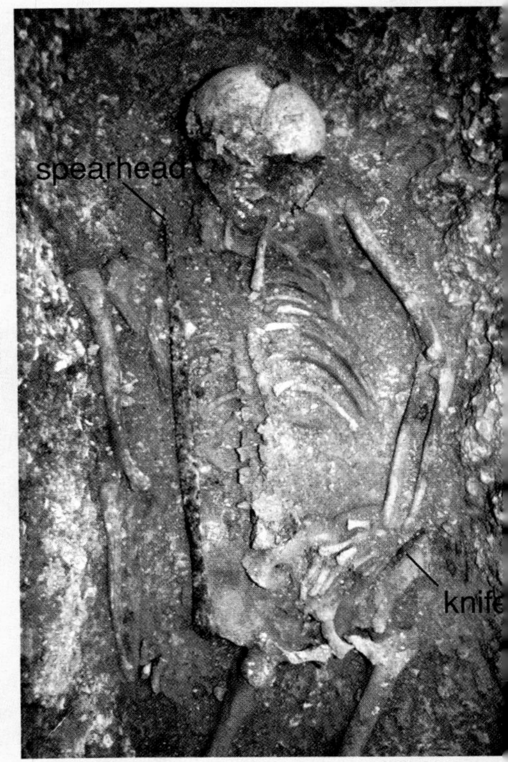

The building of Esso House at Ashtead in 1985 provided archaeologists with the chance to excavate a site that had first revealed Saxon bones nearly 60 years earlier. The initial dig produced a total of about 35 burials and further examination of the site in 1989 revealed twelve more. Dating from the late 6th and early 7th centuries both normal early Saxon burials and those of execution victims were found.

The normal burials were generally laid out east–west and the graves were probably marked on the surface by a slight mound, while the bodies either lay on their backs or in a foetal position.

Three of the burials were accompanied by socketed iron spearheads (the illustrated example (right) was of exceptional size) while others had iron knives. Perhaps the spearheads signified a warrior class but, since every adult Saxon male was potentially a warrior, they are more likely to be an indicator of status.

The skeleton of a girl aged about seven, possibly the daughter of the local lord, was found with a necklace which included amethysts and glass beads that were manufactured in the Rhineland (below). The artist's impression shows her funeral (above).

However, the generally modest quantity and character of the grave goods from the cemetery and an absence of cremation burial suggests the influence of Christianity. What may seem surprising is that at least four of the adults were over 45 years old. The cemetery itself has been interpreted as being a fairly small burial ground serving just a few families.

The execution victims were probably buried in the late Saxon or early Norman periods and in some cases later burials disturbed earlier ones. The burials themselves are shallow and the bodies, some of which had their hands tied behind their backs in preparation for hanging, are placed casually.

A wooden cup with bronze bindings which accompanied a Saxon burial beneath a barrow at Farthing Down.

A Viking sword found near Chertsey. It is incised with the maker's name, ULFBERIT, between two crosses.

Farthing Down near Croydon, and Gally Hills near Banstead, males of exceptional stature 1.93–1.98m (6ft 4in–6ft 6in) were discovered. Comparatively rich grave goods have also been found, including a wooden cup, with fine bronze bindings, discovered at Farthing Down and a hanging bowl and shield boss from Gally Hills.

The conversion of the Saxons to Christianity began when St Augustine landed at Thanet in 597 and converted King Ethelbert. One hundred years later the process was largely complete and important ecclesiastical estates were established with Minster churches at places such as Chertsey and Farnham.

The English kingdoms had been Christian for about two centuries when the Vikings began to arrive in force, reintroducing paganism. Yet their invasions served only as a brief interruption to the progress of Christianity, especially in Surrey where they made no permanent settlements.

A Viking sword recovered from a former channel of the Thames near Chertsey almost certainly represents a revival of the older tradition of making offerings in the river and bears the name of the Rhenish master craftsman who made it. More than a hundred swords with his name have been found, from Ireland to Scandinavia and across northern Europe to Russia. Another similar sword from Shepperton was bent when found, probably as part of a ritual 'killing' of the object.

Preaching crosses, where a missionary had his station, sometimes preceded the building of a church and may be represented by late

Saxon fragments found at Kingston and Reigate. Only two surviving Surrey churches are thought to be truly Saxon in origin: St Peter's, Godalming and St Mary's, Guildford.

The early Minster churches such as those at Chertsey and Farnham served very large territories. More local provision of churches often began when a lord built a private church next to his manor house, as happened at Wisley, Walton on the Hill, and Titsey. Between the 11th and 13th centuries, the modern parish system was developed in order to provide churches for all manors.

The tower of St Mary's, Guildford has projecting stone strips, which may have been used to imitate timber framing. They are characteristic of late Saxon building. Other parts of the church are of many different dates.

MONKS AND FRIARS

The first of Surrey's monasteries was at Chertsey and, by the time of their Dissolution in the 16th century, several orders had long-established houses in the county. All these orders had been founded in mainland Europe and their teachings had taken many years to reach England.

The Cluniac Order built Bermondsey Abbey in 1082. The far more numerous Cistercians founded their first church in Britain at Waverley in 1128 on the low-lying land where the northern branch of the River Wey loops lazily through a secluded valley. As revealed by excavation, the first church truly reflected the austerity of the early Cistercian philosophy but was totally replaced by a second, much grander, although still severe, building begun in 1203.

The 13th century vaulted interior of part of the refectory range of Waverley Abbey.

CHERTSEY ABBEY

Bishop Earconwald, later Bishop of London, established the monastery at Chertsey around 666. Soon afterwards it was endowed with extensive lands by Frithuwold the 'King' of Surrey which, at that time, was a subordinate Kingdom of Mercia. The church was sacked by the Vikings in about 871, the Abbot and 90 monks were killed, the buildings burned and the lands laid waste. Later in the 10th century it was refounded as a Benedictine Abbey. By Domesday the possessions of Chertsey Abbey were considerable and in 1110 a major rebuilding was begun under Abbot Hugh.

The Abbey site was excavated in 1855, in 1861 and again in 1954, and although very little evidence could be found of pre-Conquest buildings, it was possible to reconstruct the later precinct in some detail. A photograph taken in 1855 (below left) shows the tombs of Abbots buried in the Chapter House of the Abbey and may be the world's oldest photograph of an archaeological excavation. The photographic record of the 1861 work is an almost equally remarkable survival. The photograph (below right) shows the 13th century Lady Chapel, with a stone seat and columns.

In the 13th century the Abbey was responsible for the production of the finest pictorial tiles made in medieval England. The example (above) shows Richard I fighting Saladin — the most famous combat of the Crusades.

As expected of a Christian site, the burials were generally without grave goods yet one coffin, formed of a solid block of Purbeck marble hollowed out to receive the body, contained a metal chalice and paten placed at the left shoulder. These objects indicate that the occupant was a priest.

THE DOMINICAN FRIARY AT GUILDFORD

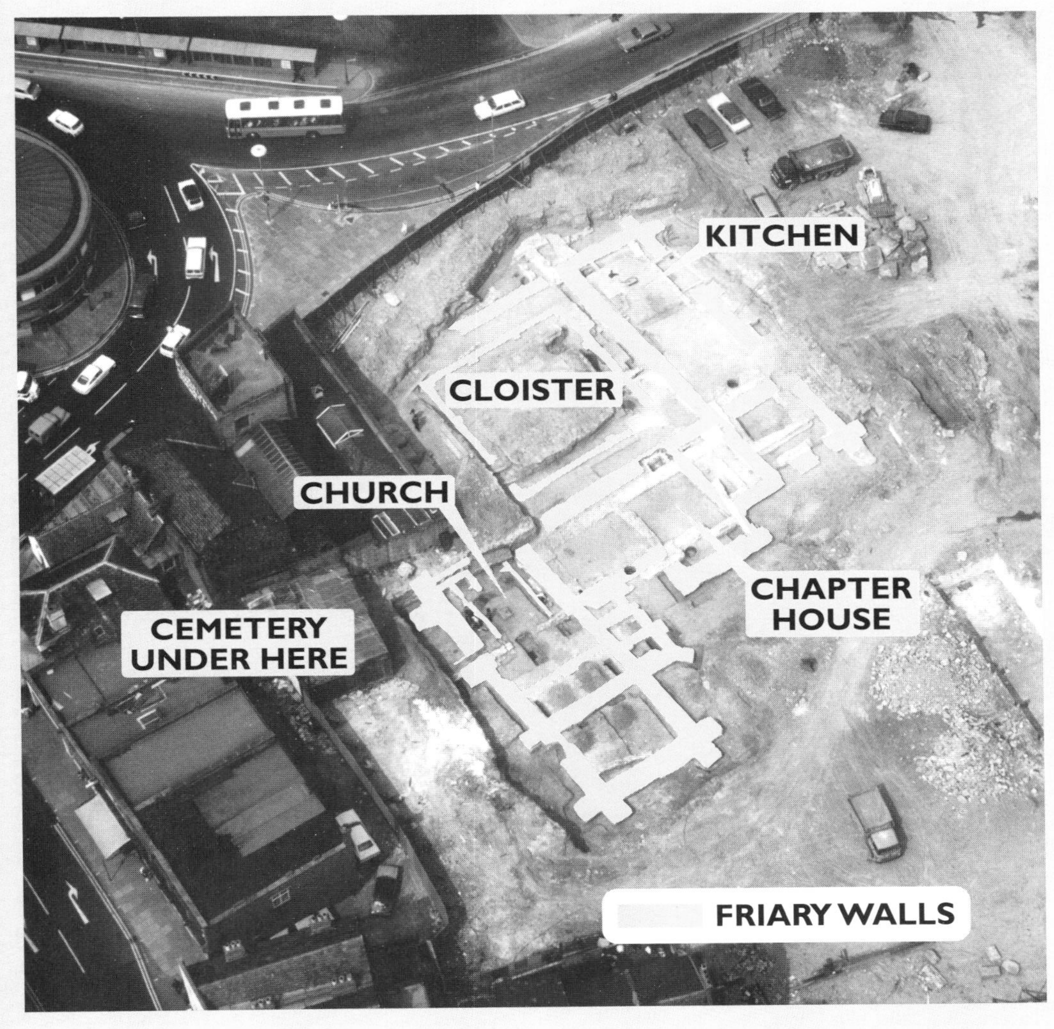

Essentially urban, friars were enthusiastic preachers, collecting alms and building churches with spacious naves. In Guildford, lying on the site of a lost friary, the name of the Friary Meux brewery preserved their memory.

Today, in the hustle and bustle of The Friary shopping centre, it is hard to believe that one is standing on a religious site but, before the present development, two large-scale excavations were carried out in 1974 and 1978. As a result many artefacts and a large number of medieval burials were discovered along with the plan of the Dominican Friary, founded in 1275, which is clearly shown in an aerial photograph (left).

In size it exceeded the parish churches of Guildford but, for a friary, it was small. The nave and churchyard yielded some 65 formal interments while scattered bones showed there had been at least 113 other burials. Most were single burials, as is normal in Christian cemeteries, but an unusual multiple burial (below right) may be the result of plague (the white tags mark the position of bronze fastenings for shrouds or other clothing).

Most intriguing was the examination of a lead coffin contained in a tomb made from neatly cut chalk blocks that lay in the nave. The coffin had a green painted border and cross and incised in the lead was the name 'Margareta Daubeny'.

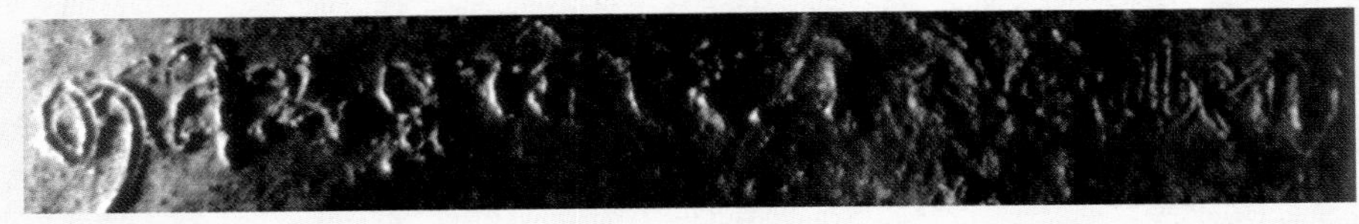

The skeleton inside was that of a young woman aged about twenty who had been wrapped in a good quality shroud. Small fragments of probably foetal bone suggested that she died in childbirth. The only Daubenys known in the Guildford area in medieval times were a West Country family.

The Carthusians built at Sheen, while the Augustinian order had five houses in the county, Southwark and Merton being the most important. The remains of their priory at Newark still stand gaunt in a pastoral landscape beside the waters of the Wey near Ripley.

MODERN DEVELOPMENTS

Throughout the Middle Ages the church and the feasts, festivals and rites associated with it played a huge part in everyday life. Following the Dissolution of the Monasteries in Henry VIII's reign

These late 12th century wall paintings at Chaldon Church were covered by whitewash, under Puritan influence, in the 17th century. The upper part represents the salvation of souls, while the lower part shows the torments of the damned.

THE END OF THE LINE

In Victorian London available space in the old parochial burial grounds was fast running out. Thus was born the idea of forming commercial companies with the intention of building new cemeteries outside the capital.

The London Necropolis and National Mausoleum Company purchased some 800ha (2,000 acres) close to Woking at Brookwood. The first 'coffin train' steamed out of the company's private station at Waterloo in November 1854; it carried both mourners and coffins. Anglicans travelled in a different portion of the train to Roman Catholics and Nonconformists and the latter disembarked within the cemetery grounds at the north station while the former continued to the south station.

Brookwood Cemetery is still in use and huge trees stand sentinel shading avenues where chapels, mausolea and simple graves are testament to a Victorian ideal.

many ecclesiastical buildings were laid waste. Some were quarried for their materials, with the stones of Chertsey Abbey being used to build Henry's palace at Oatlands and stone from Waverley employed in the building of Loseley House.

While humble parish churches have survived, many were greatly altered by the Puritans and underwent enthusiastic 'restoration' in Victorian times. In the graveyards, increasing prosperity is reflected in more elaborate monuments to the dead and headstones, not just of stone but of iron and wood have been set up over the centuries.

The Shah Jehan Mosque, Woking, was built for Dr Gottlieb Leitner, who founded a centre for oriental studies in the town.

The reform movement of the 19th century saw the establishment of large municipal cemeteries. Worship became more varied with an increasing mix of cultures and faiths, and in Woking the onion dome and minarets of the Shah Jehan Mosque catch the sun. Built in 1889, it is the oldest mosque in Britain.

In the 20th century, war on a scale never before envisaged entered people's everyday lives. The Flanders' poppy came to symbolise the loss of loved ones and, before memorials and cenotaphs across the county, young and old alike pay their respects in a ritual moment: a placing of a wreath, a solemn bowing of the head, a silence lest we forget.

5 POWER & PROTECTION

Accounts of marching armies, conquest and heroic conflict litter the pages of history but, through the centuries, the underlying cause of such actions is invariably the protection or extension of territorial rights. Control and response are aspects of all our lives whether it is to do with where we build a garden fence or where a nation has its borders. Ethnic, religious and social groups are likewise affected and a clash of cultures can be profoundly damaging be it on the world stage or in the school playground.

Frequently the resulting scars and disharmony lead to rapid changes in relationships and attitudes both in individuals and whole populations. In the widest sense they can have a direct effect on trade and industry and, in the long term, profoundly influence language, customs and culture.

PREHISTORIC SOCIETIES

In the earliest period a single band of between ten and forty hunter gatherers may have exploited the area that is now Surrey and would possibly have been part of a larger 'tribal' unit with which they would have exchanged raw materials and 'marriage' partners.

Archaeological evidence can reveal little of such transitory happenings. It is assumed that, because of their low numbers, these

The War of the Worlds. *This 1814 painting shows a Saxon chief standing over a defeated Roman and was intended to symbolise territorial conquest. The effects of the change were, though, far more pervasive since the Saxon world was pagan and illiterate, and replaced a highly organised Christian empire.*

nomadic Mesolithic people lived fairly peacefully but they would, no doubt, have protected their 'families' from both other hunters and wild animals while 'territorial' disputes must have been about access to fundamental resources.

With the establishment of farming practices, which spread from the Continent or grew up through indigenous development during the Neolithic period, cultures merged and opportunities for trade increased. Change possibly came rapidly, as it has countless times since, through conquest or an influx of 'foreigners' due to war or travel.

A dramatic insight into the organisation of Neolithic society is given by the grouping of large communal monuments such as the causewayed camp and the *cursus* in the Stanwell area.

Even with the earthmovers of today's mechanised age, these collective undertakings are hardly trifling, yet it is difficult to appreciate the enormous and concerted effort involved to achieve them some 5,000 years ago. Along with a common will, a loose tribal identity must have prevailed with either an elected leader or one with absolute power who had the ability to control the territory

BATTLE AXES

Bronze Age battle axes, or shaft-hole axes as they are sometimes known, probably served as much for ceremonial adornment and prestige as for use in battle. Their design differs from that of other simpler axes and must have involved considerable work since, as well as general shaping and sharpening, a hole had to be made through the stone to take the wooden shaft. Battle axes are generally made from imported stone, and the illustrated examples, which were both recovered from the Thames are made from stone from the highland areas of Britain. They are contemporary with the earliest bronze axes, which replaced the common types of flint and stone axes for all practical purposes, leaving only these highly prized objects to be made from stone.

and bring together the large numbers of people required.

There is little other sign of land or settlement enclosure and, with the population still small and resources comparatively plentiful, territorial disputes and conflict presumably did not loom large.

The emergence of metalworking in Britain has often been associated with the arrival from the Continent of the 'Beaker people' — a name derived from a specific type of pottery beaker found with their burials.

Beaker artefacts, comprising a pot and a series of barbed-and-tanged flint arrowheads from Ham, and a flint dagger from the Thames at Barn Elms.

Stone battle axes, flint daggers, and barbed-and-tanged arrowheads also occur in Beaker grave groups and this had led in the past to the suggestion that these people formed an aristocratic warrior elite.

Such objects are however found much more widely than just in Beaker burials and it is now generally believed that the arrival of metalworking in Britain was the result of new cultural influences rather than an invasion of new people.

This seems likely because, despite the new technology and objects, the organisation of society seems to be little changed from the Neolithic period. During the earlier Bronze Age communities seem to have remained very mobile and people moved within an unenclosed, lightly farmed landscape.

With the Middle Bronze Age comes evidence of a dramatic change. Regular field systems, perhaps mostly related to control of animal pastures, were created over a large area and it seems likely that this change occurred as an expanding population put pressure on the availability of good land. In effect, competition for resources now developed and this must have involved a change in the

BRONZE AGE ENCLOSURES

In the earlier part of the Bronze Age there is little hard evidence for enclosures with a military purpose. The emergence of these features in the later Bronze Age is probably a reflection of increased pressure on resources due to a rising population, soil exhaustion and climatic deterioration.

Requiring considerable investment of labour in their construction, some new sites in the later Bronze Age served as regional centres of power which presumably not only functioned as defensive sites but also reflected the prestige of the occupants. At Queen Mary's Hospital, Carshalton, a circular enclosure 150m (492ft) across bounded by a ditch and bank was discovered in the early part of the 20th century. The reconstruction (above) shows the fort looking down on a patchwork of fields in the valley of the River Wandle. A very similar site was discovered more recently by aerial photography at Nore Hill, Chelsham (left).

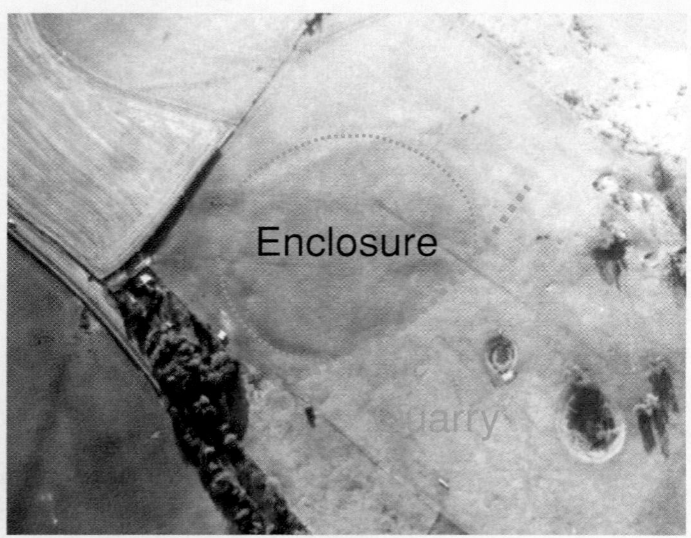

It is assumed that ramparts stood within the ditch and that settlement occurred inside the enclosure while the area outside was used for activities such as metalworking. Finds of metalwork in the Carshalton area point to it being a zone of comparative wealth and power so it may have had a pivotal role.

structure of society.

A sufficiently organised social structure to ensure the maintenance of the land and food supplies was now required. Distinct tribal areas no doubt emerged linked to enclosed settlements where stock, people and goods could be protected

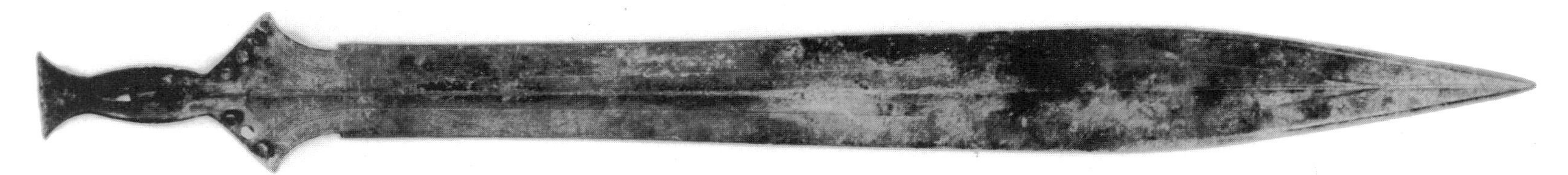

Bronze cavalry sword of the 7th century BC recovered from the River Thames, near Mortlake.

against animals and also military attack.

Clear indications of a military elite come from impressive cavalry swords and shields which also reveal the intimidating nature of the horse-riding Bronze Age warriors.

The clear division between the many hoards of metalwork so far discovered in Surrey gives direct evidence of tribal or regional territories and varying local customs or economic conditions during the Late Bronze Age. Clearly falling into two groups, the hoards have differences in their size, contents and the condition of the objects they contain.

Dominant and occurring in three distinct areas — Thames-side districts, the eastern North Downs and central-southern Surrey — are the hoards that included obsolete, worn out or miscast objects and frequently copper ingots.

In contrast the hoards found in south-west Surrey are small with just two to five objects and they contain either axes or spearheads which are generally complete and give the impression of being personal armouries or tool-kits.

It is not clear how exactly such territories relate to the defensive strongholds that have been found in upland situations, such as Nore Hill, Chelsham, as well as next to the Thames at Runnymede.

Here, where the M25 crosses the Thames near Egham, archaeologists discovered a defensible Bronze Age trading post. Structural evidence and debris indicate that the site of some 2ha (5 acres) appears to have been intensively occupied and perhaps acted as a regional centre of power. Exploiting the natural advantage of being on an island between two main streams of the

Bronze shield of about 900 BC found in a gravel pit at Chertsey.

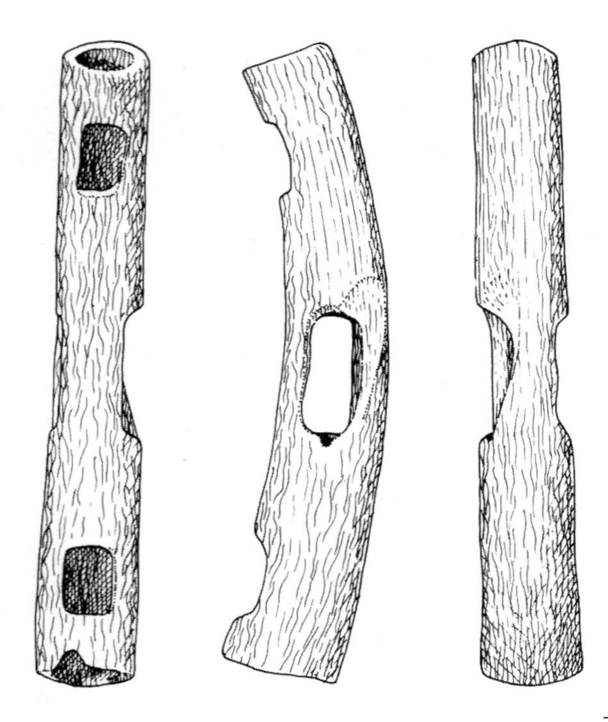

A drawing of some antler cheek pieces from Runnymede Bridge, Egham. The reconstruction shows how they worked with leather straps to form a bridle.

Thames, a pile-driven palisade was constructed along the ancient riverbank. The site also revealed evidence of the importance of the horse since a concentration of antler cheek pieces was found which would once have been attached to horse bridles.

Successors to the defended upland sites at Queen Mary's Hospital and Nore Hill were built at St George's Hill, Weybridge, and at St Ann's Hill, Chertsey. Both have some evidence for their initial development in the 8th or 9th century BC, but seem to have been used in different ways. A number of investigations at St George's Hill have failed to discover evidence for regular occupation, while, in contrast, testing of a small area at St Ann's Hill suggested it may have been intensively occupied throughout the Iron Age. The contrast shows a difference in daily use but the sites may, nevertheless, have shared a more fundamental purpose as symbols of the power and prestige of their local communities.

They offered commanding views over the well-populated valleys of the Thames and Wey and formed part of a more extensive system that included forts at Caesar's Camp, Wimbledon, and those at Mucking in Essex which overlooked the Thames estuary.

HASCOMBE HILLFORT

Hillforts dating from the Iron Age have been excavated on the edge of the Weald at Hascombe and at Holmbury, Felday and Anstiebury near Dorking, as well as in the east of the county, at Dry Hill Camp, Lingfield. Caesar's Camp, Farnham, stood on what is now the Surrey/Hampshire border and nearby was Hillbury, Puttenham, while the only hillfort on the chalk was at War Coppice Camp, Caterham.

Defended by banks, ditches and palisades, the exact role served by hillforts is still unclear and appears to vary depending on their location. Some were densely occupied while others, like those on the greensand of Surrey's southern hills, are much less so and were perhaps stock enclosures or refuges in times of crisis and would have controlled seasonal grazing lands and access to the Weald.

Pottery and coins found during the excavation of the hillfort at Hascombe point to a period of use from around 200 to 50 BC. While Anstiebury and Holmbury hillforts had two ramparts, Hascombe had only one complete rampart and part of a second, enclosing an area of about 2.5ha (6 acres). The diagrammatic reconstruction (above, looking south) shows how this second rampart may have been used to protect the entrance, which was sited to face the only gentle slope away from the fort. Stone was used to protect the out-turned banks at the entrance where there were front and rear wooden gates (left). The presence of clay sling-bullets and pebbles used as sling stones (below) suggests that a fusillade of these projectiles would have been used in defence.

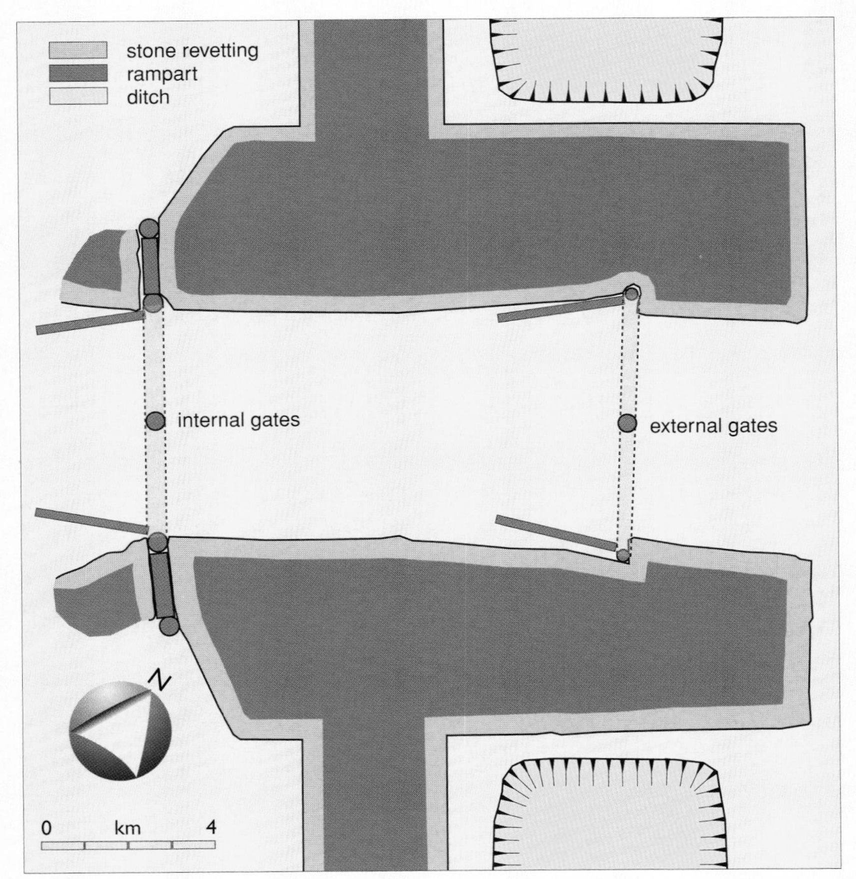

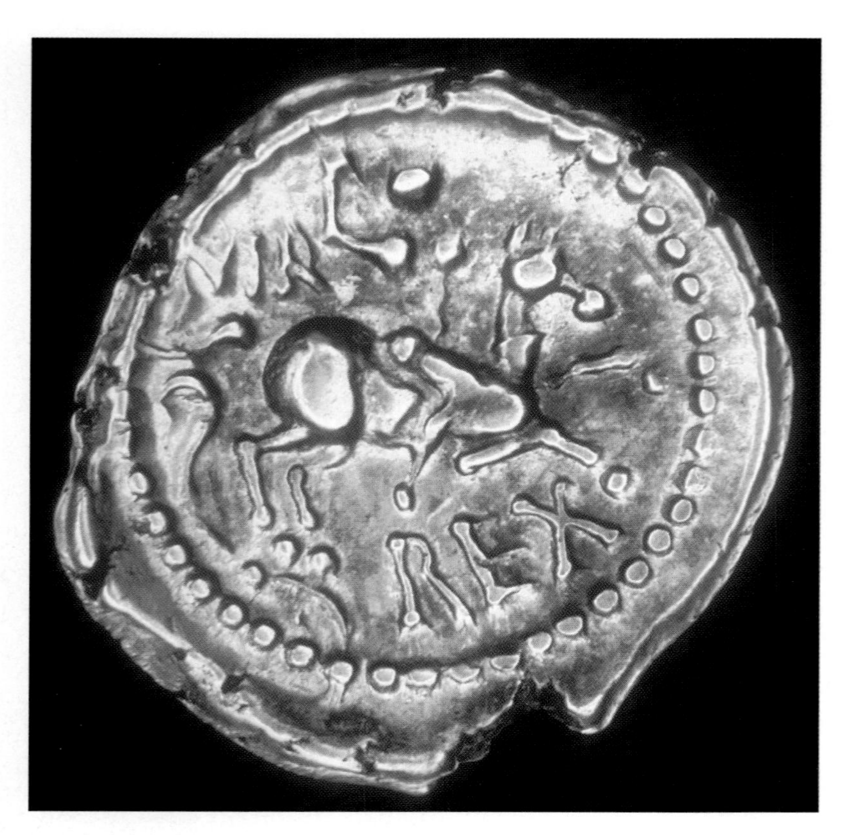

Gold coin issued by Verica, king of the Atrebates, in the period prior to the Claudian invasion. It shows a mounted warrior, and gives his title 'REX', which means king in Latin. The coin was found at Wanborough.

The expansion of the hillfort system in the Thames Valley coincided with changes in prehistoric societies right across Europe as technological advancement resulted in bronze giving way to iron. In Britain, the transition was under way by the 7th century BC, although the use of iron to make weapons and tools was probably caused not only by economic or technological factors but also by a much more general upheaval as the whole framework of society changed.

The Late Bronze and Early Iron Age periods are likely to have seen a close economic relationship between rivers, hillforts and settlements. A river was used to transport goods, animals and people; the hillforts served multiple functions and were collecting and redistribution centres, as well as being places where manufacture could take place, while farmsteads related to both and were used for agriculture and possibly other forms of production.

The introduction of coinage during the Iron Age provides the first positive clues to the tribal territories of the time since coins found by archaeologists bear the names of the rulers of the principal tribes of the area which is now Surrey.

During much of the Iron Age Surrey faced northwards, being influenced by the Thames Valley as part of an eastern region. Towards the end of the period considerable re-grouping of people occurred and it became associated with Sussex, Hampshire and parts of Berkshire — the territory of the tribe known as the Atrebates.

Evidence for warriors and weaponry includes items such as the Battersea and Chertsey shields, but they appear to be parade armour, which was never used in battle, since a sword would easily have penetrated the thin metal.

ROMAN RULE

Regarded as a distant barbaric place by Rome, south-east Britain first fell under Roman influence with Caesar's campaigns in 55 and 54 BC. Archaeological evidence for these campaigns has proved hard to identify and there is no direct sign of his presence in Surrey.

Soon after, however, tribal warfare appears to have resulted in the area coming under the control of either the Trinovantes or the Catuvellauni as they drove the Atrebates to the south, into their heartland around what is now Chichester.

As a result Verica, king of the Atrebates, eventually fled to Rome to appeal for help and it was this, and the fact that Claudius was in need of military prestige at home, that was the spur behind the Roman invasion of AD 43.

The Atrebates' alliance with Rome points to the possibility of the landing having occurred in the Chichester area. The South-East was quickly pacified with the eleven so-called kings surrendering to Claudius's forces once they could be certain that the invasion had been successful and protection would be offered.

Led by Aulus Plautius, the Roman army is believed to have passed through Surrey on its way to a crossing point on the Thames somewhere close to London prior to its great victory near Camulodunum, now Colchester.

London was established by the Romans around AD 50 and, just as now, would have exerted its influence over the surrounding areas. This, for example, resulted in the establishment of Southwark

A fully-equipped Roman legionary soldier of the 1st century AD.

Excavation at Southwark revealed a building that may have been a military guild headquarters, within which 27 fragments of a stone inscription were recovered. Soldiers of the guild may have erected the inscription, with their names listed under the cohort to which they belonged, in honour of the Emperor Severus (AD 193–211).

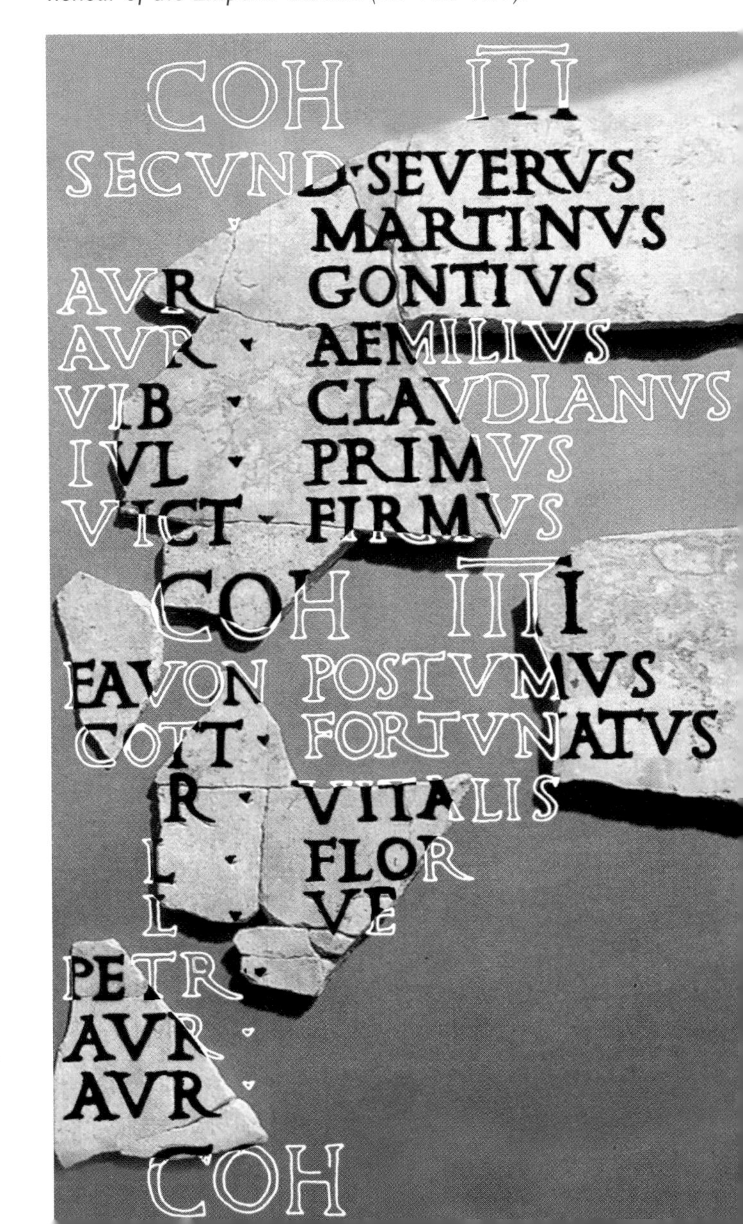

on the southern side of the Thames, where military finds include part of a *lorica segmentata*, a type of flexible body armour.

It is becoming increasingly clear that the South-East became a peaceful part of the Roman Empire very soon after the Conquest. It seems that there was only the briefest military presence and this has left little trace. While it is unclear how the South-East was controlled in the early years after the Conquest, it is likely that Surrey became part of a client kingdom as it quickly settled down as part of the new province of Britannia. The ruler of this kingdom may have been Togidubnus, who is believed to have built the palace at Fishbourne.

Finds of military objects are very few in number. They include a horse fitting or cavalry pendant from Westcott, near Dorking, and an early cavalry helmet cheek piece from Staines. It used to be thought that there was a fort at Staines, but excavation has revealed no evidence for it, so the helmet probably belonged to a soldier temporarily billeted there.

The bronze-plated iron cheek piece of a cavalry helmet was only identified, with the aid of X-rays, some time after it was excavated at Staines. It is shown here with a reconstruction of an almost complete helmet found near Koblenz, Germany.

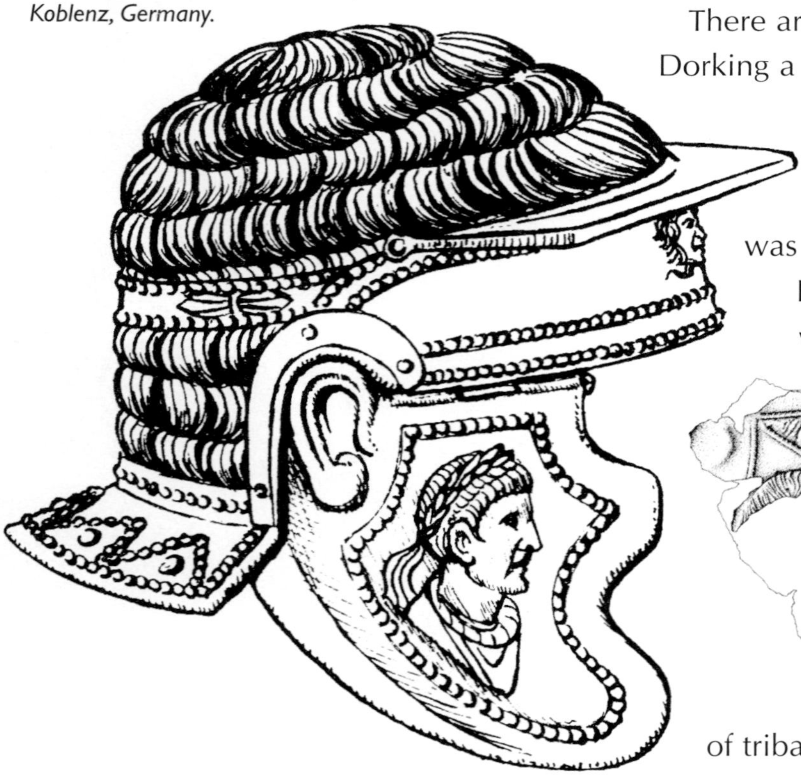

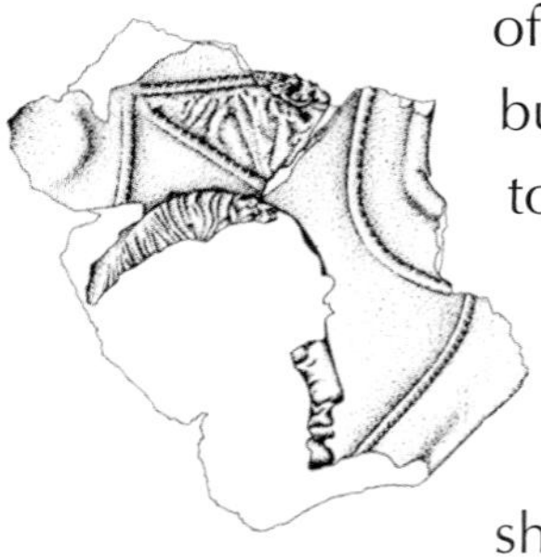

There are no certain Roman military earthworks although west of Dorking a cropmark seen from the air is suggestive of a Roman marching camp, implying campaigning along the Tillingbourne valley. Another possible military site is at Petters Sports Field, Egham, where a harness mount was found associated with a military-type ditch. Both sites could relate to the Boudiccan revolt of AD 61 when there was widespread destruction by fire and much of London was reduced to ashes, leaving a burnt layer still very evident to archaeologists today. Indeed, at Southwark Samian pottery has been discovered that had been blackened by the fire.

The client kingdom of Togidubnus was short lived, and soon absorbed into the Roman province, with its territory being split between a number of tribal areas. This probably led to the administration of the

Surrey area being largely under the control of the Atrebates, whose capital was Silchester. The Cantiaci, with their chief town at Canterbury, occupied the area of modern Kent. The Roman boundary may have corresponded to the later border between the two counties, although it has also been suggested that it may have respected a pre-existing tribal boundary lying somewhere between the rivers Wey and Mole. In the Weald, especially to the south in Sussex, the military ran the iron industry.

The hillforts fell into disuse and the towns were open and undefended as the long period of peace under the Roman Empire resulted in something of a golden age.

THE COMING OF THE SAXONS

In the later 4th and early 5th centuries the Roman Empire was in turmoil largely as a result of attacks by barbarian tribes. Britain was initially less affected than other provinces but came under threat from the incursions of Pict, Saxon and Irish raiders in the latter part of the 4th century.

Our historical sources tell us that, in the early 5th century, the last rulers of Roman Britain recruited Saxon troops to help defend the province against these threats, including those from their own kinsmen.

This may not have been such a radical move as is

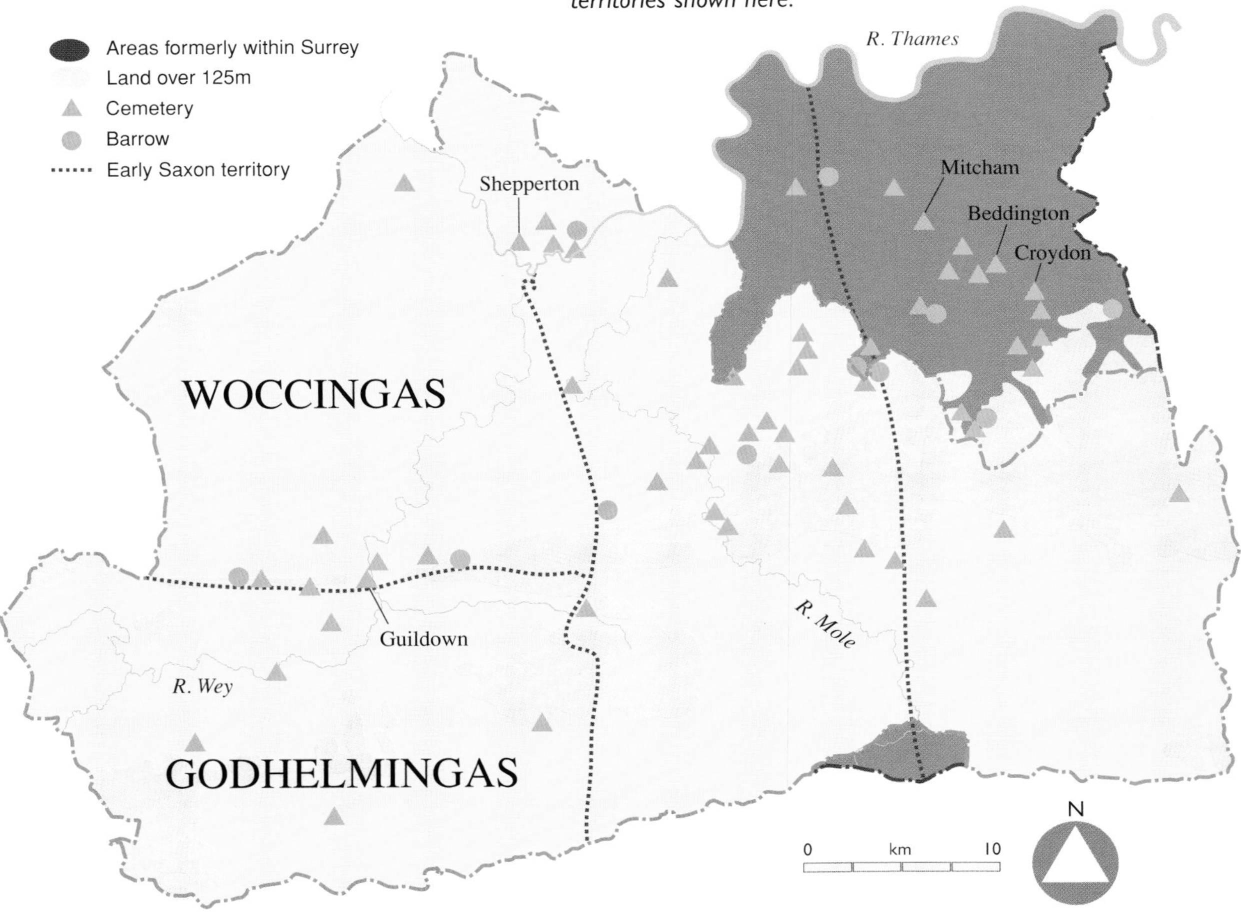

Early Saxon Surrey. The 5th century cemeteries are named. The other, later, cemeteries reveal Saxon customs spreading along the dip slope of the North Downs, but not, apparently much more widely. Surrey may have developed as a kingdom by combining the four earlier territories shown here.

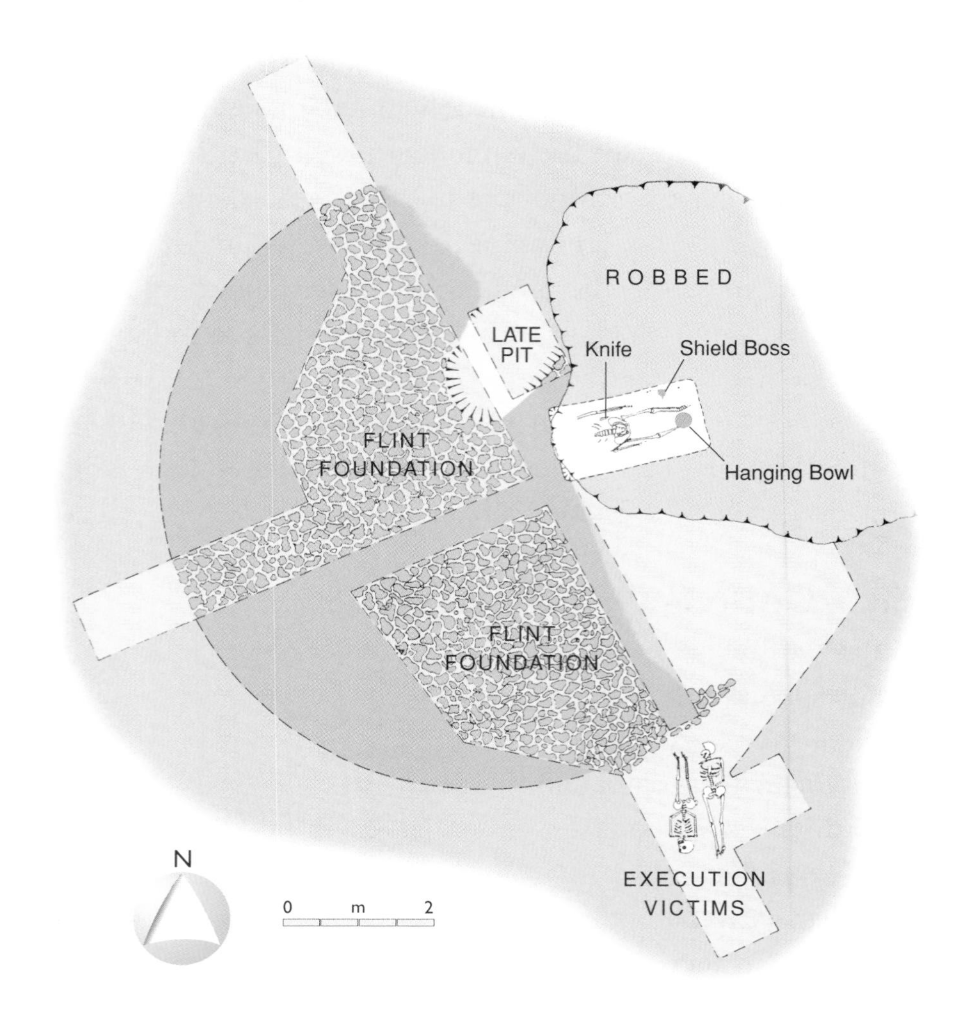

Saxon burials at Gally Hills, Banstead. The skeleton under the barrow had been damaged but enough survived to show that it was of a man, 1.93m (6ft 4ins) tall and well built, about 30 years old, who was buried wearing a twill cloak and soft leather boots. The bronze hanging bowl (below) had been filled with crab apples. On the margins of the barrow are the late Saxon burials of people hanged on the gallows which stood on top of the barrow, and from which the name Gally Hills comes.

often thought. The popular image of the Roman army is one of smart and austere uniformed soldiers, but by the late Roman period most of the regular troops were recruited from outside the Empire, and often fought under their own leaders. These troops may have inhabited settlements that formed a ring around Roman London to guard the major approach roads. The evidence for this having happened is the discovery of 5th century Saxon cemeteries including Mucking, north of the Thames in Essex, Shepperton to the west, and Croydon and Mitcham to the south.

The Anglo-Saxon Chronicle and other sources tell the story of the conquest of Britannia by the Saxons, and the gradual emergence of numerous kingdoms.

One of these was Surrey, which existed with something like its medieval boundaries by the later 7th century.

A bank visible on either side of the A25 near Westerham still marks the eastern boundary established soon after AD 568 but the southern boundary was possibly less clearly defined since much of the Weald was open pasture land. Evidence from charters points to the boundary to the west being largely established by 685–8 while, to the north, the obvious boundary was the River Thames.

Forming a frontier zone, especially in the 7th and 8th centuries, the Surrey area was variously under the control of Wessex, Mercia and Kent. The evidence for warfare is less obvious in the archaeological record. Cemeteries show that Saxons were established along the dip slope of the North Downs as far as Guildford by the end of the 6th century, but it looks as if elsewhere the native population remained in place. At this local level peaceful co-existence is more obvious than conflict.

The latest burials in this Saxon tradition date to around 700 and are of high-status males interred under barrows, such as that at Gally Hills, Banstead. The barrows appear on the boundaries of territories, perhaps the components from which Surrey was created. The dead men had been the rulers of these miniature kingdoms.

Towards the end of the Anglo Saxon period a network of *burhs* — fortified places or refuges — was established in response to Danish incursions which are graphically illustrated by the sacking of Chertsey Abbey in the 9th century.

The *burhs* included both towns and purely military sites. One, probably established by Alfred the Great some time after 880, occupied a strong defensive position away from major route-ways in the area above the bridge at Eashing.

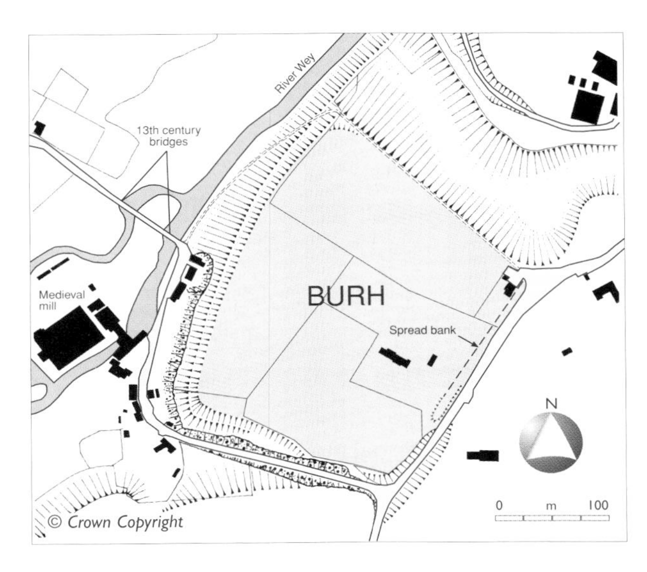

The location of the 9th century burh *at Eashing, occupying a natural strong point, above a river cliff and overlooking the Wey.*

A coin of Cnut (popularly known as King Canute, who ruled England from 1016 to 1035), which was minted in Guildford. Mints were always sited in towns in late Saxon England.

LAW AND ORDER

Lawlessness was probably no worse than in earlier times but the late Saxon kings were tough and the law ferocious with many offences such as theft, robbery, rustling, counterfeiting as well as murder frequently attracting the death penalty.

Tried and sentenced at local courts by two judges, one representing the king and the other the church, it is suggested that in each generation possibly as many as two people in every hundred were executed.

For those condemned, death was frequently by hanging. The gallows may have been a crudely constructed affair, as in the artist's impression (below right) of a late Saxon execution. The body was often left swinging in the wind as a gruesome warning to others before being finally cut down from the creaking gibbet to be buried in a shallow unmarked grave, often shared with fellow criminals. At Staines an execution cemetery included a grave with three criminals, hands tied behind their backs, buried at the same time (below left).

Surrey has at least four execution cemeteries and, since execution frequently took place at the edge of territories, a location also favoured for pagan burials, it is not surprising that many former graves are overlaid by the bodies of those condemned, as is the case at Guildown near Guildford (above). Here the execution burials are mostly grouped around a barrow, on which the gallows tree would have stood. The barrow had been raised over a pagan burial.

This appears to have been intended to act purely as a fort without any commercial importance and rapidly went out of use, to be replaced in the 10th century by the defended commercial centre which is now Guildford. This was part of a general reorganisation of the defences of Wessex in which forts at a distance from settlement centres were abandoned. Guildford was effectively a new town, and the aim was to provide the security it needed to foster its economic development.

Guildford's existence at this time is attested to by silver pennies of Edward the Martyr (975–9) and later kings, while the Domesday Book records that 'King William has 75 sites whereon dwell 175 men', making it a considerable town of some 750 people in 1086.

Southwark was the second of Surrey's two *burhs* and is listed as *Suthringa geweorche* or 'the defensive work of the men of Surrey' in the Burghal Hidage. This remarkable Anglo-Saxon document assesses the town at 1,000 hides of land, each of which was to provide one man for its defences. This was calculated from a formula which said that each pole (about a 5m/16½ft length) of man-made defences — boundaries covered by

Late Saxon burhs *(fortified places: Eashing was replaced by Guildford, so is omitted from this map) and Norman castles in south-east England. The routes, to either side of and avoiding the Weald, taken by William's army are also shown.*

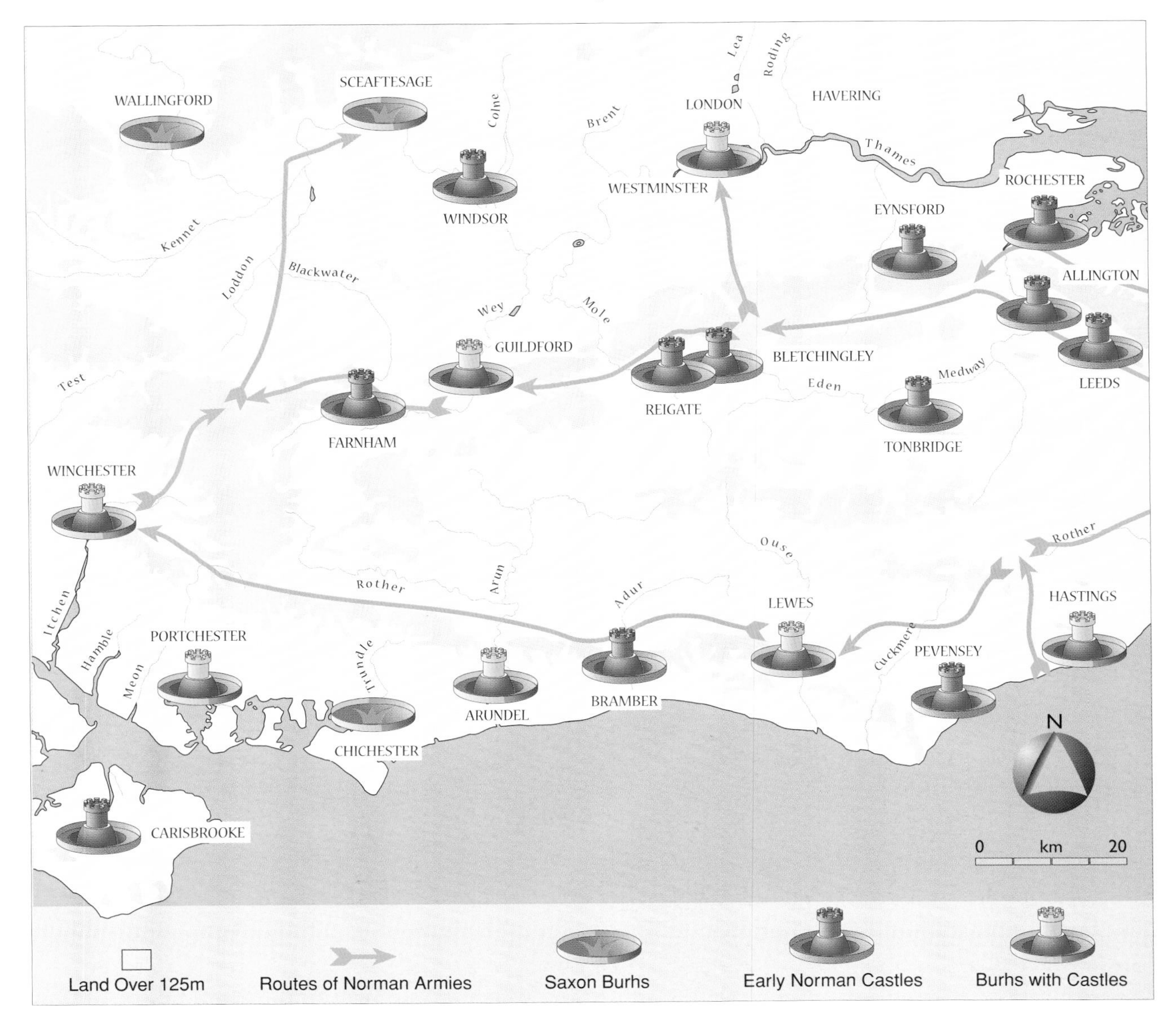

natural features such as rivers were excluded — required four men to maintain it, and hence this means that the constructed defences were some 1,250m (1,367yds) in length.

The successful organisation of such defences against the Vikings provided a platform from which the kingdom of Wessex was able to transform itself into the kingdom of England. The Domesday Book shows how prosperous the country rapidly became — not the least of its attractions for the Normans.

THE IMPACT OF THE NORMANS

It was at Hastings on Saturday, 14 October 1066, that the fate of Saxon England and its people was determined. Following their victory, King William and his followers created a state so powerful that its lands would never again be conquered.

His army marched on London but was rebuffed and then appears to have followed roughly the line of the present A25 through Surrey. The evidence for this is the reduced value of the estates along this route as recorded in the Domesday Book in 1086, compared with

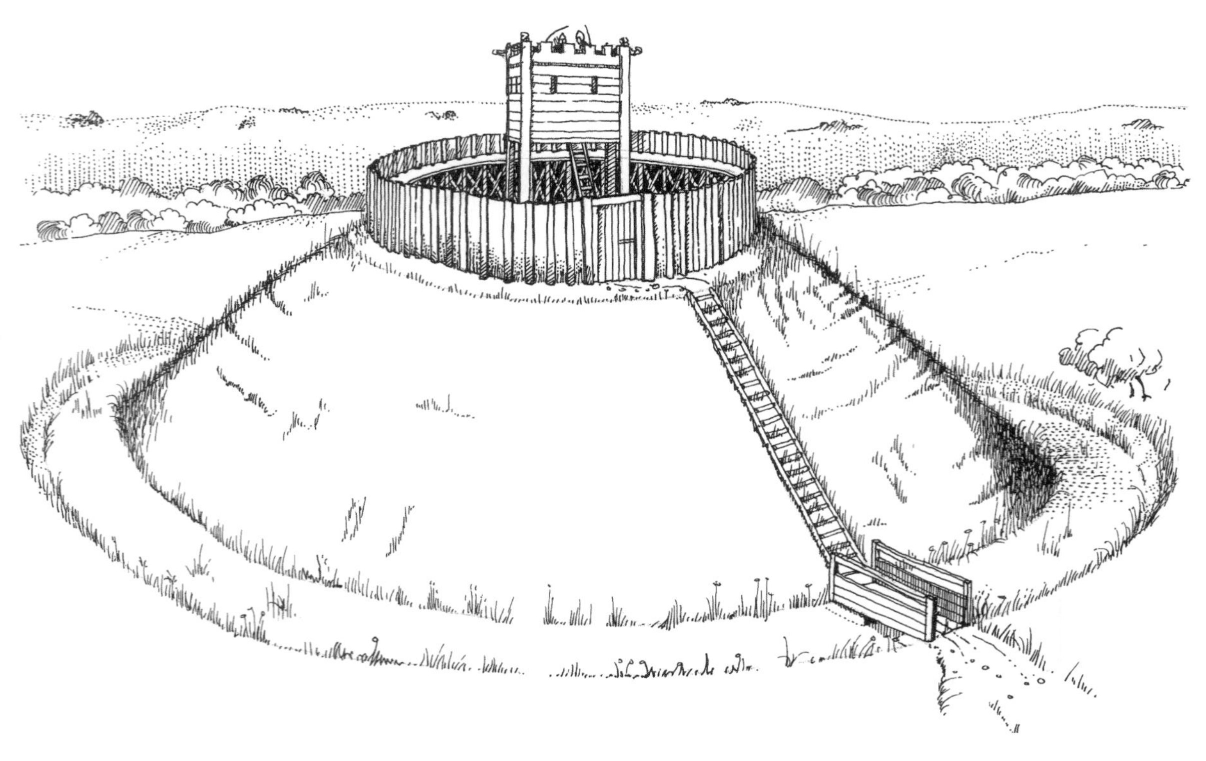

The motte at Abinger was the stronghold of a minor noble, and its timber tower and palisade were never replaced in stone. Next to it the Manor House still stands, probably the successor to the first residence in the bailey attached to the motte.

that at the time of Edward the Confessor, because of pillaging by the invading army.

Having conquered, William administered his new kingdom by replacing the Saxon lords with Norman barons and distributing land between his followers in return for military service whenever it was required.

The nobility were encouraged to build castles in defence of the realm. Simple enclosures with a rampart and ditch providing a continuous defensive circuit were constructed, with the most usual form being the motte-and-bailey castle.

The motte was an earthen mound thrown up to provide a defensive strong point and at first had a wooden tower and in later cases a stone keep. The bailey was the lower area of open ground which provided a place for storage, stabling and the mustering of troops.

Castles were built at Walton on the Hill and Abinger by relatively minor nobility. At Bletchingley and Reigate, by contrast, the castles were erected for two of the greatest families of Norman England, the de Clares and the de Warennes, while Farnham Castle was of similar status, belonging to the Bishop of Winchester. Royal castles such as that at Guildford were constructed not just for defence but to act as an ever-present symbol and reminder of the monarch's power.

Guildford Castle. In the mid-12th century the stone keep replaced earlier timber structures, and offered sophisticated yet secure accommodation for the king and his retinue on several floors.

Guildford Castle was built alongside the Saxon town on a ridge commanding both the river crossing and the possible approach to the Thames Valley through the river gap. It was the only castle in royal hands in either Sussex or Surrey, which was why it became the residence of the sheriff, the chief agent for royal administration. As with many castles, when more resources became available greater use was made of stone for building, which improved security, and attention was also given to providing comfort.

In the wider history of England Guildford Castle's only notable

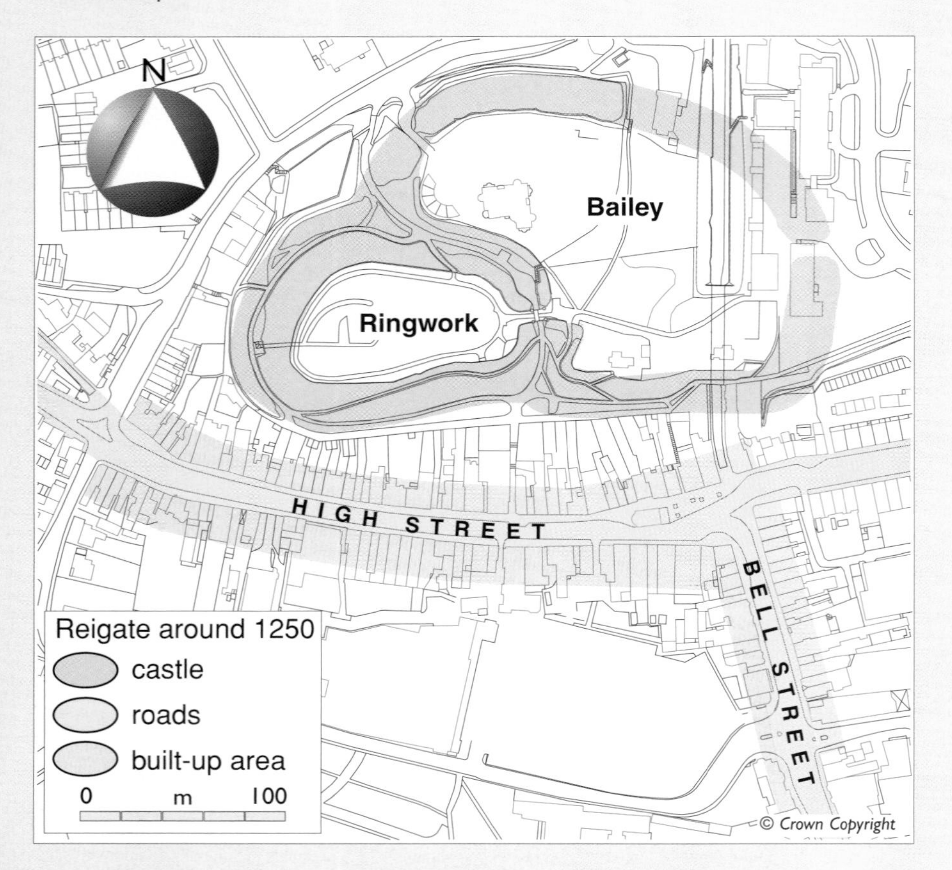

REIGATE

The relationship between castles and towns is highly varied. At Guildford the castle was carefully sited on the edge of the town. At both Farnham and Reigate the castles were originally established well away from any settlement, taking advantage of elevated locations. In the late 12th century the decision was taken to create new towns on the lower ground below them. The new towns, as the plan of Reigate (left) shows, were small but laid out in a neatly symmetrical fashion.

The remains of Reigate Castle occupy a natural sandstone hill, artificially scarped to form a plateau. The date of the castle is not known but it was probably constructed soon after 1088 when William de Warenne was created Earl of Surrey and received a grant of Reigate from the king. The castle was strongly fortified by the Earl of Arundel in the late 14th century, but by 1441 the houses within it were ruinous, and the survey of 1622 calls it 'a decayed castle with a very small house'.

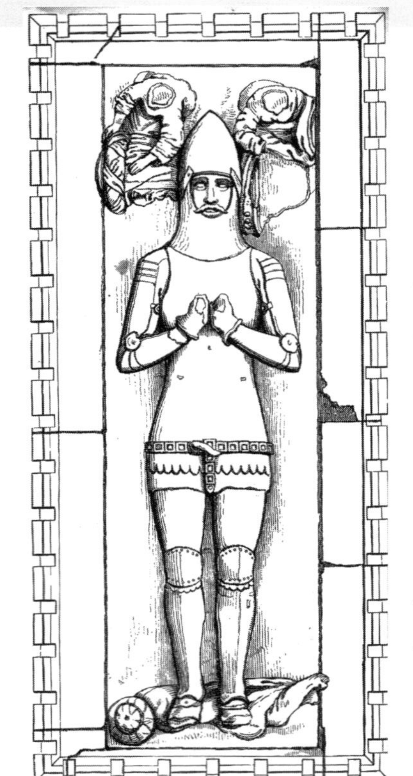

Effigy of Reginald, first Lord Cobham of Sterborough (died 1361), on his marble altar-tomb in Lingfield Church. He was the builder of Starborough Castle.

military event was its capture by the French heir to the throne, Dauphin Louis, in June 1216.

Later, Warwick Castle at Kingston was built. Known only from documents and maps, it may have been erected to defend the river crossing shortly before it was captured by Henry III in 1264.

At Lingfield, Starborough Castle had substantial fortifications along with a water-filled moat. Licence to crenellate was granted to Sir Reginald Cobham in

1341 and a drawing by Hollar shows a building not unlike Bodiam Castle in East Sussex, with four towers and a gatehouse.

INTERNAL PEACE, EXTERNAL THREATS

Internally, England became a more peaceful place with a framework of law and justice so the defences offered by castles became steadily less important.

Many homesteads and manor houses seem to have acquired moats in the 13th century. This was a means of emphasising the social standing of the house and its occupants. Undoubtedly moats would have provided some security against criminals or even local unrest, but they were not regarded as defences in a military sense. Some 150 such sites have been identified in Surrey.

The medieval moated homestead at South Park Farm, Witley, was probably originally the manor house of Ashurst but may later have declined to become the keeper's lodge of Ashurst Park. Excavation revealed finds

An artist's impression of the moated homestead at South Park, Witley, as it may have appeared about 1350.

Esher Place. The fine brick gatehouse to his palace by the River Mole was erected for Bishop Wayneflete of Winchester in about 1480. It was altered by William Kent in about 1730, and this engraving shows it soon after his work was completed.

Farnham Castle in the 18th century. It was owned by the Bishops of Winchester from its beginnings in the late 11th century until 1927, and had been a formidable residence and stronghold in the Civil War.

indicating occupation during the early 14th century and possibly pre-moat settlement in the area. Around the mid-15th century Ashurst manor was absorbed into the nearby royal manor of Witley and the house on the island could have been abandoned during the latter part of the 15th century.

Another feature, the castle gatehouse, also continued to be incorporated into high-status buildings, as at Oatlands Palace, Weybridge, in the 16th century. Others were constructed by Bishop Waynflete at Farnham and Esher and by Cardinal Moreton at Lambeth. Even Abbot's Hospital in Guildford with its gatehouse built in the early 17th century reflects the tradition.

Surrey's castles played a final military role during the Civil War and at Starborough the castle was dismantled in 1648 after being garrisoned by Parliamentary troops at the

SURREY'S SEMAPHORE

Hilltop beacons had long been used to provide warning of invasion but, in the 1790s, Britain was at war with France and the Admiralty was in urgent need of a more reliable system by which it could communicate with the major ports. As a result, having conducted trials on Wimbledon Common, an experimental line of shutter telegraphs was begun in 1795.

Ten of these stations, each consisting of a wooden hut with large wooden shutters or signals hanging above it, were built on hilltops on the route to Portsmouth to enable messages to be relayed from one to another. They were finally abandoned in March 1816, nine months after the victory at Waterloo.

Two years later a new route was surveyed and this time a semaphore system was employed and a total of fifteen stations were built on the Portsmouth line. When completed in 1822 the system was reputed to be capable of sending a time check each day in less than a minute over the 112km (70 miles) from the Admiralty in London to Portsmouth!

Some of these stations have been converted into private homes but the one standing on Chatley Heath, near Cobham, has been restored. It was in use until 13 September 1847 when it was superseded by the electric telegraph.

outbreak of the conflict. The destruction appears to have been thorough and, as at Reigate, was probably intended to prevent the site from becoming a rallying point for Royalist sympathisers.

Farnham Castle was captured by Parliamentary forces and the garrison stationed there was involved in a number of battles and skirmishes while at Chilworth the gunpowder mills supplied the Parliamentary side.

During the later 17th and most of the 18th centuries external influences had little effect on Surrey, but the fear of French invasion, that had provoked the establishment of the semaphore system at the end of the 18th century, gripped the country again in

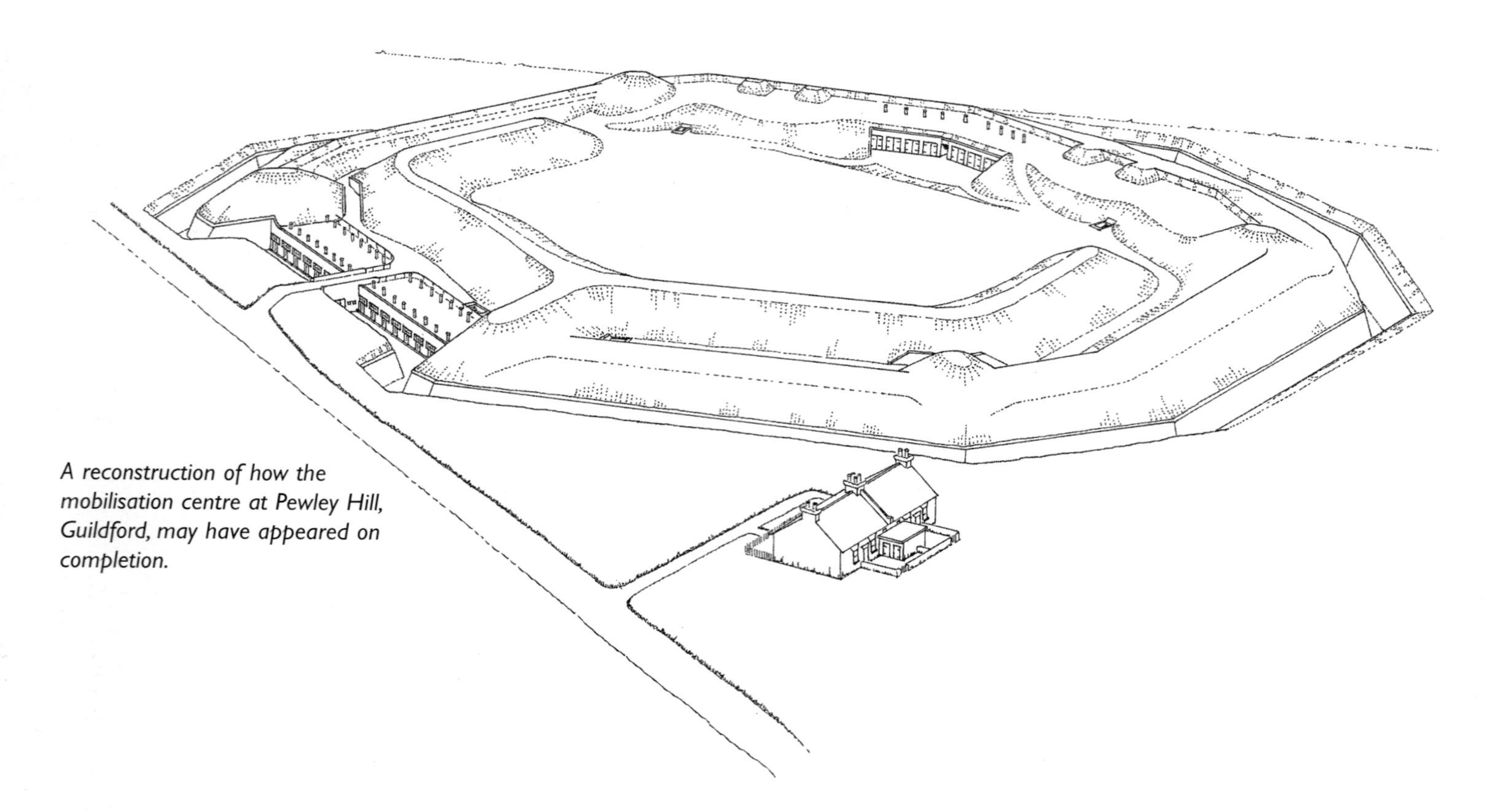

A reconstruction of how the mobilisation centre at Pewley Hill, Guildford, may have appeared on completion.

1859. The patriotic effort that followed led to the formation of corps and rifle clubs across the country. As a result a National Association was established and its first National Rifle meeting was held on Wimbledon Common in July 1860. Annual meetings were held there for the next 29 years until the National Rifle Association moved to a site at Bisley, adjoining the Pirbright rifle ranges already established for the Brigade of Guards.

Bisley became the mecca of rifle shooting with teams coming from most parts of the world. Club houses with verandas were built and dormitory huts were erected for members and through both World Wars Bisley served to train the forces in marksmanship.

The military have long used the heath and common land of Surrey and, although the key establishments of Aldershot and Sandhurst are just over the Surrey border in Hampshire and Berkshire respectively, ranges, training grounds and military establishments can be found around towns and villages such as Camberley and Ash.

CROYDON AIRPORT

Corn stood in the fields around Beddington when, in August 1914, the storm clouds of the First World War finally broke over Europe and the War Office took control of land in the area to establish an aerodrome as part of the air defence of London. Airmen and soldiers were compulsorily billeted with local households and what became the National Aircraft Factory No 1 was built close by with a railway branch line to supply it.

On 29 March 1920 Beddington Aerodrome was renamed Croydon Airport, the Customs Airport of London, and civil aviation flourished until 1939 when the prospect of war once again loomed. Croydon's role changed from civilian airport to that of military aerodrome when, as a satellite to nearby Kenley Aerodrome, it became the Royal Air Force Station Croydon.

While the aerodrome played a front-line role in the Battle of Britain, the town of Croydon suffered huge damage from bombing and the war spelt an end to Croydon's reign as a leading civilian airport since it could not accommodate the larger planes of the new era. Airport House (the original passenger terminal) still survives (right).

Britain's island status was long seen as sufficient protection from invasion but late in Queen Victoria's reign doubts were raised over the ability of the Royal Navy to give absolute protection. In an echo of the late-Roman defence of the approach to London, a plan to protect the capital from an enemy advance was introduced into Parliament in 1889 based on the construction of a line of mobilisation centres.

The last of these thirteen 'forts' was finished in February 1902 and in Surrey they stood along the North Downs from Guildford to Woldingham but their employment was brief with the scheme being abolished in 1906.

A 1932 poster advertising motor racing at Brooklands, Weybridge. In the Second World War this famous site was adapted as an aircraft factory and runway.

Second World War defences were based on anti-tank obstacles and did not follow the same path as the Victorian forts. This 'GHQ Line' was built during the early summer of 1940 and consisted basically of a continuous tank trap defended by a line of small infantry pillboxes or gun emplacements. The objective was to slow down the leading elements of the enemy's motorised columns to allow time for reserve troops to counter-attack them.

Many people in Surrey were involved in the war effort and at Brooklands the race track was closed and Vickers expanded their operations on the site with thousands of aircraft being produced including 2,500 Wellington bombers. At Kingston, where Sir Thomas Sopwith had founded a factory on an old skating rink to build aircraft in the First World War, the Hawker Engineering Company stepped up production and built, among other planes, the Hurricane and Typhoon.

RAF stations were established not only at Kenley and Croydon but at Dunsfold and Redhill, with various other landing strips created across the county.

Fortunately the huge effort in countering the German war machine paid off and the defences set up across Surrey were never needed but, even today, many of the pillboxes still stand bleak and inhospitable in the countryside as a reminder of the once all too real threat.

6
MARKETS & MANUFACTURING

Billowing smoke and the relentless thud of hammers do not immediately fit with our pastoral vision of Surrey yet, through its history, the county has served a role as something of a workshop for England. Iron, glass, cloth, paper, wool and gunpowder have all, at one time or another, been produced in the county, for it had the principal assets of fast-flowing rivers and a plentiful supply of timber.

While the county became a major centre of industry in the 16th and 17th centuries its natural resources have long been exploited and communication and trade with the Continent have occurred throughout history.

Despite this, the area was something of a rural backwater until the Victorian era when, with the coming of the railways, the process of widespread gentrification began and large parts of the county became part of the great commuter belt that encircles London.

Betchworth limeworks, with their tall Hoffman kilns, seen around 1900. Chalk was dug from the North Downs to make lime for building and agricultural use from at least the Roman period onwards.

Flint axes from Swanscombe, Kent, dating to around 400,000 BC. The same site produced the oldest human skull found in Britain. Acheulian-type handaxes are found widely across Europe. They share common methods of production but were produced locally from the nearest suitable material.

While it is natural to assume that London has always played a key role in Surrey's life this has not been the case. It is the River Thames that has been the constant; an artery along which populations have settled and traded while its tributaries threaded through the valleys supplying the need for power and transport.

PREHISTORY

Travel back to the Palaeolithic period and, around 400,000 BC, we find the first use of handaxes in Surrey. These include the distinctive teardrop-shaped Acheulian handaxes which, although giving no evidence of trade, do indicate, in the consistency of their shape and style, that ideas were communicated widely.

The small numbers of nomadic Mesolithic people who came to inhabit the area at the end of the last Ice Age around 10,000 years ago presumably exploited the resources close to hand, moving on when these were exhausted with the result that a single hunter-gatherer group might travel considerable distances.

Self-sufficiency must have been central to virtually every aspect of this hunter-gatherer existence although presumably each group formed part of larger 'tribal' units with which they exchanged both materials and marriage partners.

They used equipment and implements made with materials close to hand such as wood, bone, antlers, flint and stone and, rather than establishing 'workshops' near to the source, they appear to have carried the raw materials from place to place and worked them when required.

Interestingly, radiocarbon dating gives a hint as to the reality of the long distance communication of ideas. It has revealed that around the first quarter of the 7th millennium BC, new styles of flint tools appeared in England presumably 'imported' via a narrow land bridge connected to mainland Europe.

Whether new ideas were adopted by the existing population or were the result of an influx of newcomers taking control is

A Mesolithic core adze of around 5,000 BC from Leatherhead, which shows an elegant shape and fine workmanship.

uncertain. What we can be sure of is that the varying habitats provided by the underlying geology of the Surrey area were already being exploited and the tracks they wore into the Mesolithic landscape would eventually form the basis of some of the roads and paths we use today.

Holloways such as this one near Hambledon betray the effects of the passage of countless people, animals, and vehicles in wearing down the soft greensand. It is easy to demonstrate that they existed by the medieval period, but many are likely to be of much greater antiquity. Such a route, once established, would only be abandoned with great reluctance.

Towards the end of this period the population increased. Immigrants introduced Neolithic farming practices or alternatively the indigenous hunter-gatherers adopted the concept of farming from the Continent, and bartered for seed and domesticated animals.

The more organised society which, of necessity, developed is illustrated by the presence of sites such as the *cursus* monument and the causewayed camps. These would have required leadership and manpower in their construction and the causewayed camps may have functioned as trading centres, markets or some sort of exchange point at territorial boundaries. The fact that similar monuments exist elsewhere in the country shows that ideas were communicated widely.

That such far-reaching contact happened is indisputable since stone implements found in Surrey come not only from Britain but also from the Continent, with the Thames functioning as one of the main trade routes.

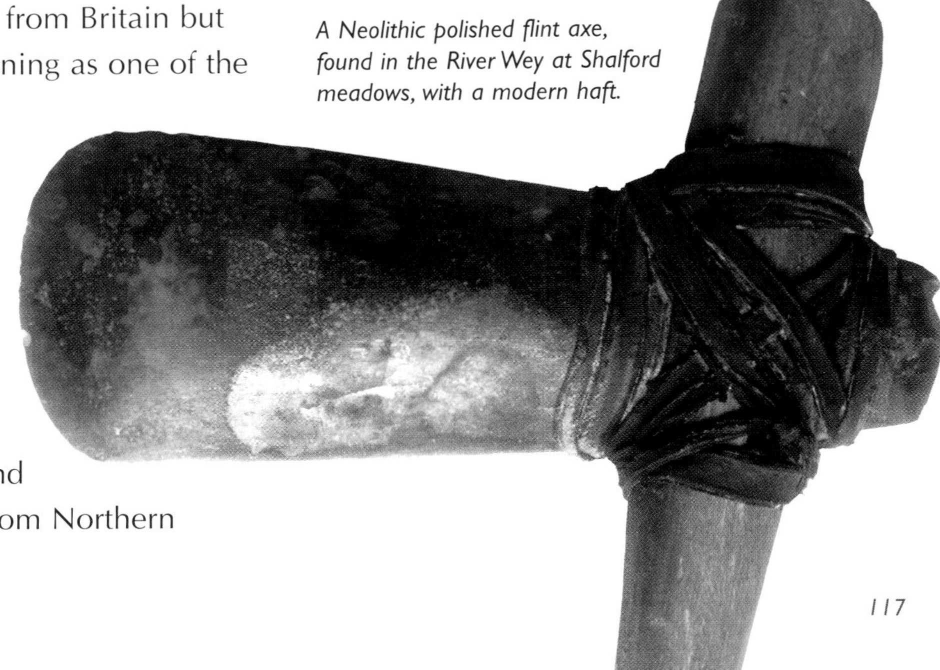

A Neolithic polished flint axe, found in the River Wey at Shalford meadows, with a modern haft.

The butt of a jadeite axe from the southern Alps was found on Staines Moor a short way from the Stanwell/Heathrow *cursus* complex and the causewayed enclosure at Yeoveney, Staines. Over half the stone axes found in Surrey whose source is known came from Cornwall. Others come from the Great Langdale–Scafell Pike area of the Lake District and from Penmaenmawr in North Wales as well as from Northern

An unusually large assemblage of Neolithic Grooved Ware pottery was found at Betchworth.

Ireland, Leicestershire, Dyfed, Northumberland and Perthshire.

The system that was employed for passing goods from place to place is unclear but, certainly among the upper echelons of society, there appears to have been the birth of a 'consumer economy' where aesthetic values, quality of product and simple materialism were as important as pure practicality. Some of the stone and flint axes discovered are obviously prestige items that marked personal status since they

FLINT MINING

During the early periods most or all of the flint used in Surrey appears to have been 'imported' or gathered from the surface in the areas of Clay-with-Flints on the North Downs. In other parts of England there is clear evidence of flint mining with perhaps the best-known mines being those discovered at Grimes Graves in East Anglia, while the nearest mines to Surrey were those on the South Downs in Sussex.

It has been claimed that evidence for Neolithic mining within the county was discovered during an excavation led by Commander K R U Todd (left) at East Horsley in 1949. There appeared to be two major shafts surrounded by spoil heaps but only one was excavated and this had a diameter of some 3m (10ft) and a depth of about 3.65m (12ft).

Although fragments of pottery and a large quantity of flint-working waste (a few pieces of which are shown right) and flint tools from the Neolithic period were discovered, it eventually became clear that the mineshafts were predominantly medieval. A stairway of six steps had been cut from the solid chalk running down the wall and had marks in the stone matching those of a medieval metal pick, while nearby there was pottery of a similar date. It seems probable that the Neolithic working involved the exploitation of a surface outcrop of flint. People have speculated however that the rubble and debris left by the Neolithic workings may have attracted the later workers to the spot when they required materials for building work at nearby Rowbarns Manor.

exhibit superb craftsmanship which is clearly much more to do with show than use.

By their very nature, many commodities used by Neolithic people were ephemeral since they were made of wood and other materials that quickly rot, but tools such as crown-antler mace-heads have been recovered from the Thames.

Although probably made locally, pottery of similar styles is very widely spread across the country and the Grooved Ware type of pottery discovered at Betchworth in Surrey has been found as far away as the Orkney Islands in Scotland.

For the Bronze Age to develop, both trade and industry were vital since bronze is made using tin and copper which only occur in limited geological areas: copper is found with tin in Cornwall and in North Wales at Great Orme, while tin also occurs on Dartmoor. The two metals therefore had first to be extracted in sufficient quantities to supply the needs of the British Isles and then distributed for use.

Undoubtedly the production of Bronze Age goods fell to skilled craftsmen for, while it is easy to suppose that most people could, given time, turn their hand to fashioning a flint axe, few could undertake the production of bronze or make bronze items without knowledge of the processes involved.

Over a relatively short period of time the Bronze Age saw a revolution in technology as simple metal versions of the stone axes that had gone before gradually evolved into more sophisticated versions, with improved arrangements for hafting and more efficient blades.

Swords, knives, chisels and other tools followed and it is assumed that, as in Neolithic times, these advances and the constant evolution of styles were driven by Continental influences and also, perhaps, immigrant smiths. The Thames corridor again acted as a conduit for ideas and trade and has in turn given archaeologists many clues to Bronze Age traditions through the recovered artefacts.

With the bonus of good soil and consequently agricultural wealth, the Thames-side region had something of a monopoly on the metal

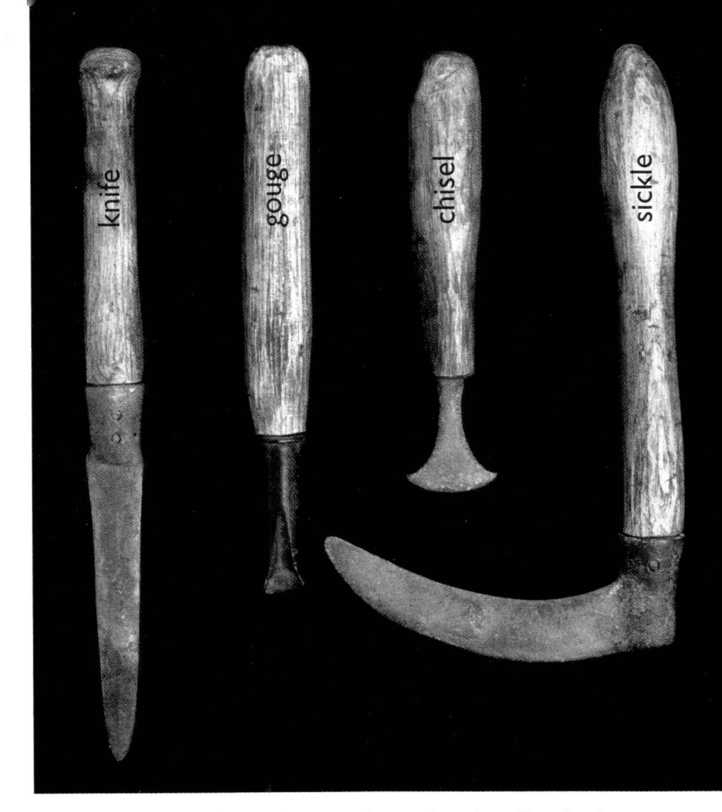

Bronze Age tools, here shown with modern handles. Such tools became increasingly diverse over time and were adapted to a wide variety of industrial and agricultural uses.

Stone mould (left) for use in manufacturing bronze axes, found near Egham. A hoard of bronze objects found at the same site included some (right) which were of very similar form, though not produced from the same mould.

supply and the quantity and variety of the products suggests that a productive and technologically advanced local industry flourished.

Hoards associated with metalworking occur in the Thames-side districts, the eastern North Downs and central–southern Surrey and contain scrap implements, copper ingots and less frequently metal-working waste and mould fragments.

Analysis of a large hoard from excavations at Petters Sports Field at Egham, which included weapons, tools, vessels and ornamental attachments, indicates that local smiths were recycling a stock of

RUNNYMEDE BRIDGE

Like a site further down the Thames at Kingston, the one at Runnymede Bridge was strategically placed. While the extensive excavations (right) revealed evidence of occupation during Neolithic times, in the Late Bronze Age the site appears to have been a trading post of quite considerable importance, illustrating the increasing development of trade and exchange.

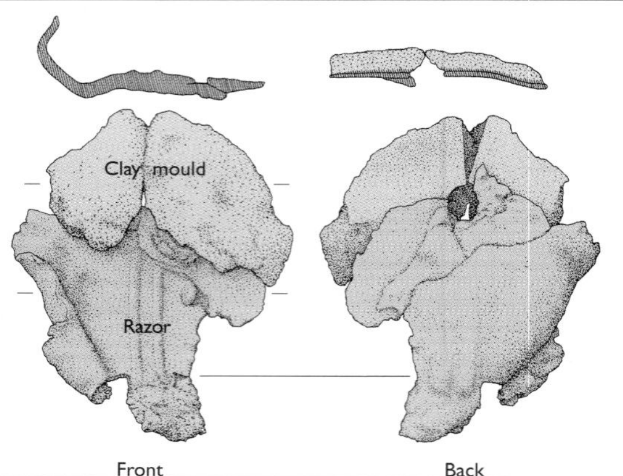

Chosen because of the natural advantages of being an island between two main streams of the river (left), and improved by a palisade of wooden stakes driven into the river bed to provide landing stages and some fortification, it would have controlled the flow of resources and finished products along the waterway.

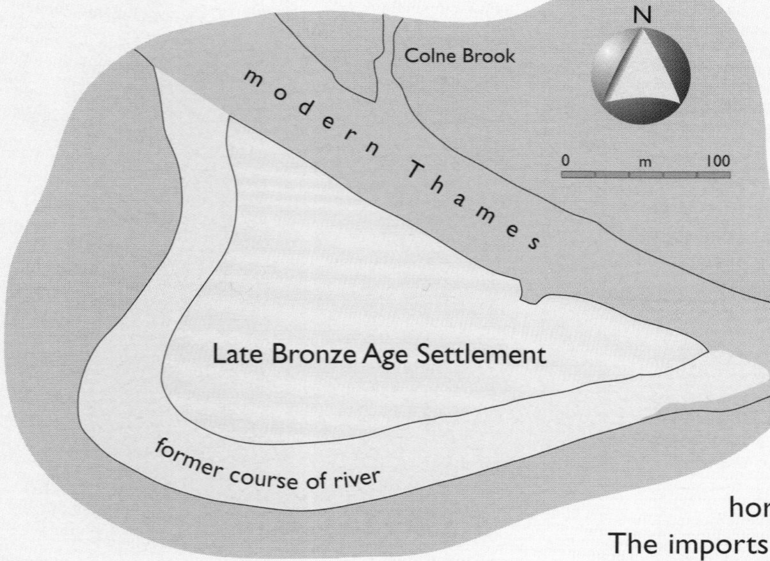

There were a number of buildings on the site and the unusually large quantities of pottery discovered point to a high degree of activity. Metalworking appears to have been a major specialist activity with evidence of tools and weapons being cast.

Among the many items found that are connected with manufacture was a discarded razor still in the clay mould that had been used to make it (above right). Other finds included trimmed antlers and a blank for the manufacture of horse bridle equipment as well as fine polished antler cheek pieces. The imports included shell bracelets and amber beads.

scrap metal which had its origin in northern France but was becoming adulterated with metal from other sources.

The finds included a stone mould used for making a socketed axe of a type not normally found in Surrey, so giving a clear indication that the bronze smiths of the period were peripatetic.

Excavations also give clues to the other industries practised at different sites: clay loomweights and spindlewhorls are not uncommon and attest to textile production while animal bones were made into basic tools and pottery was beginning to take on forms much more distinctive to particular areas.

A new metalworking tradition arrived in Britain around 800 BC. This was the beginning of the Iron Age — an age upon which the Industrial Revolution would build more than two millennia later. Ironworking technology was probably present on the Continent long before its widespread adoption and political, economic and technical factors must all have played their part in a period of upheaval and advance.

In Surrey low-grade iron ores were worked and processed to produce tools and weapons at places like Brooklands and Ewell, where a smithing hearth was found together with slag, but the main source seems to have been to the south of today's county boundary. As in the Bronze Age, specialists visited

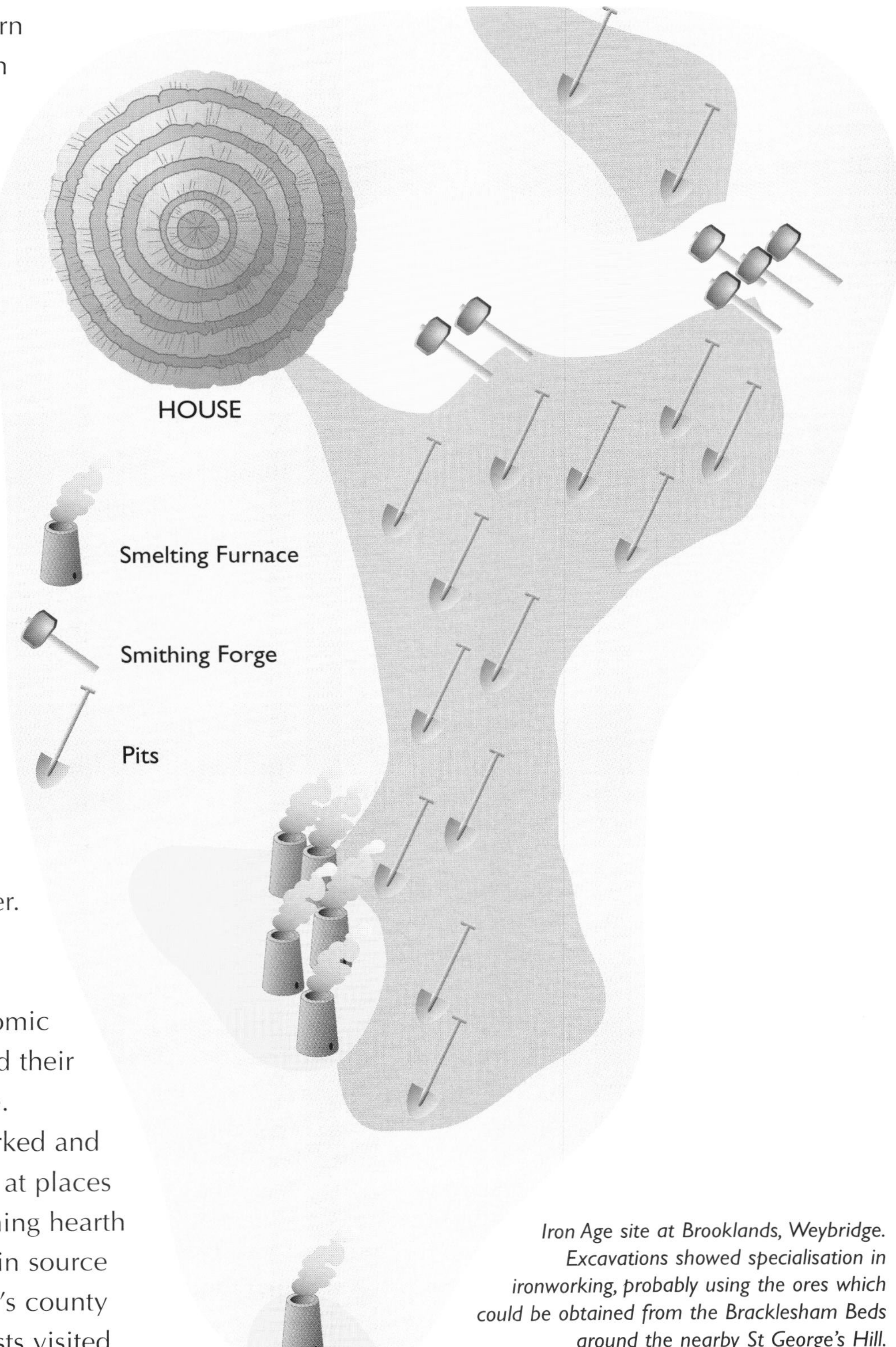

Iron Age site at Brooklands, Weybridge. Excavations showed specialisation in ironworking, probably using the ores which could be obtained from the Bracklesham Beds around the nearby St George's Hill.

manufacturing sites on a seasonal basis and probably undertook much of the production and working of iron.

Perhaps chosen because of the ready availability of iron ore and timber for charcoal, the Brooklands site may have been the homestead of an ironworker and his family and presents a clear picture of small-scale ironworking technology in the Iron Age. The key processes of smelting and forging occur in different areas of the site and bowl-shaped indentations in the ground probably represent all that remains of the more substantial structures of the smelting furnaces.

It is likely that the Late Bronze and Iron Age economies centred on the hillforts that were strung out across the county. While their function is not fully understood they were almost certainly central to trade and served not only as centres for the collection and

QUERNS

Querns — stones for grinding corn — were traded from the Iron Age, if not before. Suitably rough but hard stone was available only in certain areas but querns, coming from various sources including the Hythe Beds in the Petworth–Midhurst area, have been widely found around Godalming.

The industry in querns is important as it gives firm evidence that even heavy goods could be transported considerable distances. Excavation of the main ditch around the hillfort at Holmbury (right) produced a number of querns. Some were made from quite local stone while others had been brought to the hillfort from a site 25km (16 miles) away, suggesting that the hillfort was trading in or redistributing these products. A quern found on an Iron Age site near Ewell (left) was also made from stone from the Hythe Beds. In the Roman period stone even came from the Rhineland.

redistribution of goods but also as places of manufacture. In the valleys below, the rivers offered a means of transport for goods, animals and people, while farmsteads related to both river and hillfort were used mainly for agriculture and possibly other forms of production.

A clear indication of long-distance trade during the period is given by the remarkable swords and daggers yielded by the Thames. Ideas were also plied back and forth along this route and it seems highly likely that British smiths would copy and modify examples from the Continent and then sometimes export their products.

The beginnings of coinage in Britain also belong to the final century or so before the Roman Conquest. At first imported from Gaul (France), the coins were soon manufactured locally. Initially, it seems unlikely that they were used as currency in the modern manner, but they did form part of the system of trade and exchange of goods. These were changing rapidly at this time, largely in response to the development of the sophisticated economy of the Roman world.

This hoard of tin-bronze (potin) coins was found inside the pottery vessel, at Sunbury. The motive for burial can only be guessed at, but an offering to a god or gods is the most likely explanation.

ROMAN

On the fringe of the Roman Empire, Britain formed part of a trading network even before the Roman invasion of AD 43. Indeed, the level of trade was sufficiently established for the Greek writer Strabo to comment on the close relationship between some of Britain's 'chieftains' and Rome: 'They pay dues which yield a large revenue on imports from Gaul and on their own exports (corn, cattle, gold, silver, iron, hides, slaves, and hounds), so that the island does not require a garrison.'

Once Britain became part of the Roman Empire, it saw its first true industrial age while at the same time there was the birth, certainly amongst the higher echelons of society, of a commercialism that was helped by a money economy.

How much the ordinary people benefited is hard to quantify.

A 19th century illustration of finds from the Roman villa at Titsey reveals the widely spread sources of the pottery found there, as well as painted plaster suggesting some of the varied trades (painters, plasterers, perhaps interior designers?) that served such establishments.

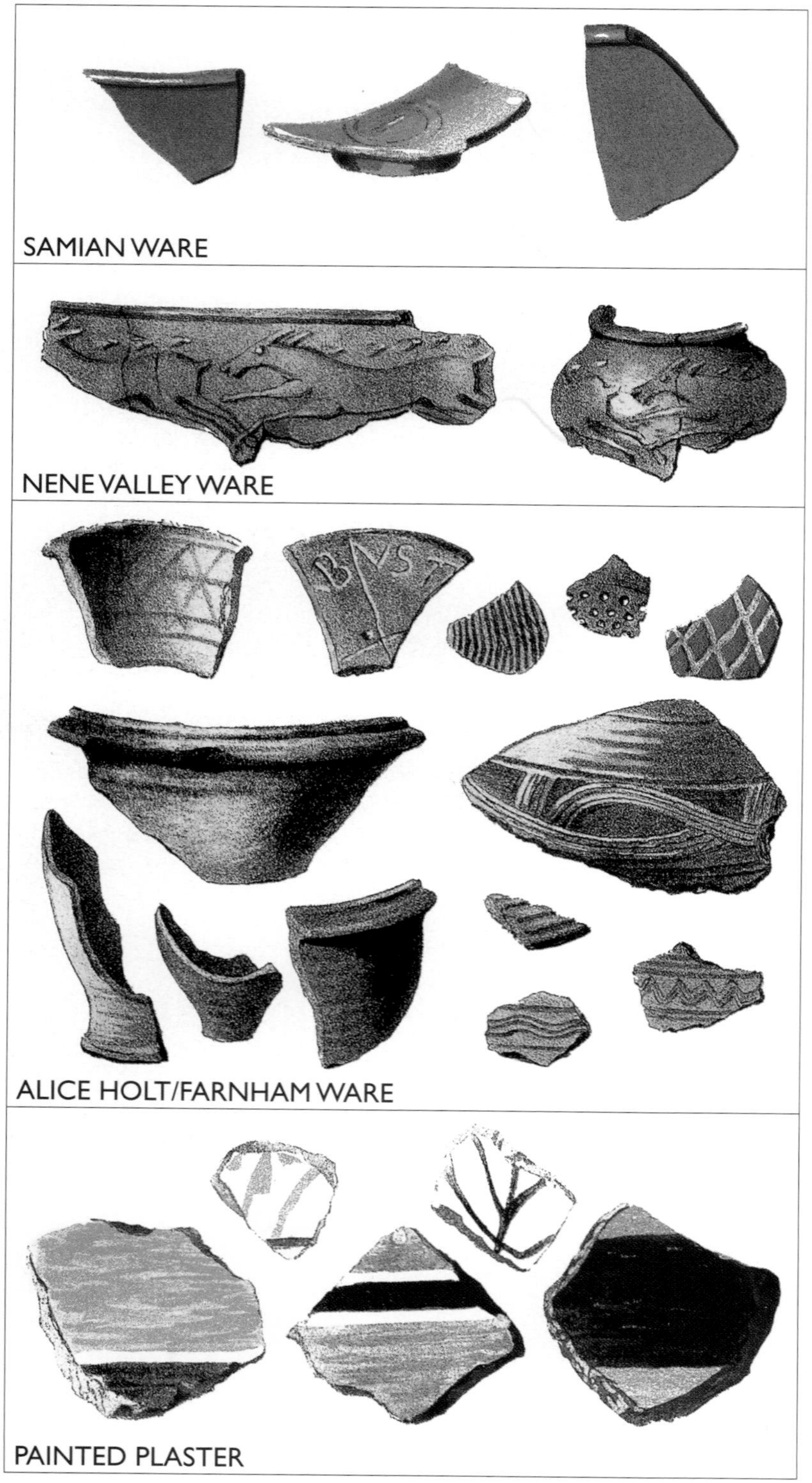

SAMIAN WARE

NENE VALLEY WARE

ALICE HOLT/FARNHAM WARE

PAINTED PLASTER

There were towns at Staines and Southwark and smaller market centres such as that at Ewell, but the focus of power lay outside the county boundaries, especially at the major trading centre in London which was founded at this time.

More specialist exploitation of the countryside is illustrated by the importance of the villa sites. The primary role of these significant houses was as the centre of estates organising the production of arable, pastoral and woodland resources. The remains of Spanish pottery storage jars (*amphorae*) from Chiddingfold show that fish paste or oil could even reach such an apparently isolated spot. Other villa sites reveal high-quality pottery including the glossy Samian ware imported from places such as south Gaul, while, at Rapsley, near Ewhurst, a piece of fine glass was found that came from a vessel made in Cologne.

Other goods came from closer to home, with fragments of pots from Pulborough in West Sussex being found at the villa sites of Rapsley and Chiddingfold, while examples also came from centres in the New Forest area and Oxfordshire.

Evidence of conspicuous consumption is clear with villa owners surrounding themselves with beautiful and sought after objects and decorating the interiors of their buildings with wall paintings and mosaic floors.

Items like roof tiles were often transported some distance by road. Tiles made at Ashtead have been found in London and tile making was also practised at Horton near Epsom, Wykehurst Farm near Rapsley and possibly at Doods Farm near Reigate, production from which seems to have reached London in some quantity.

Firing of a reconstructed kiln at Alice Holt (left). The experiment was aimed at producing pottery of a quality to match the hardness and high quality of the original Alice Holt/Farnham ware, which has been widely found in settlements such as London (below).

Pottery was a key industry in Roman Britain and one of the major production centres was on the Surrey/Hampshire border. It is generally called the Alice Holt pottery industry, from the numerous discoveries there, but Farnham was also an important production area. This centre was responsible for a vast range of mostly grey domestic ware — large storage jars, bowls and the like — used in everyday life, with much of it going to the London market throughout the Roman period. It is almost always the commonest pottery type found on Roman excavations in Surrey. Other pottery kilns are known to have existed at Farley Heath and near Wisley while there was probably a production centre in the Leatherhead area.

Pottery oil lamps from Staines. Even minor objects like these were standardised in Roman Britain. The one on the left is stamped with the manufacturer's name.

Agricultural industries existed to supply London with animals for both meat and transport but also served the requirements of the leather industry and the need for bone to make items like spoons and hairpins. While the Wealden Clay and London Clay were little used for agriculture they were exploited for growing trees since wood was required for everything from fuel to building.

Underlying what must have been an almost insatiable demand for goods was a money economy with coins of all denominations and there is good evidence that, later in the period, there were official attempts to fix prices.

The economy itself worked on an Empire-wide basis and large-scale production was not uncommon with many items, from mixing bowls to timber, carrying a maker's or originator's stamp. London itself appears to have been built as a centre for trade and rapidly expanded with the settlement at Southwark growing up around the bridge on the opposite bank of the Thames.

Excavation of a Roman warehouse in Southwark. The drawing shows the joists which underlay the wide floorboards visible towards the bottom left of the photograph.

The perfectly preserved timbers of the floor of a Roman warehouse discovered in Southwark indicate that the port was involved in the import and export of goods along the Thames. The warehouse itself would have been cool and dark — perfect for storing wine or foodstuffs.

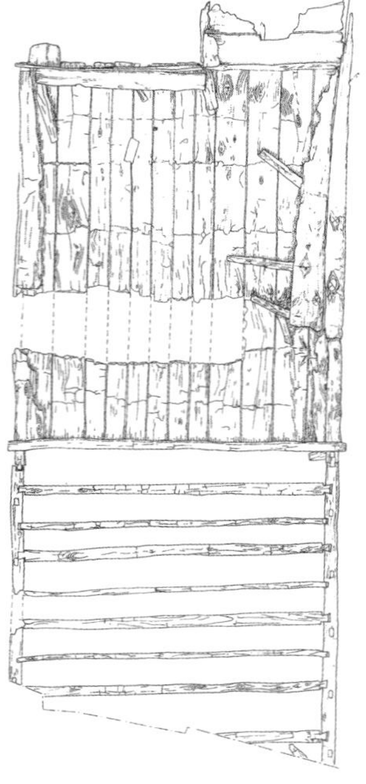

With the need for an infrastructure to ensure contact and trade and allow the movement of goods, materials and people over long distances, roads were built. In Southwark logs were laid side-by-side where it

ROMAN TILE WORKS

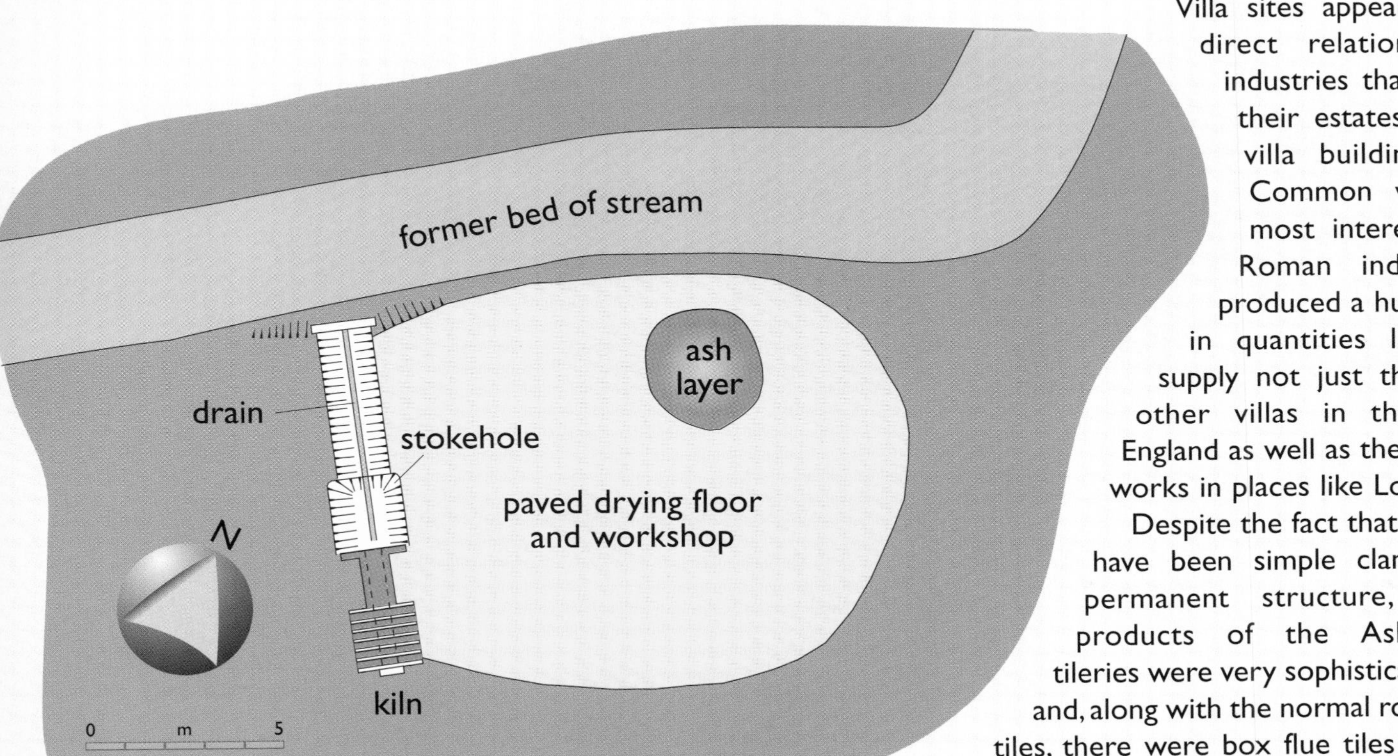

Villa sites appear to have had a direct relationship with the industries that formed part of their estates and around the villa buildings on Ashtead Common was one of the most interesting of Surrey's Roman industrial sites. It produced a huge variety of tiles in quantities large enough to supply not just the local area but other villas in the south-east of England as well as the needs of building works in places like London.

Despite the fact that the kilns seem to have been simple clamps involving no permanent structure, some of the products of the Ashtead tileries were very sophisticated and, along with the normal roof tiles, there were box flue tiles for hypocaust heating systems (right centre). Although such tiles were plastered some were highly unusual and were decorated using wooden or bone combs or stamps (near right) to create patterns on the outer faces to act as a key for the plaster.

Also produced at Ashtead were small bricks used in herringbone-pattern floors, quarter and semi-circular tiles for columns and elaborate chimney pots (far right) or lamp columns.

At Wykehurst Farm, Cranleigh (above), the tile works was used for only a short period of time. It was probably established to produce tile and brick for construction of the villa at nearby Rapsley, and its simple products have not been widely identified elsewhere.

An artist's impression of a detachment of the Roman army marching along Stane Street.

was necessary to cross marshy ground. Elsewhere the famous straight 'Roman roads' were constructed with a degree of engineering competence and organisation not witnessed again until the 18th century.

Generally surfaced with gravel, often on a flint cobble base, these roads included Stane Street which was laid out some ten years after the Conquest. Linking London to Chichester in Sussex it headed into Ewell on the same route as the present A24.

Panther Cowrie shell (right) found near the left elbow of a female burial (left) at the Esso House site, Ashtead.

SAXON

As Roman power ebbed away from the province of Britannia, the money economy collapsed as the shores of the island saw ever increasing raids from the barbarians, Picts, Saxons and Irish.

The Saxons and other Germanic tribes, including Angles and Jutes, settled in England during the 5th and 6th centuries and gradually assumed control over the whole of England.

What exactly happened in these 'Dark Ages' is very difficult to verify. Undoubtedly the period brought a reversion to self-sufficiency and a small-scale localised economy with rule by Kingdom rather than Empire. What has to be remembered is that

The border between Kent and Surrey is marked by a boundary bank, probably established while both were still independent kingdoms in the 6th century AD.

the Saxon period — stretching from 410 to 1066 — is longer than that of the Roman influence and so, out of what might have been early disarray, there eventually grew the much more stable economy described by the Domesday Book.

While trade and travel certainly declined, there is evidence that it still went on and nowhere is the reality of this revealed more clearly than in excavations of early Saxon graves where pagan rites had led to the deposition of artefacts.

*Excavations (left) at Shepperton revealed an ordered settlement, perhaps a small village, established in the late Saxon period. Its emergence reflects an economic upsurge in late Saxon England, which includes the development of coinage for trade. This silver penny of King Eadred (*Eadred Rex*) of Wessex (946–955) was found at the same site.*

At the Ashtead cemetery site one of the unusual finds accompanying a male burial was a Panther Cowrie shell of a type found only in the Red Sea area, a remarkable illustration of the distance that an object, valued purely for its protection against evil, might travel. Buried nearby, a six or seven year old child wore a necklace formed of three small beads from a Panther Cowrie as well as two amethysts and two glass beads, one of which, with red polka dots on a blue background, may have been manufactured in the Rhineland.

The waning of Roman influence must have caused what we might today term urban decay. London's importance in the 5th and 6th centuries is difficult to assess but it appears to have ceased to function as a heavily populated market and port, though it may have remained an official and administrative centre. Elsewhere the Roman stone and brick buildings fell out of use and decayed and the skills needed for their repair were lost. For example, the art of brickmaking was not revived until the Middle Ages.

A water-mill was probably first established at Elstead in the late Saxon period, when the technology became widespread in England. The existing structure is largely of 18th century date, a period when many Surrey mills were rebuilt to cope with increasing demand.

Across Britain the Roman heritage included almost 8,000km (5,000 miles) of roads and it is likely that in Saxon times both these and the riverways remained in use. In addition, trackways continued to serve the needs of both local people and travellers.

Such routes seem to have converged on the meeting places of the Hundred Courts and a bank and ditch between Epsom and Ashtead is almost certainly of Saxon origin and relevant to the Copthorne Hundred. Clearly designed to control the route, a Saxon origin has been argued for the massive boundary bank which still marks the border between Kent and Surrey where it is crossed by the A25.

In the medieval period Kingston Bridge was the first across the Thames upstream from London. The seemingly flimsy old bridge (above) was pulled down in 1828. Its foundations were exposed by excavation in 1996 (below), which showed that repair works to the original medieval fabric had taken place on numerous occasions.

The economic upsurge in late Saxon times saw a revival of trade and markets with Guildford and Kingston among the places that began to grow as trading centres. At the same time a money economy once again developed and coins were produced at a mint in Guildford by the 10th century.

Many Surrey villages begin their recorded history with an entry in the Domesday Book. In essence the survey captured a snapshot of England at the Norman Conquest and reveals a generally flourishing economy.

Perhaps most noticeable amongst the entries are the water mills. These formed a vital part of life; indeed they represented the lifeblood of many communities for the grinding of corn provided an important staple of the diet: bread.

MEDIEVAL

Most of Surrey's towns are medieval and date from the 12th and 13th centuries. London was again dominant, with Southwark as its suburb, and trade flourished both at home and abroad with

KINGSTON POTTERY

Pottery kilns were in use both in the main towns and in many rural locations with the goods frequently being transported considerable distances. In the late medieval period the Whiteware kilns of north and west Surrey became important in supplying the growing London markets.

In Kingston the excavated debris of medieval times hints at the craftsmen and traders who worked there: potters, blacksmiths, bronzesmiths, tilers, masons, butchers, hornworkers, leathermakers and hurdlemakers. The craftsmen worked close to the market area while the dirty industries and those with a high fire risk were situated further from the centre.

This was clearly demonstrated with the discovery of four 14th century kilns which were excavated in Eden Street (right) along with pottery that included jugs, cooking pots, crucibles, cups and bowls (below).

Kingston was an ideal location for the potters who had probably relocated from London. Not only did it offer closer availability of the white-firing clay but it was conveniently situated on the Thames for transport. It also had a market of some standing which drew traders from both local and regional areas and so offered the chance to increase distribution; Kingston-type Whiteware has been recorded in Hertfordshire and Essex.

Large orders would have required several kilns to operate simultaneously and three of the kilns were dug into the natural brickearth with some of their structure below ground. The surrounding brickearth mantle presumably promoted good heat retention, hence avoiding the need to build a substantial part of the kiln chamber.

Continental influences significant, particularly from Flanders and the Rhineland.

Guildford was an important market centre for corn, cattle and cloth and the town's suburbs grew up to the west of the River Wey and at the east end of the High Street. This growth and the wealth of the town are illustrated by evidence of 13th century chalk undercrofts which were used as shop premises.

A fair granted to the rector of St Nicholas in 1308 must have increased further the flow of goods into Guildford and, although the castle fell into decay at the end of the 14th century, the town itself continued to thrive.

While the peasantry were presumably a reasonably static element of the population, the rural markets were a focus for trade so there was a steadily shifting community of traders and merchants as well as those who chose to migrate more permanently from country to town or vice versa. The ruling classes and their retinues travelled widely and, as a conduit of communication and ideas, the clergy also undoubtedly played a vital role both at home and abroad.

Despite this movement of people across the medieval landscape, the road network was largely undefined and far from good, so travellers hired guides on unfamiliar routes, while travelling monks compiled itineraries to help their brethren.

Although settlements frequently grew up at river crossings a ford was often the only means for the traveller to get to the other side. Bridge building generally relied on the goodwill of wealthy landowners or religious houses and stone bridges built at this time across the River Wey by the monks of Waverley Abbey, such as those at Elstead, Tilford and Eashing, still survive.

The increasing evidence of trade and industry in medieval times includes the first mention of Chiddingfold's connection with glassmaking in the early 13th century when the techniques of manufacture were brought to the area by French glassworkers.

Glasshouses — oblong buildings containing furnaces — were established in the woods and, fuelled by charcoal made from local

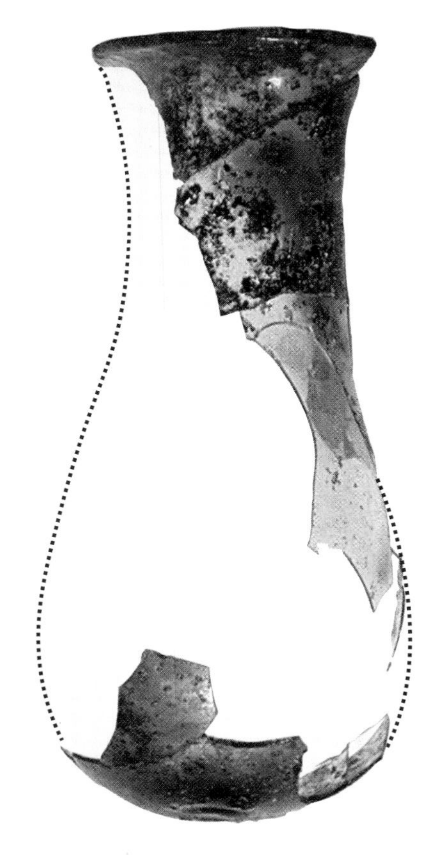

A 13th century glass urinal (used as an aid to medical diagnosis), found at Guildford Castle, shows the high-quality, thin, transparent products of which the early Wealden glass industry was capable.

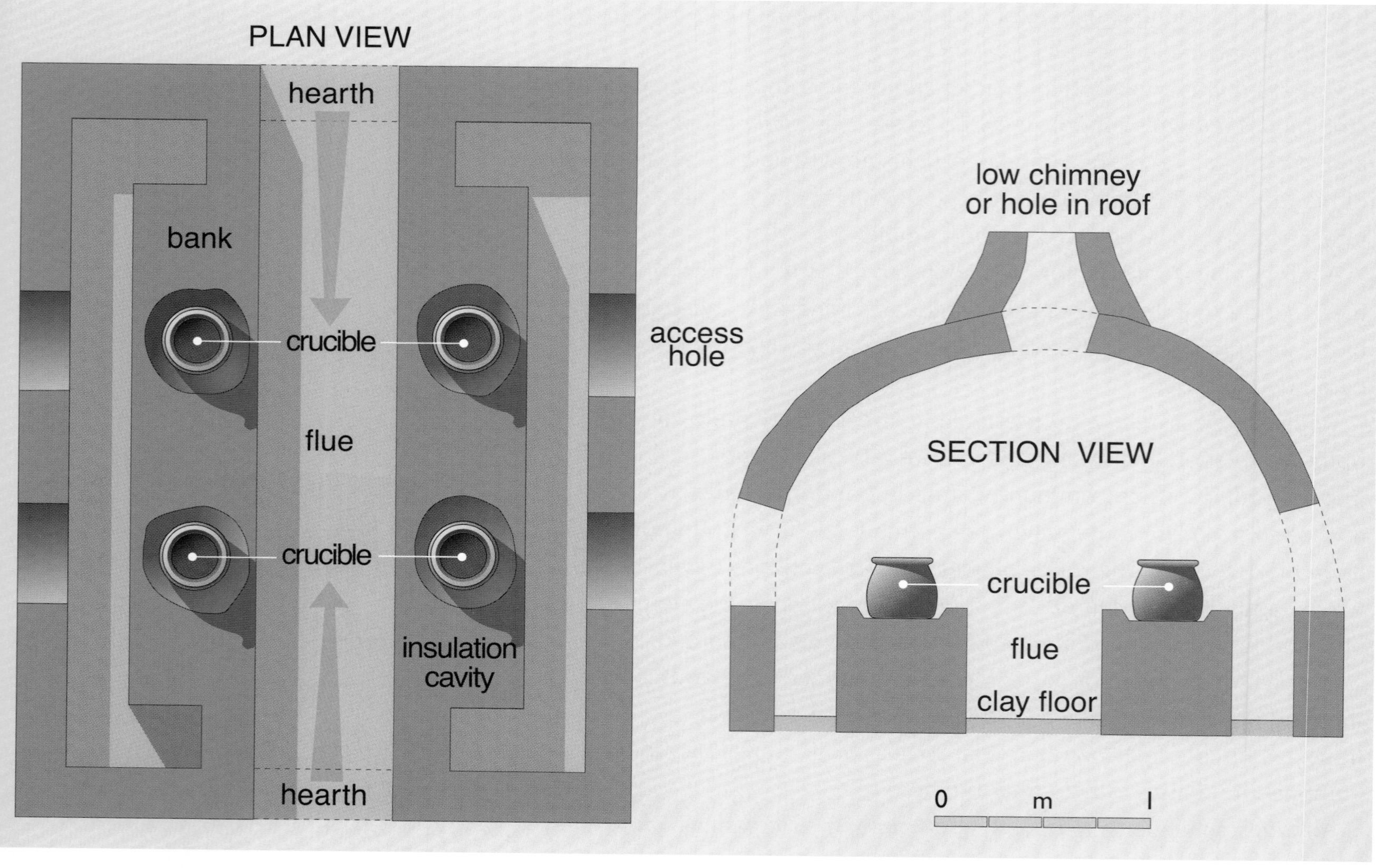

Reconstructed plan and section of the 14th century kiln for the production of Wealden glass, which was found in Blunden's Wood, Hambledon, in the 1960s.

timber, appear to have been the source of white and coloured glass supplied for use in Westminster Abbey in 1240. The village remained at the centre of English glassmaking for some 400 years until, in 1611, furnaces were established in London which used 'sea-coal' from Newcastle. In addition, the use of charcoal for glassmaking was prohibited and Sir Robert Mansell was granted a monopoly for coal-fired glass in 1615.

Evidence in Southwark from the 14th and 15th centuries indicates that it supplied London with goods and services and that there were shops, taverns and accommodation for travellers passing through.

As well as having a market, Southwark was granted the right to hold a fair in 1444 and objects recovered by excavation include leather shoes along with garments that may have come from a workshop or leather market near Bankside. Evidence of pilgrims survives in the form of pewter and silver badges purchased at shrines like Canterbury.

Southwark's well-established immigrant population included people from France, Holland and Flanders who put their skills to use and turned the area into a centre for stone-cutting and weaving while wharves, coal and timber yards grew up along the river front.

From the 13th century, and for more than 400 years, the manufacture of cloth formed the main industry of many villages across Surrey, but Guildford and Godalming were the key centres and consequently both still have wool-packs incorporated in their coats of arms.

Indeed, Guildford cloth was sufficiently highly regarded for the 'Merchant of Prato', the 14th century Italian, Francesco di Marco Datini, whose interests extended throughout the western Mediterranean, to buy Guildford cloth (*panni di Guildiforte*) in various colours.

While Surrey's soil was generally poor for agriculture it was highly suitable for the grazing of sheep and, in addition, there were rich beds of fuller's earth, a substance used for processing wool to remove oil and grease that would otherwise hinder its cleaning and dyeing.

As with the other Surrey industries, the rivers contributed to the establishment of the industry by supplying water for scouring and dyeing and to drive the hammers of

The framework knitting workshop in Godalming was purpose-built in about 1860. It housed 25 knitting frames on the ground floor, which had seven wide windows to maximise natural light. There was a packing room upstairs.

the fulling mills which shrunk and strengthened the cloth.

Whole families were involved in the process with the children preparing the wool, the mother spinning and the father weaving. At the same time, subsidiary industries such as leather dressing and glove making grew up.

The importance of the cloth industry diminished in the 17th century but continued in a reduced form until the middle of the 19th century. In the Godalming area the framework knitting industry provided a partial replacement from the late 17th century. It spread from London, and was at first concerned with luxury goods in silk and worsted.

OUTWOOD WINDMILL

Early windmills were of the post-mill type deriving their name from the massive wooden post upon which the upper part, containing the machinery and the millstones used for grinding the corn, was balanced so that it could be turned into the wind. The post mill at Outwood is said to have been built in 1665 and it is claimed that in the following year the miller, Thomas Budgen, watched the Great Fire of London as it raged beyond the Thames to the north.

Outwood post mill stood alone until around 1790 when Ezekiel and Isaac, the two brothers who by then owned the mill, quarrelled and Ezekiel built a new windmill close to the first. This second octagonal mill was a smock mill, so called because of its likeness to the smock which was the traditional dress of the countryman.

The smock mill had a rotating cap to which the sails were fixed, thus avoiding the need to turn the entire body of the mill to face the wind. Opposite the sails was a fantail that provided the power for the automatic gearing that turned the sails into the eye of the wind.

POST-MEDIEVAL

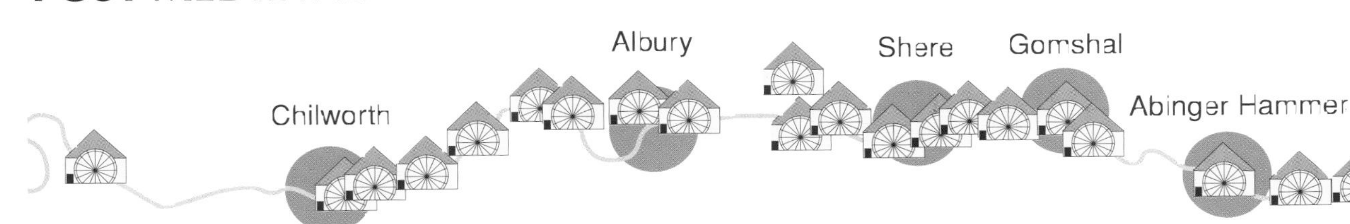

The number and variety of mills on the Tillingbourne in the 17th and 18th centuries is astonishing. There were corn, fulling, wire, gunpowder, paper and brass mills, and also an iron forge and tanneries.

The Wealden iron industry was not as extensive in Surrey as in Sussex, yet iron making was an important activity in the south of the county. At first iron could only be smelted in relatively small quantities in simple bloomery furnaces but around 1500 the blast furnace was introduced from France. This produced cast iron which was cast into guns or converted into wrought iron for the market by beating out carbon with great forge hammers. Both blast furnaces and forges were situated on fast-flowing streams which powered the bellows and hammers. To harness the water effectively streams were diverted and dammed to create 'hammer' ponds which acted as reservoirs.

In north Surrey, at Cobham, Byfleet and Weybridge, iron mills produced a huge range of manufactured goods, and village blacksmiths operated everywhere. At Abinger Hammer, the figure of a blacksmith who strikes his hammer against the bell of a clock makes a romantic play on the name of the village, which from 1557 to 1787 was the site of a Wealden iron forge.

Timber was essential to produce the charcoal needed in iron manufacture and other industries so, amongst the woods lived the charcoal burners or colliers who cut timber and built it into heaps which they covered in turf before firing. To smelt one ton of iron two tons of charcoal were required and to produce two tons of charcoal four tons of wood were consumed.

From 1555 each parish was responsible for the upkeep of its roads but many were so deeply rutted that they were virtually impassable to wagons and many horse riders struck out directly across farmland.

When these photographs of charcoal burners in West Surrey were taken in the late 19th century, they captured the final years of an industry whose modes of production (top) and packing (bottom) were probably little altered from the medieval period.

Cart Bridge over the Wey Navigation at Send. It was built in 1759 to replace an earlier timber bridge.

A new trade route was created with the construction of the Wey Navigation which opened in 1653 on the initiative of Sir Richard Weston of Sutton Place and was soon carrying goods such as corn, timber, coal, malt, hides, skins, lime and gunpowder. Later it was linked to the Basingstoke Canal which was completed in 1796.

At last, in the mid-17th century, the problems with the roads were recognised as being an obstacle to trade and the first 'Turnpike' Act was passed in 1663. Usually backed by landowners, merchants and farmers, the turnpike trusts put up barriers and levied a toll which paid for the maintenance of the roads.

The first such road in Surrey was a 16km (10 mile) stretch between Reigate and Crawley. Authorised in 1696 as a saddle horse road, it had a row of wooden posts down the centre to prevent wheeled traffic from using it.

When it was improved for carriages in 1755 it linked with the

The tollgate at Tadworth on the turnpike road to Reigate, from a watercolour of 1881.

GUNPOWDER AND OTHER MILLS

Gunpowder was an important industry in Surrey from the 16th century and there were early mills at Tolworth, Godstone and Wotton but the site at Chilworth lasted longest.

It was in 1626 that the East India Company, which was licensed to produce gunpowder for its own use, established the first gunpowder mills at Chilworth and these were expanded by Charles I and given a Crown monopoly in the 1630s. By 1677 the mills stretched for about a mile along the Tillingbourne valley and during the period of the Dutch and French wars were the largest in the country, but subsequently some were converted to the production of paper.

When, in November 1822, William Cobbett visited Chilworth he wrote that the valley had been 'so perverted as to make it instrumental in effecting two of the most damnable of purposes … the making of gunpowder and of bank-notes!'

At their peak the mills employed as many as 400 people. Significant expansion of the works began in the 1860s, when steam power was introduced. In 1885 the Chilworth Gunpowder Company was formed, as a subsidiary of a German company, to manufacture an improved gunpowder. Most of the surviving buildings belong to this era, including the gatehouse.

In 1888 a tramway, of which parts still survive, including the swing bridge across the river (below left), was built linking the works with Chilworth and Albury railway station. Prior to this the materials needed for manufacture — saltpetre and sulphur — as well as the finished gunpowder had been transported by barge along the Godalming and Wey Navigations.

Further expansion of the site occurred during the First World War but in 1920 the gunpowder works closed. The photograph shows the Incorporating Mills of 1885, and demonstrates how overgrown the site has become since the works closed.

For sheer concentration of industry the River Wandle is worthy of note. Just 18km (11 miles) long from its source at Croydon to the Thames at Wandsworth it drove 68 waterwheels in the early 18th century. Even in the 13th century the calico-bleaching and hat-making industries had used its waters and by the second half of the 17th century Wandsworth was notable for its brass mills and later brewing became established.

Most famous of the works along the Wandle were the Liberty site at Merton, where textiles were printed for the famous Regent Street shop, and the Merton Abbey workshops of William Morris's company, Morris & Co, which were a centre of production from 1881.

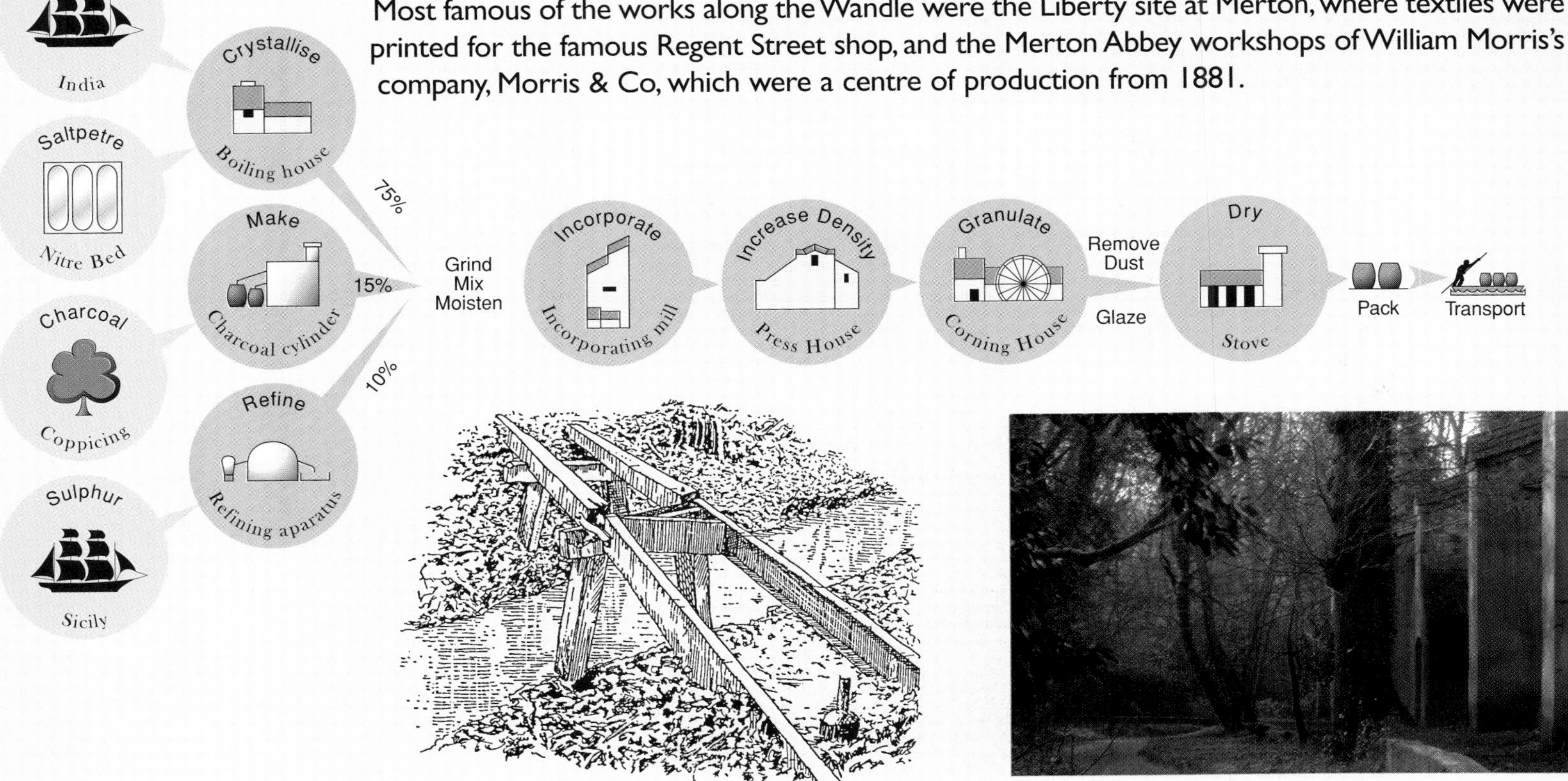

The Angel, in Guildford, was a well-known 19th century coaching inn.

London to Sutton road which had been turnpiked in 1718, making it possible for wheeled carriages to run on decent roads for the first time from London to the resort of Brighton.

The route from London to Portsmouth became linked in similar stages with its full length finally open in 1749. Up to then the 112km (70 mile) journey from London to Portsmouth had taken fourteen hours, which often led to an overnight stay in one of the inns along the way. The turnpike road cut the time to as little as nine hours, with the coaches changing horses at 16–19km (10–12 mile) stages.

Coaching inns such as The Bear at Esher, which is said to have boasted stabling for 100 horses, grew up alongside the roads in a similar way to the motorway services of today and, as a consequence, the economy of many villages and towns was boosted.

THE MODERN ERA BEGINS

When on 26 July 1803 the Surrey Iron Railway opened it was the first public railway in the world. The Parliamentary Bill authorising it stated that it should run from 'a place called Ram Field in the parish of Wandsworth, to or near to a Place called Pitlake Meadow in the Town of Croydon, and a Collateral Branch … to a place called Hack Bridge in the Parish of Carshalton'.

A lock and basin were built at the confluence of the Wandle and the Thames at Wandsworth and the cast iron rails were laid along the route. Horses pulled the 'train' and the high upturned flange of the rails guided the wagon wheels, which meant that the wheels could have a flat rim so that the wooden wagons could be hauled to their final destination by road.

A toll was charged per mile which permitted merchants or carriers to use their own wagons and horses. The toll sheet of 1804 lists dung at 1d per ton per mile while coal per chaldron (just over a ton) was 3d. Passengers were not generally carried but the wagons were sometimes cleaned out and used for excursions or

THE FARNHAM POTTERY

Literally dozens of modest-sized potteries and brickworks once existed in the Farnham area, making use of the ready supply of easily dug red-firing and white-firing clays as well as local wood and turf. In addition, the proximity of the area to London meant their cheap and serviceable wares could easily be transported to the capital by barge and later by wagon.

The Farnham Pottery (left), one of the last to be established, was founded by Absalom Harris in 1872 at a time when the existence of country potteries was becoming threatened by the Victorian age of factory production.

Despite this, Absalom built a workshop and designed his own up-draught kilns which had loading chambers of some 28 cubic metres (1,000 cubic feet). Each took about three days to load and once full was fired, using coal and wood, to a temperature of 1,000 degrees centigrade (1,800 degrees Fahrenheit). This process took a further three days and then the kiln was allowed to cool for a week before being unloaded.

The Pottery used both pole-powered wheels (below right) and treadle wheels, some of which were geared to rotate very fast, making possible the economic production of small flowerpots. Skilled potters, who were on piece work, could produce three 9-cm (3½ inch) plant pots per minute — more than 1,000 per day.

By the 1920s, the Pottery had become an integral part of the Arts and Crafts movement in west Surrey and at one point produced a range of 'art' pottery (below left), tiles and architectural mouldings of such quality that they were supplied to the Queen Mother and Gertrude Jekyll.

A watercolour of 1823 shows a train of wagons, pulled by a horse along the Surrey Iron Railway, as it crosses the Chipstead Valley Road.

organised outings. The following year the line was extended to carry materials from the fuller's earth pits and chalk quarries at Nutfield and Merstham to the Thames. Later a further section was built to link with the Croydon Canal but, with the coming of steam railways, it could no longer compete and the Surrey Iron Railway closed in 1846.

By the 1840s the iron tentacles of the railway system were spreading rapidly across Surrey and eventually led to the abandonment of the canals as a means of carrying goods. The impact of the railway is clearly illustrated by the growth of

Stripping of the ground for the Clacket Lane service station on the M25, revealed the patches of black soil which indicated the site of pottery production (left). Further excavation revealed the distinctive kilns of the Limpsfield medieval pottery industry. The reconstruction (below) is of the kiln and associated work areas at Vicar's Haw, Limpsfield.

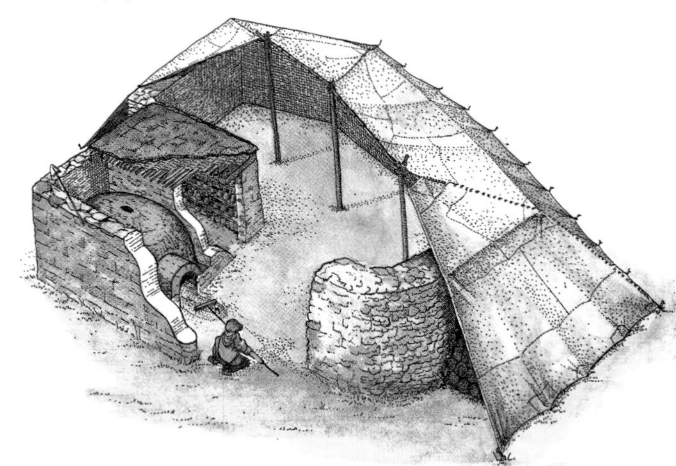

Guildford's population. Between 1739 and the beginning of the 19th century it had increased from about 2,500 to only 2,639 yet by the end of the century it was 9,000, with the London and South Western Railway having reached the town in 1845.

From 1862 local highway boards began to take over from the unprofitable turnpike trusts. The Brighton turnpike became the last to be a free road in 1881 and within a hundred years motorways were being built across the landscape. Today the county has the M3, M23 and M25, the construction of which was begun in 1972 and ironically led to the discovery of archaeological finds that make it possible to tell some of the history of the county.

7 THE FUTURE OF THE PAST

FINDING THE PAST

From archaeology emerges the story of man. It is a tale fabulously rich in intrigue and mystery and the piecing together of evidence sometimes has all the suspense of the best detective fiction.

As with any good mystery the amateur can play an important role but, today, highly sophisticated analytical and scientific techniques are also vital keys in unlocking the exciting kaleidoscope of history.

However ephemeral we may think our lives to be it soon becomes clear that we all leave our imprint on the landscape. Whether it is the discovery of a coin buried in the ground or signs of field systems revealed by aerial photography it is impossible to escape the lives of our ancestors.

Speculation about the past is nothing new and the first archaeologists were enthusiastic amateurs. Even the most scholarly amongst them lacked the skills and techniques that the modern archaeologist is able to employ so, although well meaning, they often unwittingly destroyed evidence or did not make the necessary formal records.

For this reason early discoveries are now often hard to explain and, although modern techniques can sometimes be applied to old finds, it

A report on the excavations at Chertsey Abbey appeared in the very first volume of the Surrey Archaeological Collections *in 1858. This stimulated further investigations, most of the work being done by the three labourers (Mason, Jack and Bob) shown in this 1861 photograph.*

is mostly recent work that we rely upon today for our understanding of the past.

It was not until the middle of the 19th century that the discipline of archaeology began to be established. The Surrey Archaeology Society itself was formed in 1854 'for the investigation of subjects connected with the history and antiquities of the County of Surrey'.

Members were soon involved in properly organised excavations and the findings were published, as they still are today, in the *Surrey Archaeological Collections*. These volumes form the main record of archaeological work in the county, and the basic data for future research.

MODERN METHODS

Key facets of modern archaeology are accurate recording and investigation followed by the publication of results — it is only then that the real importance of any discovery becomes apparent and can be related to the wider picture that helps us form a better understanding of Surrey's past.

There are many processes involved in the progress from the initial discovery of archaeological evidence to its analysis and presentation to the public. Each of these stages relies not just upon a huge range of techniques, but also on the expertise of specialists from a wide range of backgrounds, including computing, medicine and natural history.

Systematic fieldwalking is used to locate evidence disturbed by the plough and may be followed by the mapping and planning of sites and their settings. Geophysical surveys are also employed using sophisticated electronic equipment to obtain data to reveal the pattern of buried remains by computer analysis.

A hearth of hard-fired clay at Thorpe Lea Nurseries, Egham, is being sampled for archaeomagnetic dating by the late Dr A J Clark, who pioneered the technique. The direction and strength of the Earth's magnetic field varied considerably in the past. When clay is fired, the iron oxides within it preserve a record of the Earth's magnetic field at the time of heating. Laboratory measurements showed that this hearth was fired in the 4th century AD.

Interestingly though, digging itself — with the archaeologist's tools of trowel, mattock, brush, and shovel — remains resistant to technological progress. At the heart of the work, the interaction of people directly with the remains of their ancestors is of crucial importance.

Nevertheless, the use of computers and electronic surveying instruments is of increasing importance for all the recording work involved in excavation, with data recovered in this way being analysed by ever more sophisticated means.

Finds, too, are made to yield up their secrets by a battery of scientific techniques. Their diversity is vast, ranging from the microscopic study of wear patterns on flint tools to determine how and what they were used for, to the use of a nuclear reactor for neutron activation analysis to determine the concentration of different elements and hence the source of raw materials.

Similarly, when skeletons are recovered, examination using X-rays and other scientific techniques can provide a wealth of evidence about the prevalence of diseases, such as TB and osteoporosis, diet, and life expectancy.

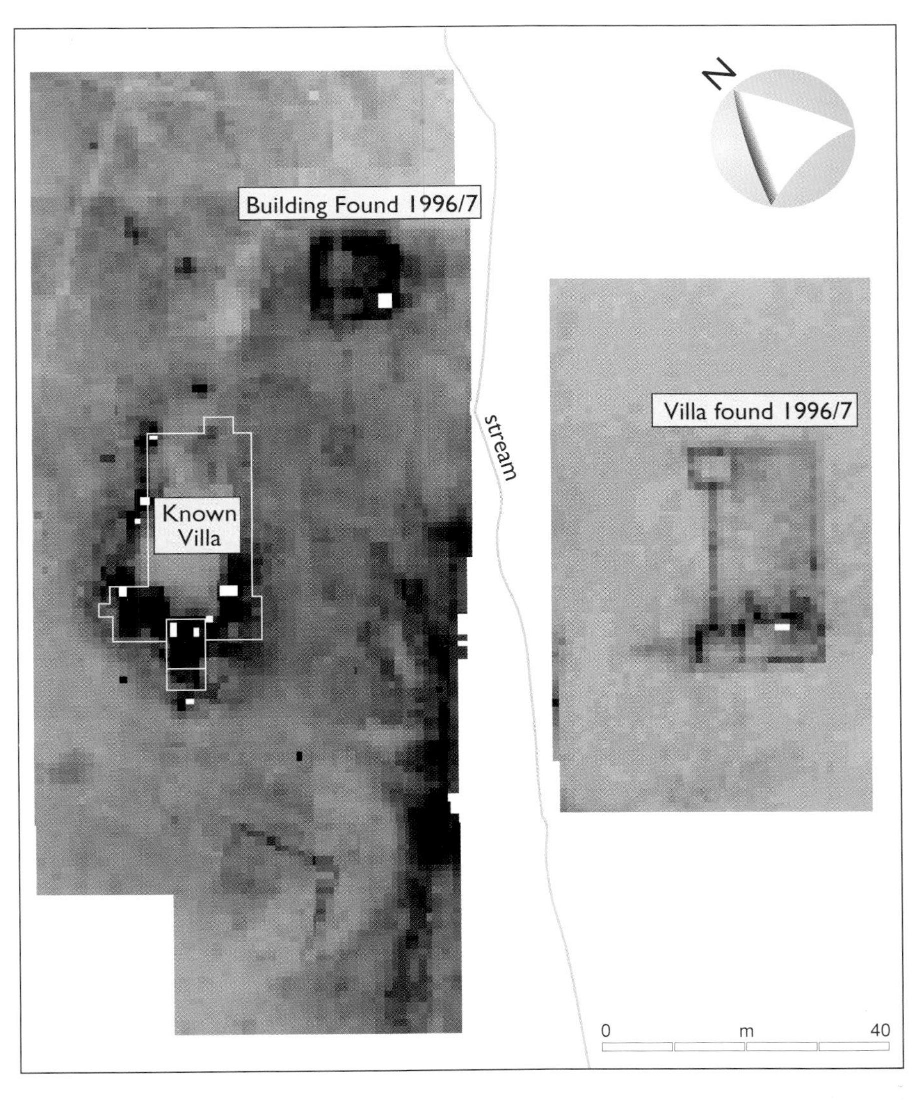

The 'twin' Roman villas at Titsey, as revealed by geophysical survey in 1996–7 and by earlier investigations.

LOST AND FOUND

The ability to put evidence into context is vital and this is why damage to historical sites by treasure seekers is so disastrous. Removing just one item or interfering with evidence in its context can forever destroy our chance of understanding a piece of history.

At Wanborough, near Guildford, in the 1980s, the site of a Roman temple was severely damaged when treasure hunters dug holes all over it to recover Iron Age gold and silver coins. In response to this, The Surrey Archaeological Society became closely involved in efforts

A 5,500 year old ceremonial monument (a henge) was found and excavated at Shepperton prior to gravel extraction. As soon as the archaeological work was finished, the ditch and all other parts of the monument were bulldozed away so quarrying could continue.

to change the law. As a result, the Treasure Act became law in 1997 and has succeeded in ensuring that more objects of archaeological importance find their way into museums. Co-operation between metal detector users and archaeologists has also improved.

Nature can also play a significant role in distorting the interpretation of the past, since rivers and changing sea levels have, and continue to have, a dramatic impact on the landscape and sometimes move artefacts from their original context in the process.

Unfortunately the loss of our heritage has accelerated rapidly. Aerial photographs taken of Surrey before the Second World War reveal patterns indicating the remains of ancient buildings and field systems. Now these traces are being devastated because of the effects of ploughing and erosion.

Ironically the impending destruction of archaeological evidence through housing or office development, gravel extraction, road building or even the laying of water mains or gas pipes means that there is a chance to learn because archaeological investigation may be undertaken as part of the work.

Archaeology has now become firmly established as a factor to be considered in the planning process. The aim is to ensure that evidence for the past is preserved, or, if that is not possible, to make sure it is properly recorded.

ARCHAEOLOGY AT WORK

The work that arises through the planning system is mainly carried out by professional archaeological teams, usually working on behalf of the developer, agreeing the best way forward at each stage of the process with the planning authority.

Such work is about far more than digging. The first stage in many investigations is detailed desk-based appraisal of available information. Sample excavations may be made to evaluate the

PROTECTING OUR PAST

Our heritage is still not as well protected as it should be. Monuments of national importance are protected by law (scheduled monuments), as are listed buildings (in three grades, I, II* and II). Otherwise protection is only provided through the planning process, which means that much can be lost to activities not regulated in this way, such as farming or forestry.

The government Planning Policy Guidance notes (PPG 15 and 16) have had a major impact on the management of the historic environment. They have led to the development of planning policies in County Structure Plans and District Local Plans which form the basis for the current system of rescue archaeology, including the recording of historic buildings. These helped, for instance, to ensure the proper recording of a 17th century wall painting, showing a dragon, at Bagshot, when it was unexpectedly discovered during office refurbishment (below right).

As a result, developers are asked to provide information about the potential effects of their proposals on aspects of the historic environment, such as buried archaeology or the fabric of historic buildings. Where necessary, if permission is given, the developer will be required to make arrangements for archaeological excavation or building recording in advance. Many of the important discoveries mentioned in this book have been made as a result of this system. For example, archaeological excavation was made possible on a constricted urban site in Swan Lane, Guildford (above left). The photograph shows Swan Lane on the left, with the chalk foundation of a long-demolished 14th century building revealed alongside it.

The planning process also provides some extra protection for historic buildings through the creation of Conservation Areas and local lists of significant buildings. Historic parks and gardens entered on a Register created by English Heritage are also taken into account and work is under way to create lists of locally important historic gardens.

A category of Areas of Special Historic Landscape Value has also been created in Surrey in an attempt to seek better management for historic landscape features. Recently some measure of protection for historic hedgerows has also been introduced at a national level.

Volunteers helping to carry out a survey of the historic landscape at Mickleham.

archaeological potential of sites and can be followed by more intensive investigation to provide a detailed record.

Much still remains to be done even after evidence emerges above ground, since the records and finds need to be ordered, analysed and interpreted and the results made available to everyone.

In the end, all the finds and records are deposited in museums, which have the expertise to conserve and protect them for the future. Of equal importance is the fact that these materials can then be used to develop the displays and interpretations that the museums provide.

'Rescue' excavation, the work that takes place during new developments, is only one aspect of modern archaeology. Research of many types is also being carried out. Often this may involve the re-examination of old finds and records, using the broad range of modern scientific techniques.

Equally, it may involve fieldwork, looking, for example, in detail at the local landscape and identifying the factors which reflect its shaping by people over many centuries.

There is a great opportunity for the involvement of volunteers, and this has been particularly the focus of the Community Archaeology Programme, which has been developed by Surrey County Council and Surrey Archaeological Society in recent years.

There is an increasing emphasis on training and the Surrey Archaeological Society has been instrumental in establishing adult education courses in archaeology and the provision of training digs. Literally hundreds of people now have some basic knowledge of the

This dug-out boat was found in the River Wey at Wisley in 1907. Thanks to its preservation in Guildford Museum it has recently been possible to use radiocarbon dating to show that it was made in the 12th century.

disciplines needed such as stratigraphy, recording, photography and environmental sampling.

In this way a body of people of all ages has been established who, although not completely qualified, have the basic skills to be able to join excavation teams, make discoveries and assess what they have found.

ARCHAEOLOGY IN THE FUTURE

Undoubtedly the uncertainty and excitement involved with predicting the future and interpreting the past helps explain the attraction of these activities.

There can be no doubt that in the 21st century archaeologists will employ an increasing variety of ever more sophisticated scientific techniques to help them. These, in combination with new fieldwork, will produce the fresh data which will inevitably change many of the interpretations put forward in this book — in archaeology no case is ever closed.

It is not only new facts which change our understanding of the past; very often it is different ways of looking at things which alter interpretations.

For example, almost invariably, archaeologists used to regard the artefacts they found as the rubbish which people threw away. Increasingly, now, it is suspected that many objects were deliberately deposited, and this gives an interesting glimpse into people's attitudes to the natural and spiritual worlds.

There is no doubt that there has been strong growth in the amount of archaeological work being done in recent years and that this will continue in the foreseeable future.

In the final decades of the 20th century this growth was sometimes frantic, and certainly fragmented, with the involvement of many different organisations. Efforts are now being made to ensure better co-ordination and to

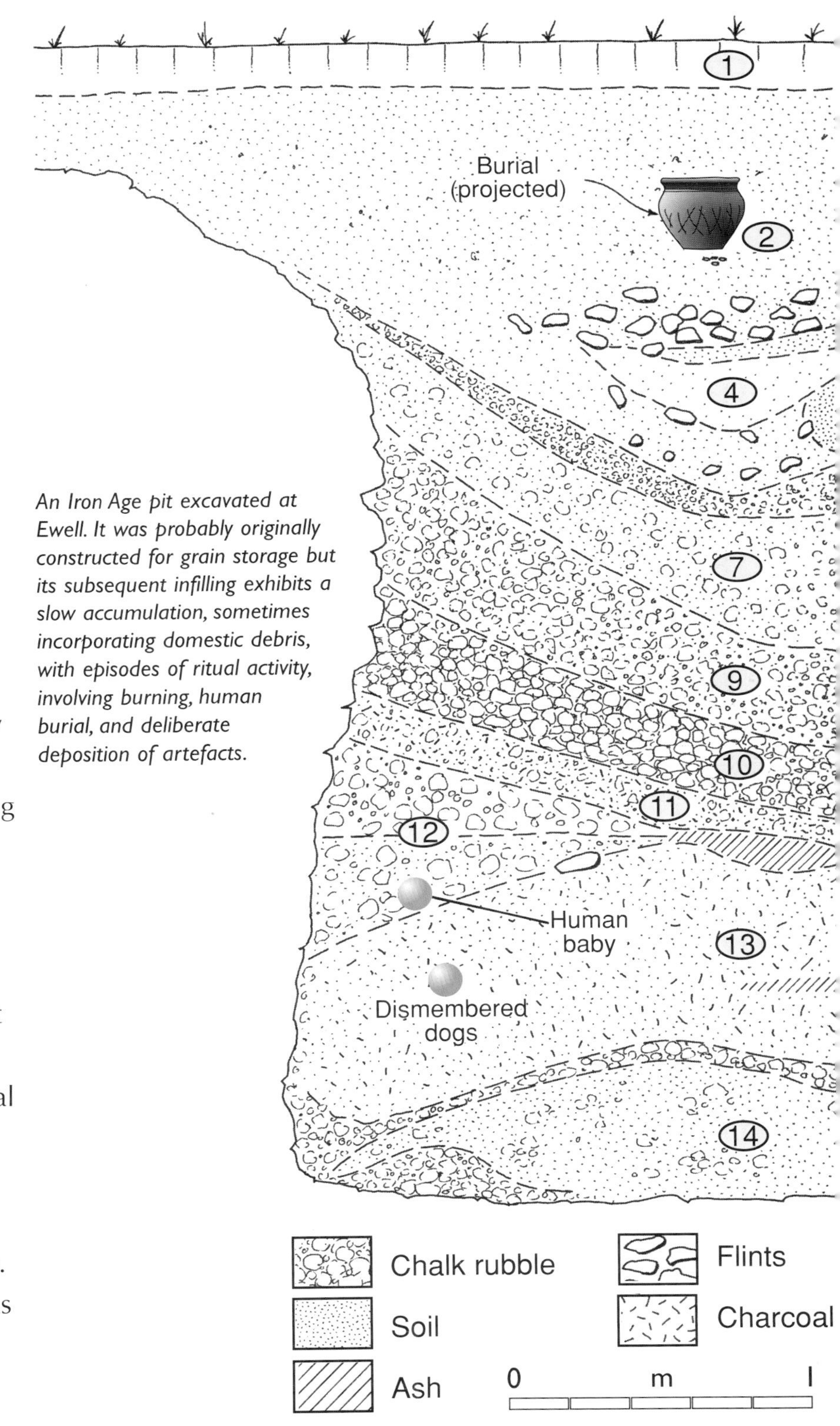

An Iron Age pit excavated at Ewell. It was probably originally constructed for grain storage but its subsequent infilling exhibits a slow accumulation, sometimes incorporating domestic debris, with episodes of ritual activity, involving burning, human burial, and deliberate deposition of artefacts.

Displays at the busy Clacket Lane Services, on the M25 near Westerham, record the archaeological finds made during their construction, including medieval pottery kilns. The photograph shows a visit by Sir Geoffrey Howe, the local MP.

develop a strategy for the future.

It is very important that this strategy should address the needs of the increasing numbers of people whose interest in the past has been stimulated by a variety of television programmes.

The results of archaeological work must be made more widely available so that they can be appreciated by everyone through exhibitions, heritage trails, interpretation boards, schools and adult education classes, as well as books.

However, it is not only a matter of communication but also one of involvement. The Surrey Archaeological Society and numerous museums and local societies provide opportunities to participate. The level of interest in our heritage has never been higher and people want and need to be informed, so that they can help preserve their local environment in the face of a multiplicity of changes.

Whether you wish to join in or simply find out more, the following pages should help. Greater knowledge and more participation will together form the best safeguard for the future of the past.

The 18th century mill at Stoke, near Guildford, is now home to the Surrey Advertiser, showing that preserving our heritage need not be in conflict with change.

glossary

Acheulian Palaeolithic culture characterised by certain types of hand axe. Named after the site at St Acheul in France, it occupied the time span roughly from 500,000 to about 70,000 years ago.

Amphora A large two-handled vessel used for the transport of wine or olive oil. It had a distinctive narrow base to allow ease of stacking.

Apse A semicircular structure, often with a semi-domed roof, situated at the end of a building.

Ard A type of primitive plough with no mouldboard to turn the soil over.

Artefact An object made by a human being.

Ashlar Square-cut stone; masonry constructed of such stones laid in horizontal courses with vertical joints. Also used as a facing to rubble or brick walls.

Atrebates A late Iron Age tribe whose capital was at Silchester and whose territory is thought to have included parts of Surrey.

Aurochs The wild ox (now extinct) which was the ancestor of domestic cattle in Europe.

Banjo enclosure An Iron Age circular ditched enclosure with a long entrance, similar in shape to a banjo.

Baron A minor aristocrat who held his lands from the king or other feudal lord, usually in exchange for military service.

Barrow — Bell A circular Bronze Age burial mound with a slight flat area (berm) between the mound and the surrounding ditch.

Barrow — Bowl A circular Bronze Age burial mound where the ditch immediately surrounds the mound.

Barrow — Disc A Bronze Age burial monument consisting of a round external bank with an internal ditch enclosing a circular flat area (berm) with a small mound at the centre.

Beaker people Early Bronze Age culture characterised by a particular style of pot.

Broom squires 19th century name given to people who lived on the commons and made their living from making and selling brooms of birch or heather bound with hazel.

Burghal Hidage 10th century list of *burhs* in Wessex (the kingdom of the West Saxons).

Burh Saxon defensive earthwork enclosure, some surrounded towns.

Cames Lead strips used to hold panes of window glass in place. The cames had grooves into which the pieces of glass were fitted.

Capital messuage Lord of the manor's principal house.

Causewayed camp Early to middle Neolithic enclosure consisting of one or more concentric circles of banks and ditches crossed by numerous causeways.

Celtic Generic name given to the Iron Age peoples of Western Europe and continuing in use in the post-Roman period to describe the population of the western fringes of the Continent — in Britain the peoples of Cornwall, Wales, Scotland and Ireland.

Chaldron A medieval unit of weight, approximately one ton, usually applied to lead and later to coals.

Chapter House The building where the business of the monastery was conducted.

Cist A prehistoric burial-chamber made with stone slabs.

Clamp (kiln) Early structure for firing pottery. The pots were stacked and baked in a pit beneath a bonfire.

Cluniac Monastic order with its mother house at Cluny, near Mâcon in France.

Cohort A unit of the Roman army. Each legion was divided into ten cohorts and each cohort in theory consisted of 480 soldiers.

Cremation The burning of human remains which may then be placed in a container before burial (see also inhumation — below).

Crenellate A means of defending walls by leaving openings through which arrows or guns could be fired at attacking forces.

Crown-antler mace-head Neolithic antler object resembling a mace-head, but of uncertain function.

Crucible A pot, usually of earthenware, for melting metals or glass in a furnace.

Cursus A long narrow enclosure bounded by parallel ditches, usually with a central bank, sometimes several miles in length. Neolithic in date, they are often close to henges and are therefore probably intended for some religious purpose — perhaps as processional ways.

Cybele A Roman goddess referred to as 'The Great Mother of the Gods'.

Daub A mixture of mud and hair used as plaster and particularly to cover wattle panels in timber-framed buildings.

Dendrochronology The science of dating by means of the comparative study of the growth rings in timber.

Dip slope Gentle slope of the land that approximately follows that of the underlying geological strata.

Dissolution (of the Monasteries) Action by Henry VIII dissolving the monasteries, friaries and abbeys by Acts of Parliament of 1536–9.

Domesday Book A survey of landholdings carried out by the order of William the Conqueror, and completed in 1086.

Dominicans The order of Friars Preachers (Black Friars), founded in 1215 by the Spanish priest St Dominic (c1170–1221).

Environmental sampling Microscopic examination of soil samples used to reveal the remains of ancient animals and plants that can give clues to the past uses of a particular area of land.

Feudal A medieval system of administration, jurisdiction and land holding. It was based on the relationship between a person who worked the land and his superiors, the highest lord of which was often the king, and by which land was granted in return for allegiance, military service, and other duties.

Fibula Latin name for a brooch, usually used for either holding clothes together (like a safety pin) or for decoration or for both.

Flint blade Longitudinal piece of deliberately struck flint, sometimes used as a knife or scraper.

Framework knitting The manufacture of hosiery and other items of clothing using developed forms of the stocking frame invented in England in 1589.

Fuller's earth A fine clay used to clean and degrease cloth.

Garderobe A privy or lavatory.

Geophysical survey A method of detecting below-ground features using scientific techniques.

Greensand Geological deposits comprising the Upper and Lower Greensand separated by the Gault Clay.

Grooved Ware A type of pottery made during the Neolithic *c*3000 –2000 BC. The pots were bucket or flowerpot shaped with thick walls and were decorated with grooved lines.
Hammer pond An artificial pond built to provide power to drive a hammer in an iron works.
Henge A Neolithic ceremonial site. Usually circular in shape with a ditch and external bank.
Hide An area of land that varied with soil quality and could be between 24 and 72ha (60 and 180 acres). In the Domesday survey of 1086 it was used as a basis for tax assessment.
Holloway A sunken track, usually the result of erosion caused by the passage of traffic and animals over the years.
Hundred A Saxon and medieval land division with its own court system. Basically an area capable of providing a hundred fighting men — the actual physical size varied depending on the agricultural productivity of the land.
Hypocaust An under-floor heating system used in the Roman period.
Infra-red photography Uses a type of film that records heat given off by vegetation. This shows the health of each plant which is affected by the underlying soil. The technique can reveal buried archaeological features.
Inhumation The practice of burying a human corpse (see also cremation — above).
Keep A tower, sometimes built on a raised mound and which functioned as the most heavily defended part of a castle.
Loomweight A type of weight used to hold warp threads taut during the weaving of cloth on a vertical loom. In prehistoric and Saxon times loomweights were often made of clay and shaped like doughnuts.
Lorica segmentata Roman armour made of iron strips.
Mace-head A weapon resembling a hammer. In the prehistoric period maces may have been ceremonial as well, but in medieval times they were mainly used as weapons, particularly by bishops who were forbidden by the Bible to use weapons that had a cutting edge.
Manor House Generally the largest house in the manor and home of the lord. Manors form one of the basic landholding units within the feudal system.
Midden A rubbish heap or pit.
Minster The church of a monastery; the term is also used for a large or important church.
Moat A water-filled ditch surrounding a castle or dwelling.
Mortlake bowl A type of Neolithic ceramic pot with a rounded base.
Motte and bailey A type of Norman castle, with an outer bailey, enclosed by a ditch, which contained a range of buildings and an earth mound, or motte, which formed the most strongly defended part of the castle.
Opus signinum A hard waterproof Roman cement coloured red by the addition of crushed tile.
Palisade A fence of closely spaced, pointed, wooden stakes fixed deeply in the ground, as a defence.
Pillbox A defensive concrete shelter, often containing a machine-gunpost Large numbers were built during the Second World War.
Pot boilers Stones heated in a fire and then dropped into water to heat it.
Potin coins Bronze coins containing a high proportion of tin. They seem to have been used in Kent and the Thames valley area as small change in the late Iron Age and early Roman period.
Quern A hand-mill consisting of an upper and a lower stone for grinding corn to make flour.
Quoin An external angle of a wall or building or any of the stones or bricks forming this angle; the term is also used to describe a cornerstone.
Radiocarbon dating A dating technique based on carbon 14 — a radioactive isotope which is present in all living things and which decays at a known rate after death.
Roundhouse Name for a circular hut. Occasionally quite large and usually of Bronze Age or Iron Age date.
Saddle quern Iron Age type of quern which consisted of a lower stone (saddle) on which the grain was placed and an upper stone (rider) which was pushed backwards and forwards on top to grind the corn into flour.
Saltpetre Potassium nitrate, the major ingredient of gunpowder.
Samian A type of glossy red Roman pottery. Often highly decorated, it was imported into Britain from Gaul in the 1st, 2nd and early 3rd centuries AD and used as fine tableware.
Sarsen A large boulder or block of grey sandstone or conglomerate. Such stones were frequently used as boundary markers and also in the construction of prehistoric monuments.
Semaphore A mechanical system of signalling by pivoted arms which passed messages between the Admiralty in London and the naval base of Portsmouth. It opened in 1822 and replaced the 18th century shutter system dismantled in 1816.
Sherd A fragment of pottery.
Spelt A type of primitive wheat grown in the prehistoric and Roman periods.
Spindle-whorl Rotating weight on a hand–held spindle or pulley on the spindle of a spinning wheel.
Stratigraphy The relationship between archaeological layers and features. In general terms, where one layer or feature overlies or cuts through another, the upper one is later in date.
Temenos Boundary surrounding the precinct of a Roman temple.
Truss A framework of rafters, posts, and struts, supporting a roof.
Turnpike A road built by private financiers who charged travellers to use it.
Undercroft The room beneath the main accommodation of a medieval building; often used to store merchandise or foodstuffs.
Vernacular Name given to buildings or styles based on local tradition.
Villa A high-status Roman building, usually the main house on a country estate and normally built of stone with a tiled roof.
Wattle and daub Branches or thin rods (wattles) woven together and covered with a mixture of mud and hair (daub). These panels were used to infill the spaces between timber uprights in walls of buildings.
Whiteware A type of medieval pottery made from white-firing clay. It was in widespread use in the 13th century and the main area of manufacture was on the Surrey/Hampshire border.

further reading

Some of the books on the list may no longer be in print, but should be available through public libraries, the Surrey History Centre at Woking, or the Surrey Archaeological Society library at Guildford.

SURREY

The Archaeology of Surrey to 1540, J & D G Bird (eds), Surrey Archaeological Society, 1987

Surrey's Industrial Past, G Crocker (ed), Surrey Industrial History Group, 1999

Surrey: Ordnance Survey Historical Guides, D Turner, 1988

The Churches of Surrey, M Blatch, Phillimore, 1997

In Pursuit of the Picturesque, J Percy. Surrey Gardens Trust, 2001

Farmsteads and Farm Buildings in Surrey, P Gray, Surrey County Council, 1998

Watermills of Surrey, D Stidder, Barracuda Books, 1990

The Royal Castle and Palace at Guildford, R Poulton, Surrey Archaeological Society, 1999

The Victoria History of the County of Surrey, H E Malden (ed) 4 vols, 1902–12

Buildings of England: Surrey, I Nairn, N Pevsner, B Cherry, 1971

Surrey Railways Remembered, L Oppitz, Countryside Books, 1988

Surrey Archaeological Society publishes the *Surrey Archaeological Collections*, *Bulletin*, and many other individual publications.
Catalogue of publications available from: Surrey Archaeological Society, Castle Arch, Guildford, GU1 3SX.
web: www.surreyarchaeology.org.uk
Surrey Industrial History Group publishes guides to the industrial history of the eleven administrative districts in the county.
web: shs.surreycc.gov.uk/sihg/

GENERAL

Archaeology: an Introduction, K Greene, (RKP) 1996

Discovering Timber-framed Buildings, R Harris, Shire Publications, 1979

Historical Britain, E S Wood, The Harvill Press, 1995

The History of the Countryside, O Rackham, J M Dent, 1986 (1st edn)

Oxford Illustrated Prehistory of Europe, B Cunliffe (ed), (OUP), 1994

Batsford Companion to Local History, S Friar, 1991

Shire Publications produces popular books on a wide range of subjects.
Catalogue available from: Shire Publications Ltd, Cromwell House, Church Street, Princes Risborough, HP27 9AA.
web: shirebooks.co.uk/

English Heritage publishes the *Gatekeeper Series*: a range of highly illustrated books that reconstructs daily life in ancient monuments such as castles and villas.
Catalogue available from: English Heritage Postal Sales, Knights of Old Ltd, Kettering Parkway, Kettering, NN15 6XU
web: www.english-heritage.org.uk/

Sources of information

Surrey History Centre
web: shs.surreycc.gov.uk/ (see page 172 for more information)

Surrey Sites & Monuments Record
Database held at County Hall in Kingston providing information about known archaeological sites and finds in the county. Bona fide researchers are welcome; contact **020 8541 9083** for an appointment.

gazetteer

A list of all museums and a selection, based on recommendations by local people, of publicly accessible sites of archaeological and historical interest. It is arranged by local authority area with districts in the present administrative county listed first, followed by those south-west London boroughs which were formerly part of Surrey (see map). National grid references are given where sites may otherwise be difficult to locate.

Up-to-date information on Surrey museums can be obtained from: *www.surreymuseums.org.uk/*

ELMBRIDGE

Museums

Brooklands Museum

Occupies 30 acres of the original 1907 motor racing circuit, featuring the steepest section of the old banked track, and the 1 in 4 test hill. Many of the original buildings, including the Malcolm Campbell sheds, have been restored. On show is a unique collection of Vickers & Hawker aircraft, including the Wellington bomber R for Robert, which was rescued from Loch Ness in 1985. Don't miss the collection of historic motorbikes and the new 'Fastest on Earth' speed record exhibition.
Facilities: *Interactive displays; audio tours; video introduction; gift shop with wheelchair access; tea rooms, toilets; special event days, Friends Group; events/lectures; library access by appointment.*
Museum open: Summer, Tuesday–Sunday 10:00–17:00;
Winter, Tuesday–Sunday, 10:00–16:00
Tel: *01932 857381*
Webpage: *www.motor-software.co.uk/brooklands/*
Address: *Brooklands Museum, Brooklands Road, Weybridge KT13 0QN*
How to get there: *Train – 15 minutes walk from Weybridge Station. Bus – 15 minutes walk from bus stop. Car parking on site with special parking for disabled visitors.*
Admission: *Adults £7, senior citizens and students £6, children £5, family £18*

Cobham Bus Museum

Where can you find the largest collection of historic London buses in the world? At this working museum — where some of the unique exhibits represent the last surviving examples of their kind. The oldest vehicle dates from 1925 and the youngest from 1973, clearly showing the remarkable advances made in just under fifty years. The museum building dates back to the Second World War, and is believed to have been the base from which Barnes Wallis developed his famous 'Bouncing Bomb'.
Facilities: *Interactive displays; gift shop with wheelchair access; special events on selected dates; toilets.*
Museum open: *Open most weekends, 10:30–17:00. Visitors should phone in advance to avoid disappointment.*
Tel: *01932 868665*
Webpage: *www.ibpt.org.uk*
Address: *Cobham Bus Museum, Redhill Road, Cobham, KT11 1EF*
How to get there: *Train – Weybridge Station.*
Admission: *Adults £3, accompanied under-16's free.*

Elmbridge Museum

A museum which caters for a wide range of age groups and interests, the exhibits range from 18th century costume to an audio-visual film about Cecil Hepworth, Walton's pioneer filmmaker. Particularly strong in social history and old photographs of the area, this museum also contains Mary Bennet's album of sketches and watercolours painted between 1816 and 1836 portraying scenes of Walton. In terms of archaeology, there is a case dedicated to Oatlands Palace, displaying a number of fine specimens from the 1968 excavations and also displays of prehistoric, Roman and Anglo-Saxon artefacts.
Facilities: *Interactive displays; gift shop; toilets; children's play area and holiday activities for children; local history research facility; photographic reproduction service.*
Museum open: *Monday, Tuesday, Wednesday and Friday 11:00–17:00, Saturday 10:00–13:00 and 14:00–17:00*
Tel: *01932 843573*
Webpage: *www.surrey-online.co.uk/elm-mus/*
Address: *Elmbridge Museum, Church Street, Weybridge, KT13 8DE*
How to get there: *Train – 15 minutes walk from Weybridge Station. Bus within 15 minutes walk. Car parking in vicinity.*
Admission: *Free*

Sites of interest

Brooklands motor track TQ 063 618

World's first purpose-built motor racing track. Site also important for early land and airspeed records. Site is now business park but some aspects of the track can be seen at and from the Museum, accessible from Brooklands Road, Weybridge.

Chatley semaphore tower

Brick-built semaphore tower, part of the Admiralty signalling system linking Portsmouth naval base with London and dating to the Napoleonic period. Accessible from car parks on Ockham Common (in Old Lane); signposted from there. Opening times available from 01483 517595.

Claremont Landscape Garden, Esher

One of the earliest surviving English landscape gardens. Opening times from National Trust (01372 469421).

Oatlands Palace site TQ 079 652
One of Henry VIII's palaces. Surviving Tudor gate in Tudor Walk, off West Palace Gardens, Weybridge.

Painshill Park, Cobham
One of the finest English 18th century landscape gardens created in 1704–86 incorporating numerous follies. Opening times available from the office (01932 864674).

St George's Hill camp TQ 085 619
Iron Age hillfort. Private (mostly), but some sections can be viewed from roads; accessible from Golf Club Road off Brooklands Road, Weybridge.

EPSOM & EWELL

Museums

Bourne Hall Museum
Great fun for children, the museum occupies the upper floor of Bourne Hall, a remarkable 1960s building concealed among rambling gardens in the heart of Ewell village. Come and find out about the Tudor palace of Nonsuch, the Epsom Derby, and the Horton cluster of mental hospitals. Life on the London fringe of Surrey in the last 200 years is illustrated by cases of old kitchenware, tools, toys and many curious items. You can study local archaeology from prehistory and the Roman period. Historic pictures and photographs illustrate days gone by.
Facilities: *Garden; gift shop with wheelchair access; toilets; children's holiday activities; evening events/lectures; town walks by arrangement; Friends Group.*
Museum open: *Monday–Saturday 9:00–17:00, Sunday 9:00–12:00*
Tel: *0208 394 1734*
Webpage: *www.epsom.townpage.co.uk/*
Address: *Bourne Hall Museum, Spring Street, Ewell KT17 1UF*
How to get there: *Train – 15 minutes walk from Ewell West Station. Bus – within 4 minutes walk. Car park at museum.*
Admission: *Free*

Sites of interest

Ewell church tower, Church Street TQ 221 627
All that remains of Ewell's 15th century church. In 1844 the old church was described as patched and maltreated. Sir George Glyn offered a plot of land nearby and £500 to build a new church on it, but the offer depended on the closure of a footpath which ran close to his rectory, now Glyn House. Visible from the street and accessible on open days.

Nonsuch Palace site TQ 227 631
Work began in 1538 on Henry VIII's hunting lodge. Building of unrivalled splendour with lavish decoration — so much so that there was 'nonsuch' like it. Heyday in Elizabeth I's reign. Following the Civil War it was given by Charles II to his mistress the Countess of Castlemaine who pulled it down in the 1680s and sold it off as building material to pay her debts. Nonsuch Park, off London Road, Ewell.

Nonsuch Palace Banqueting House TQ 224 628
Remains of Banqueting House of Henry VIII's Nonsuch Palace. Now an earthen terrace bounded by a brick wall partly of 16th century brick. Original Tudor cellars and fireplaces filled in but intact. Nonsuch Park, off London Road, Ewell.

GUILDFORD

Museums

Army Medical Services Museum
You'll be fascinated by this welcoming and highly organized museum, with its 2,500 exhibits. For example, you can follow the progression of medical treatment from 1600 to the present day. Among the more unusual exhibits are a mummified foot, Napoleon's razor and Florence Nightingale's carriage. There are working models of various exhibits to absorb young and old alike, and the museum as a whole makes a highly enjoyable visit.
Facilities: *Gift shop with wheelchair access; toilets; Historical Society.*
Museum open: *Monday–Friday 10:00–15:30, evenings and weekends by appointment*
Tel: *01252 868 612*
Webpage: *www.army.mod.uk/medical/ams_museum/*
Address: *Army Medical Services Museum, Keogh Barracks, Ash Vale, GU12 5RQ*
How to get there: *Train – 30 minutes walk from Ash Vale station. Car parking on site.*
Admission: *Free*

Ash
A new village museum is being planned for Ash. The museum will be located in Ash Cemetery Chapel.

Guildford House Gallery
This jewel of a building, dating from 1660, is one of the most important historic houses in Guildford. There are many fine features to admire, among them decorated plaster ceilings, panelled rooms and an ornately carved staircase. There are regular new exhibitions and you can see examples of fine works from the Borough's art collection, including pastel portraits by the Guildford-born artist, John Russell (1745–1806). The collections of contemporary crafts and glass are worth a visit in themselves.
Facilities: *Gift shop; refreshments; toilets; events/lectures; Friends Group.*
Museum open: *Tuesday–Saturday 10:00–16:45*
Tel: *01483 444740*

Webpage: *www.guildford.gov.uk/pages/leisure/culture/housgall/housegt.htm*
Address: *Guildford House Gallery, 155 High Street, Guildford, GU1 3AJ*
How to get there: *Train – 15 minutes walk from Guildford Station. Bus within 10 minutes walk. Car parking in vicinity.*
Admission: *Free*

Guildford Museum

What does a Roman priest's head-dress look like? You can actually see one in the Guildford Museum, home to the largest collection of archaeology and local history in Surrey. There you'll find everything from Palaeolithic hand axes to Saxon coins, to an outstanding collection of 17th century pottery and glass. There is also an enviable collection of needlework and a huge variety of historical objects and pictures covering trades and industries, social life and well-known local characters such as Lewis Carroll and Gertrude Jekyll. The Museum building is shared with Surrey Archaeological Society whose library and research facilities are open on a limited basis to the public by appointment.
Facilities: *Toilets, Young Archaeologists Club, evening lectures, Friends Group.*
Museum open: *Monday–Saturday 11:00–17:00*
Tel: *01483 444750*
Webpage: *www.guildford.gov.uk/pages/leisure/culture/housgall/housegt.htm*
Address: *Guildford Museum, Quarry Street, Guildford, GU1 3SX*
How to get there: *Train – 15 minutes walk from Guildford Station. Bus within 10 minutes walk, car parking in vicinity.*
Admission: *Free*

Queens Royal Surrey Regimental Museum

Facilities: *Wheelchair access; gift shop; research facility by appointment; tea rooms; toilets.*
Museum open: *Re-opening in 2002 after refurbishment; Tuesday–Thursday, Sunday, Bank Holidays 12:00–17:00 April–end October.*
Tel: *01483 223419*
Webpage: *www.surrey-online.co.uk/queenssurreys/*
Address: *Clandon Park, West Clandon, Guildford GU4 7RQ*
How to get there: *Car parking (including disabled) nearby.*
Admission: *Free*

Send and Ripley History Society Museum

Possibly the smallest museum in the country! A former bank building in Ripley transported to a new site beside the village hall, has been converted to house local history artefacts, photographs and local history research material.
Facilities: *Wheelchair access. Publications by the Society and others on sale. Periodic displays on specific subjects. Toilets in the village hall when open.*
Museum open: *Saturdays 10:00–12.30 (except public holidays). Third Sunday every month 10.00–12.30 to coincide with antiques fairs in the village hall.*
Tel: *01483 224876 (Chairman)*
Webpage: *Coming soon*
Address: *SRHS Museum, The Village Hall, High Street, Ripley, Woking, Surrey*
How to get there: *Train to Woking, then bus or taxi. Parking in the village hall car park.*
Admission: *Free*

Shere Museum

A small private museum in a former maltings in this picturesque village. The extensive displays include objects of daily life: tools, toys, domestic and leisure items and wartime memorabilia, mainly from Victorian times to the 1950s. Special items include the Charles Fellows collection of Magic Lanterns and a Tudor hat found locally in a secret room. There is a wealth of information for research on the locality, especially family history, including the archives of the local history society. Visitors can sit and reminisce, or browse through the albums of old pictures in a friendly and informal atmosphere. Children are particularly welcome.
Facilities: *Gift shop; wheelchair access; interactive displays; local history research facility. Guided tours of Shere village can be arranged.*
Museum open: *Easter to 30 September, open daily except Wednesday and Saturday, 13:00–17:30. Other times throughout the year by appointment.*
Tel: *01483 203245*
Address: *Shere Museum, The Malt House, Shere Lane, Shere, GU5 9HS*
How to get there: *Train – to Gomshall Station (1 mile). Bus within 2 minutes walk. Car parking in vicinity. Disabled parking on site by prior arrangement.*
Admission: *Adults 50p, children 25p*

Sites of interest

Chilworth Gunpowder Mills TQ 029 475

Remains of historic gunpowder works dating from 17th to 20th centuries. Information boards line public open trail. Access from Blacksmith Lane, Chilworth.

Cockrow Hill, BA barrows TQ 076 591 and TQ 079 591

Bronze Age round barrows north of car park on Wisley Common (south of M25).

Eashing Bridge SU 946 438

Medieval bridge across River Wey at Eashing.

Eashing burh SU 948 437

Probable site of late Saxon fortified site, one of a number of burhs intended to serve as refuges from the Vikings. Right of way from Eashing Bridge or off Eashing Lane adjacent to eastern edge of possible fort.

Farley Heath Roman temple TQ 051 449

Site of Romano-Celtic temple; line of the walls laid out; information board. On Farley Heath adjacent to Farley Heath Road, between Shamley Green and Albury.

Guildford Castle SU 997 493

Medieval castle and royal palace including Norman keep and remnants of other buildings. Castle, Grounds and Palace ruins open during hours of daylight. Keep open April–September 10:00–16:00. Display in Guildford Museum.

Guildhall, High Street, Guildford
Magnificent 16th/17th century building, usually open Tuesday and Thursday 14:00–16:00.

Guildford treadwheel crane SU 994 494
Central Guildford on riverside, near Town Bridge. 17th/18th century in date. Exterior always accessible, interior workings on Heritage Open Days only.

Guildford Park Manor moated site SU 969 493
Visible from right of way off Beechcroft Drive, Guildford.

Guildford undercroft, 72–74 High Street
Medieval undercroft, probably originally part of a 13th century shop; Guided tours May to end September Tuesday and Thursday 14:00–16:00, Saturday 12:00–16:00. Information from Guildford Museum.

Hillbury camp SU 911 468
Hillfort, probably dating to the Iron Age, on Puttenham Common.

Loseley House and Park, near Compton
Built in 1562, the house is an outstanding example of Elizabethan architecture and is surrounded by a fine garden. Access from B3000. Opening hours available on 01483 304440.

Newark Priory TQ 041 577
Ruins of medieval priory visible from Newark Lane between Ripley and Pyrford but not accessible as on private land.

St Catherine's Chapel SU 993 481
Ruins of medieval chapel, on St Catherine's Hill at Ferry Lane, Guildford; accessible by footpath along river from central Guildford.

Soldier's Ring SU 880 462
Hillfort of probable Iron Age date accessible from Botany Hill or Smugglers Way south of Runfold.

Whitmoor Common BA barrow SU 996 536
Bronze Age round barrow on Whitmoor Common east of Guildford Road (A320).

Whitmoor Common ditch and associated field boundaries SU 986 536–SU 988 533
Early bank and ditch continuing the line of track north from Salt Box Road and just west of the railway line. Possibly part of a wider field system traces of which can be seen on the Common. Accessible from car park off Salt Box Road.

MOLE VALLEY

Museums

Dorking & District Museum
The museum's two exhibition halls are devoted to the many aspects of Dorking's past including agricultural and domestic items, paintings and products of local industry from bricks to modern antibiotics developed at a nearby research site. Among Lord Ashcombe's collection of minerals and chalk fossils you will even find the 3-metre long tail bone of an iguanodon! The library contains an extensive collection of photographs, documents, books and maps of the area, which are of considerable interest to researchers of local and family history.
Facilities: *Gift shop area; wheelchair access to most areas; toilet; local history research facility.*
Museum open: *Wednesday and Thursday 14:00–17:00, Saturday 10:00–16:00*
Tel: *01306 876591 (Museum Secretary 01306 743821)*
Webpage: *web.ukonline.co.uk/members/honor.m/visitors/museums/dorking.html*
Address: *Dorking & District Museum, The Old Foundry, 62A West Street, Dorking RH4 1BS*
How to get there: *Train – 15 minutes walk from Dorking Station. Bus – within 5 minutes walk. Car parks in vicinity.*
Admission: *Small charge*

Leatherhead Museum of Local History
Timber-framed Hampton Cottage is a 17th century listed building. For those interested in local history, it offers a comprehensive collection of exhibits from Ashtead, Bookham, Fetcham and Leatherhead including maps and old photographs.
Notable displays include The Victorian Kitchen, Ashtead Roman Villa (models and finds), Leatherhead in the Second World War and products from local manufacturers including Ronson, Goblin and Ashtead Pottery. The museum is also home to the Leatherhead & District Local History Society.
Facilities: *Gift shop; Friends Group; local research facility by arrangement*
Museum open: *April to Christmas, Thursday and Friday 13:00–16:00 and Saturday 10:00–16:00*
Tel: *01372 386348*
Webpage: *www.leatherheadweb.org.uk*
Address: *Leatherhead Museum of Local History, Hampton Cottage, 64 Church Street, Leatherhead, KT22 8DP*
How to get there: *Train – 10 minutes walk from Leatherhead Station. Bus within 5 minutes walk. Car parking in vicinity.*
Admission: *Free*

Sites of interest

Anstiebury Camp TQ 153 440
Iron Age hillfort. Accessible by rights of way off Anstie Lane and Abinger Road, Coldharbour, but land is private.

Ashtead church (near), earthworks TQ 192 581
Undated earthworks, probably medieval approach to manor house. Accessible off Park Lane, Ashtead, north of parish church of St Giles.

Ashtead Common Camp TQ 176 600
A triangular multi-vallate earthwork of uncertain date. It may be a medieval stock enclosure, but could also be of Iron Age or Roman date.

Ashtead Roman villa TQ 177 601
The site lies in woodland to the west-south-west of Flag Pond. Nothing is directly visible except the outline of ditches and spoil heaps from the 1926/27 excavations.

Betchworth Castle TQ 190 500
Ruins of medieval fortified manor and 18th century house made into romantic ruin. Distant views from right of way.

Box Hill TQ 180 512 and TQ 185 513
Bronze Age round barrows near Boxhurst and near Upper Farm Bungalow, both next to Zig Zag Road on Box Hill.

Box Hill fort TQ 177 514
19th century 'mobilisation centre' or fort, part of a defensive line around London. Partly accessible as National Trust tea rooms at Box Hill.

Holmbury camp TQ 104 430
Iron Age hillfort. Accessible from car park off Radnor Road (minor road from Peaslake to Ewhurst).

Leaser's Barn (near) TQ 111 481
Bronze Age round barrow. Accessible by road north from Crossways Farm, just south of railway.

Polesden Lacey House
Originally 1630, subsequently owned by the dramatist Richard Brinsley Sheridan and demolished 1818. Replaced by a villa built by Thomas Cubitt at the beginning of his career. Now open to the public along with extensive and attractive grounds. Opening times from National Trust (01327 458203).

St Mary's Parish Church, The Ridgeway, Fetcham
Very attractive knapped flint church, dating from 11th century, with additions from the 12th–13th centuries. 12th century tower. Roman tiles above arch in nave.

Stane Street Roman road (north of Box Hill) TQ 180 540–TQ 183 546; TQ 183 546–TQ 186 551; TQ 186 551–TQ 187 554; TQ 187 554–TQ 191 560; TQ 191 560–TQ 195 568
The line of Roman road runs north from Juniper Hall and across Mickleham Downs. A section can be clearly seen to the south of Pebble Lane just to the north of the M25. Accessible as right of way on foot.

West Humble chapel TQ 160 519
Ruins of medieval chapel. Adjacent to Chapel Lane, West Humble.

REIGATE & BANSTEAD

Museums

Fire Brigades of Surrey Preservation Trust
More than fire engines! This small private museum houses photographs, costumes, and objects illustrating the work of Fire Officers.
No facilities for the disabled.
Museum open: *By appointment and on Brigade Open Days*
Tel: *01737 224067*
Webpage:
www.surreytourism.org.uk/museums/Fire_Brigades_of_Surrey_Preser/fire_brigades_of_surrey_preser.htm
Address: *Surrey Fire and Rescue Service, Croydon Road, Reigate, Surrey RH2 0EJ*
How to get there: *Train – short walk from Reigate station. Car parking available adjacent to the museum.*
Admission: *Free*

Holmesdale Natural History Club Museum
The extensive museum collections of Holmesdale Natural History Club (founded 1857) include a large collection of stuffed birds, herbarium specimens, local history and archaeological collections. The collections include material gathered by James Brewer for the first *Flora of Surrey* which was published by the Club in 1863, and some specimens collected in the 18th century.
Museum open: *By appointment, but lectures are held monthly for members and guests.*
Tel: *None*
Webpage: *www.hnhc.co.uk*
Address: *14 Croydon Road, Reigate, RH2 0PG*
How to get there: *Train – 5 minutes walk from Reigate station; 10 minutes walk from town centre. Limited car parking.*
Admission: *Free*

Reigate Priory Museum
This museum is housed in Reigate Priory, a Grade I listed building set in open parkland with its own lake. The exhibitions are changed regularly and designed to appeal to adults and children alike. The displays specialise in local and social history with the use of domestic items and costume, and they are often arranged in scene or room settings to evoke life in earlier times. On your visit don't miss the magnificent Holbein fireplace, the 17th century oak staircase and murals by Antonio Verrio.

Facilities: *Attractive parkland; occasional interactive displays; gift shop with wheelchair access; toilets; evening events/lectures; Friends Group; school loan service.*
Museum open: *Easter to end November, Wednesday and Saturday 14:00–16:30 (term time only)*
Tel: *01737 222550*
Webpage: *Coming soon*
Address: *Reigate Priory Museum, Reigate Priory, Bell Street, Reigate, RH2 7RL*
How to get there: *Train – 15 minutes walk from Reigate Station. Bus within 10 minutes walk. Car parking in vicinity; disabled parking on site.*
Admission: *Free, charge for school groups depending on activity*

Royal Earlswood Museum
This unusual museum, based in the Royal Earlswood Hospital and home for people with learning disabilities, closed in 1997. Displays illustrating asylum life can however still be seen in the Belfry Shopping Centre on car park level 1 and the Pullen collection (a display of some of the models made by the 'Idiot Genius of Earlswood Asylum') is housed over Marks and Spencer.
Facilities: *Access for the disabled is good. Car parking and lifts available at the Shopping Centre.*
Address: *Belfry Shopping Centre in the centre of Redhill.*
How to get there: *Train – a few minutes walk from station. Bus within a few minutes walk.*
Admission: *Free*

Sites of interest

Albury Farm medieval moated site TQ 293 527
In South Merstham recreation ground, Bletchingley Close off Bletchingley Road.

Banstead Heath earthworks TQ 230 552, TQ 235 553 and TQ 235 552
Possible medieval stock enclosures on Banstead Heath. Either side of B2032 between Kingswood and Walton on the Hill.

Earlswood Common, Bronze Age barrow TQ 267 487
Accessible from Pendleton Road, Reigate.

Gally Hills (Anglo-Saxon) barrows TQ 249 607 and TQ 249 608
On public open space on Banstead Downs, near and west of the A217.

Reigate Castle TQ 252 503
Site of medieval castle; earthworks survive with 18th century 'ruins'. North of Reigate High Street.

Reigate Heath Bronze Age barrows TQ 237 504
Group of several Bronze Age barrows on a ridge. Accessible from car park in Flanchford Road.

Surrey Iron Railway earthworks TQ 287 555–TQ 287 548 and TQ 287 545
Adjacent to A23 north of Merstham.

RUNNYMEDE

Museums

Chertsey Museum
A Grade II listed Regency townhouse with a charming garden. The displays include important archaeological finds from the Thames valley such as a Celtic sword, a Late Bronze Age axe and shield and a Viking sword. Also on view are rare medieval tiles from Chertsey Abbey. A fashion gallery shows selections from the outstanding Olive Matthews dress collection. A Discovery Zone enables hands-on exploration with an archaeological trench and 3D Greek pot jigsaw puzzle. Other highlights include longcase clocks, paintings, decorative art and ironwork from the local foundry. A lively exhibitions and events programme complements the permanent display.
Facilities: *Interactive displays; toilets; holiday activities for children; evening events/lectures by arrangement; Friends Group; local history research facility (Wednesday, Thursday and Saturday).*
Museum open: *Tuesday–Friday 12:30–16:30, Saturday 11:00–16:00*
Tel: *01932 565764*
Webpage: *www.chertseymuseum.org.uk*
Address: *Chertsey Museum, The Cedars, 33 Windsor Street, Chertsey KT16 8AT*
How to get there: *Train – 15 minutes walk from station. Bus – 15 minutes from Staines or Woking. Car parking in vicinity, disabled parking outside museum.*
Admission: *Free*

Egham Museum
The museum has a small archaeological collection and holds photos, documents, objects and maps relating to the history of Egham, the Hythe, Englefield Green, Virginia Water and Thorpe.
Facilities: *Interactive displays; gift shop; toilets; research facilities; guided tours by arrangement.*
Museum open: *Tuesday, Thursday and Saturday 10:00–12.30, 14:00–16:30*
Tel: *01344 843047*
Webpage: *Coming soon*
Address: *Egham Museum, c/o 35 Trotsworth Avenue, Virginia Water, GU25 4AN*
How to get there: *Train – 10 minutes walk from Egham Station. Car parking, including disabled, in the vicinity.*
Admission: *Tuesday, Thursday & Saturday, 10:00–12:30, 14:00–16.30. There is no access for wheelchair users.*

Sites of interest

Chertsey Abbey TQ 043 673–TQ 044 672
Site of medieval abbey of which only a few fragments are visible including

the former fishponds which can be seen in the recreation ground, and parts of the precinct wall along Colonel's Lane. Accessible from Colonel's Lane, Chertsey.

St Ann's Hill camp TQ 026 676
Iron Age hillfort and site of medieval chapel. In public open space accessible from St Ann's Hill Road, Chertsey.

SPELTHORNE

Museum

Spelthorne Museum

Numerous archaeological excavations have confirmed that Staines is indeed on the site of the ancient Roman town of *Pontibus*. Situated in the old fire station, the museum's collection includes antiquities from the Roman town. Children are encouraged to try on a Roman toga and to find out what a Roman soldier wore. But there are other interesting exhibits too, including a fire engine dating back to 1738 and a small exhibition relating to the Staines linoleum industry.
Facilities: *Interactive displays; gift shop with wheelchair access; evening events/lectures.*
Museum open: *Wednesday and Friday, 14:00–16:00, Saturday, 13:30–16:30*
Tel: *01784 461804*
Webpage: *www.semuseums.org.uk/spelthorne*
Address: *Spelthorne Museum, (adjacent to) The Old Town Hall, Market Square, Staines, Middx, TW18 4RH*
How to get there: *Train – 15 minutes walk from Staines Station. Bus within 5 minutes walk. Car parking in vicinity.*
Admission: *Free*

SURREY HEATH

Museums

Basingstoke Canal Centre

The Canal Centre has an Information Point which is full of maps and information to help you get out and enjoy the canal. Fishing permits and boat licences are on sale. There is a Canal History Exhibition as well as various events along the canal throughout the year. For further information contact the Canal Centre.
Facilities: *Gift shop with wheelchair access; toilets.*
Museum open: *Easter to September: Tuesday to Sunday, 10:30–17.00; October to Easter: Tuesday to Friday, 11:00–16:00.*
It is hoped to open on Sundays in October — please phone to check first.
Webpage: *www.basingstokecanal1.freeserve.co.uk/cancent.htm*
Address: *Basingstoke Canal Centre, Mychett Place Road, Mychett, GU16 6DD*
How to get there: *Train – 30 minutes walk from Ash Vale station. Car parking on site.*
Admission: *Free*

Chobham Museum

A village museum with a wealth of objects and information about Chobham and heathland life.
Facilities: *Displays; local history publications; wheelchair access; small parties of children welcomed by appointment.*
Museum open: *Wednesday 10:00–16:00, Saturday 10:00–16:00, Sunday 11:00–16:00, or by appointment.*
Tel: *01276 858612 (Curator: Mrs Gill Willis)*
Webpage: *www.chobham.org/museum/*
Address: *Benham's Corner, Bagshot Road, Chobham, Surrey, GU24 8AB*
How to get there: *Bus – 2 minutes walk from bus stop opposite Benham's Corner. Free public car parking within 200m.*
Admission: *Free*

Surrey Heath Museum

Children will love this friendly small museum, which is largely designed to be viewed from a child's eye height. The permanent display, 'The Heathland Story', illustrates the environment and development of the district including small displays on heathland crafts, local highwaymen, archaeology and Camberley's military connections. Among the intriguing exhibits are an award-winning model roundabout from 1930, and some remarkable miniature implements less than 1cm high. A temporary exhibition gallery features a varied programme of displays of local and regional interest including art, crafts and social history.
Facilities: *Gift shop with wheelchair access; toilets; holiday activities and quiz sheets for children, evening events/lectures; talks for local groups; Friends Group; local research facility; loans of copies of old photographs.*
Museum open: *Tuesday – Saturday, 11:00–17:00 or by appointment*
Tel: *01276 707284*
Webpage: *www.surreyheath.gov.uk/*
Address: *Surrey Heath Museum, Surrey Heath House, Knoll Road, Camberley GU15 3HD*
How to get there: *Train – 5 minutes walk from station. Bus – 5 minutes walk from bus stop. Car parking in vicinity; parking for disabled visitors.*
Admission: *Free*

The Royal Logistic Corps Museum

The RLC was formed in 1993 from the Royal Army Ordnance Corps, the Royal Corps of Transport, the Royal Pioneer Corps, the Army Catering Corps, and the Postal and Courier Service of the Royal Engineers. The museum covers the history of supply and transport to the Army since the 14th century, with the emphasis mostly on the period 1800–2000. The museum opened in 1995 and is now starting a period of major redevelopment.
Facilities: *Audio tours; toilets; wheelchair access.*
Museum open: *Tuesday–Friday 9:00–16:00 (all year); Saturday 10:00–15:00 (Easter–end of September). Closed Sunday and Bank Holidays.*
Tel: *01252 340871*
Webpage:
www.army.mod.uk/ceremonialandheritage/museums/details/m033logi.htm

Address: *The Royal Logistics Corps Museum, Princess Royal Barracks, Deepcut, Camberley GU16 6RW*
How to get there: *Bus – 48 bus from Woking and Brookwood stations; 48 bus from Kingsmead, Farnborough; 530 bus from Lightwater; 530 bus from Camberley station and Frimley Park Hospital.*
Admission: *Free*

Sites of interest

Albury Bottom, Bee Garden SU 974 643
Prehistoric or later earthwork enclosure on Chobham Common. Accessible from car park on Staple Hill.

Bee garden north-west of Childown Farm SU 994 638
Small, triple-banked earthwork of unknown date but most likely medieval. On Chobham Common, accessible from Gracious Pond Road.

West End Common SU 934 613
Bronze Age barrow group.

TANDRIDGE

Museum

East Surrey Museum
Whatever East Surrey may be like today, it was very different in past times. A lively programme of regularly changing exhibitions presents an overall picture of life in East Surrey and means that there is something new to see every time you visit. A large collection of prehistoric worked flints and medieval and post-medieval pottery is available for study. There are also interesting samples of the rock, sand, clay and chalk strata and a fine collection of local fossils.
Facilities: *Gift shop with access for wheelchairs; refreshments; toilets; Friends Group; local history research facility.*
Museum open: *Wednesday and Saturday 10:00–17:00, Sunday 14:00–17:00*
Tel: *01883 340275*
Webpage: *www.surreytourism.org.uk/museums/East_Surrey_Museum/east _surrey_museum.htm*
Address: *1 Stafford Road, Caterham CR3 6JG*
How to get there: *Train – 185 metres from station. Bus – nearby. Car parking in vicinity.*
Admission: *Free, but donations welcome*

Sites of interest

Covers Farm, county boundary earthwork TQ 432 536–TQ 433 532
Possible Dark Age earthwork marking the boundary between Kent and Surrey. Visible from A25.

Dry Hill camp TQ 432 417
Iron Age hillfort. On private land, but right of way along western edge.

Flower Wood, medieval moated site TQ 356 525
Crossed by right of way; adjacent to A22 Godstone by-pass north.

Godstone Green, two Bronze Age barrows TQ 348 518
In public open space north of Bletchingley Road, Godstone. One barrow was subsequently used as a windmill mound.

Henley Wood, earthworks TQ 375 585
Earthworks of medieval enclosure. On private land but crossed by right of way accessible from Ledgers Road, Chelsham.

Holt Wood, earthworks TQ 379 592
Earthworks of medieval enclosure. On private land but crossed by right of way accessible from Church Lane, Chelsham.

WAVERLEY

Museums

Charterhouse School Museum
Look no further for an impressive collection of antiquities, including ancient Greek, Corinthian, Cypriot and even Peruvian pottery and Roman glass. All of this, as well as a small Egyptian collection has been donated by old Carthusians or others connected with the school in some way. The natural history section, in another building, houses displays of birds, eggs, butterflies, moths and beetles. Geological displays, local archaeological finds and school memorabilia make up much of the rest of the collections in this listed building.
Museum open: *By appointment only (please write)*
Webpage: *www.charterhouse.org.uk/_chweb/features/museum/museum.asp*
Address: *Charterhouse School Museum, Charterhouse, Godalming GU7 2DX*
How to get there: *Train – 30 minutes walk from Farncombe or Godalming Station. Bus – 30 minutes walk from bus stop. Parking facilities on site for disabled visitors.*
Admission: *Free*

Godalming Museum
One of the most fascinating things about this museum is the building itself: timber-framed, dating from the 15th and 16th centuries, with Georgian and Victorian additions. The museum recognises the achievements of colourful local personalities such as Gertrude Jekyll, artist, gardener and craftswoman and Jack Phillips, the radio operator on the *Titanic*. Regular displays are enhanced by touch-screen computers and include geology, archaeology and local history. The museum mounts special exhibitions and events throughout the year, including the work of local artists and craft workers. Archaeological collections include finds

from Binscombe Roman villa as well as the archives of more recent local excavations.
Facilities: *Gertrude Jekyll style garden; gift shop and refreshments, wheelchair access to ground floor; holiday activities for children, evening events/lectures; Friends Group; local history research facility with Gertrude Jekyll related material, including garden plans and planting notebooks and the Percy Woods Archive for family history researchers.*
Museum open: *Summer: Tuesday–Saturday 10:00–17:00, Winter: Tuesday–Saturday 10:00–16:00 Local studies library open 13:00–16:00*
Tel: *01483 426510*
Webpage: *www.godalming-museum.org.uk*
Address: *Godalming Museum, 109A High Street, Godalming, GU7 1AQ*
How to get there: *Train – 10 minutes walk from Godalming Station. Bus stop outside museum. Car parking in vicinity.*
Admission: *Free*

Haslemere Educational Museum

Its been described as a mini British Museum – the galleries include many rare exhibits, favourites being Arthur the Bear, an Egyptian mummy intriguingly exposing its toes and the bird migration display. Archaeology, botany, zoology and traditional displays on history are major features. There is a fresh wildflower display every day in the foyer and you can observe bees actually in the hive from where the museum's own honey is collected. Activities for children range from pond dipping to woolly mammoth workshops!
Facilities: *Gardens/grounds; interactive displays; gift shop with wheelchair access; toilets; special events; holiday activities for children; evening events/lectures.*
Museum open: *Tuesday–Saturday 10:00–17:00*
Tel: *01428 642112*
Webpage: *www.haslemeremuseum.co.uk/*
Address: *Haslemere Educational Museum, High Street, Haslemere, GU27 2LA*
How to get there: *Train.–.20minutes walk from Haslemere Station. Bus within 15 minutes walk. Town centre car parking within 2 minutes walk.*
Admission: *Free (donations welcome)*

Museum of Farnham

This award-winning museum is situated in one of England's finest 18th century town houses. Innovative displays of carefully selected items from the museum's extensive collections, coupled with the use of life-size photographs, give you the extraordinary experience of 'meeting the past face-to-face'. Another recent installation is an audio tour, which guides the visitor round the exhibitions from room to room; and no visit would be complete without a tour of the delightful garden.
Facilities: *Garden; audio tour; interactive displays; gift shop, access to ground floor for visitors in wheelchairs; toilets; children's holiday activities; evening events/lectures; Friends Group; local history research facility.*
Museum open: *Tuesday–Saturday 10:00–17:00*
Tel: *01252 715094*
Webpage: *www.waverley.gov.uk/museumoffarnham*
Address: *Museum of Farnham, 38 West Street, Farnham, GU9 7DX*
How to get there: *Train – 20 minutes walk from Farnham Station. Bus within 15 minutes walk. Car parking in vicinity.*
Admission: *Free*

Rural Life Centre, Old Kiln Museum

This is a collection of implements and devices marking a century of farming and spread over 10 acres of field, woodland and barns. On show are recreations of actual workshops and emporia as they were a hundred years ago, and there is even a narrow gauge railway. As well as displays on farming through the seasons, the social history of village life and rural life in the 1930s and during World War II, there is a fascinating arboretum giving year round colour.
Facilities: *Garden; gift shop; good wheelchair access; picnic areas; café; toilets; Friends Group.*
Museum open: *April to September, Wednesday–Sunday, 11:00–18:00. October to March, Wednesdays 11:00–16:00.*
Open Bank Holidays. Railway runs on Sundays.
Tel: *01252 795571*
Webpage: *www.rural-life.org.uk*
Address: *Old Kiln Museum, Reeds Road, Tilford, Farnham, GU10 2DL*
How to get there: *Train, then bus or taxi from Farnham Station. Bus within 15 minutes walk. Car parking on site.*

Sites of interest

Caesar's Camp, Bricksbury Hill SU 835 500

Iron Age hillfort across county boundary. Accessible from Sandy Hill Road, Upper Hale, Farnham.

Elstead Bridge SU 905 438

Medieval bridge across the River Wey. On the road to Farnham.

Farnham Castle SU 837 472

Medieval castle and bishop's palace at top of Castle Street, Farnham. Keep open to the public: 1 April–30 September, 10:00–18:00 daily; 1–31 October 10:00–17:00 daily.
Guided tours to other parts of the castle — information from Museum of Farnham (01252 715094).

Frensham Common Bronze Age barrow group c SU 853 406

Four barrows on the King's Ridge east of the A287, on Frensham Common.

Hascombe Hill camp TQ 004 386

Iron Age hillfort. Accessible by right of way around the fort (which is on private land) from junction of School Road and Godalming Road, Hascombe.

Somerset Bridge SU 921 439

Medieval bridge across the River Wey on the Shackleford–Elstead road.

South Park Farm, Grayswood, moated site SU 916 355
Best-preserved medieval moated site in the county. Maintained by Surrey Archaeological Society and open to the public at all reasonable hours. Car park, explanatory notice, picnic table. Entry: free.

Tilford Bridge, north end of Green SU 871 435
Medieval bridge across the River Wey on the Tilford–Farnham road.

Tilford Bridge, east end of Green SU 873 434
Medieval bridge across the River Wey on the Tilford–Elstead road.

Waverley Abbey SU 868 452
Ruins of first Cistercian Abbey in England (founded AD1128), laid out with interpretation panels. Accessible from the Elstead–Farnham road.

Witley Common, Bronze Age barrows SU 922 402
A group of Bronze Age barrows accessible from Witley Centre or from the road crossing the west end of Witley Common towards the A3.

WOKING

Museum

Woking Galleries
Will be opening to the public in 2006 in a brand new canal-side building. It will combine Woking Borough's only museum with a community arts centre. It will include a major exhibition area taking temporary exhibits from national institutions. The interactive history displays will be designed to appeal to all ages. Initial exhibitions will include Britain's first mosque, post-war migration, and Brookwood Mental Hospital. The collection is expanding and includes finds from recent excavations at the Tudor Woking Palace site.
Facilities: *When open, facilities will include a cafe, gift shop, toilets, education and schools facilities, research facilities, garden, canal moorings and holiday activities programmes.*
Museum open: *Will be open six days per week including evening openings from 2006. Collection can be viewed by appointment now.*
Tel: *01483 725517*
Webpage: *Coming soon*
Address: *Woking Galleries, Chobham Road, Woking, GU21 1JF*
How to get there: *2 minute walk from train and bus station. On street parking outside, including disabled parking.*
Admission: *Permanent exhibitions will be free*

Sites of interest

Goldsworth or Langman's Bridge SU 987 583
Bridge over the Basingstoke Canal. Langmans Lane, off St John's Road, Woking.

Horsell Common, Bronze Age barrows TQ 014 598–TQ 016 597
Two round barrows on Horsell Common, one on each side of Monument Road, Woking.

Woking Palace TQ 029 570
Not accessible at time of publication but the site is owned by the Borough Council which is working towards public access and a display.

SOUTH-WEST LONDON BOROUGHS

CROYDON

Museums

Birley Windmill
Built in the mid-1850s, it replaced an earlier post mill destroyed by fire. It worked until 1892 when it was abandoned. Bought by Croydon Council in 1951.
Facilities: *Guided tours, disabled parking, group visits by arrangement.*
Open: *First Sunday each month 13:00–17:00, June to October.*
Tel: *020 8654 0899*
Address: *Postmill Close, Shirley, Croydon*
How to get there: *Train – East Croydon station then bus 466. Bus-route 466 passes the mill. Car parking in Coloma Convent School, opposite the mill.*
Admission: *Free (donations gratefully received)*

Croydon Airport Visitor Centre
Housed in the former control tower is an exhibition of the airport's history and a re-creation of the radio room where air traffic control was pioneered.
Facilities: *'Hands on' models for children and the opportunity for them to dress up as 1930s passengers. Restaurant. Lift to first floor.*
Centre open: First Sunday of each month 11:00–16:00.
Tel: *020 8253 1009*
Webpage: *www.croydonairport.org.uk/*
How to get there: *Train – 15 minutes walk from Waddon station. Car – free parking.*
Admission: *Free (donations gratefully received)*

Croydon Clocktower
Lifetimes: a permanent exhibition of everyday objects from Croydon's past which lead you on a path of discovery via a series of touch screen computers. The Riesco Gallery houses a collection of Chinese pottery and ceramics.
Facilities: *part of Croydon Central Library complex which includes a cinema, café, local studies section, gift shops and tourist information centre.*
Museum open: *Monday to Saturday 11:00–17:00, Sunday 12:00–17:00*
Tel: *020 8253 1009*

Webpage: *www.croydon.gov.uk/clocktower*
How to get there: *Train – East or West Croydon stations, then short walk. Tram – George Street stop. Bus – town centre bus stops close by. Car parking in town centre.*
Admission: *Free*

Croydon Natural History and Scientific Society Museum
The museum houses the archaeological, geological and local history collections of the society which was founded in 1870 as the Croydon Microscopical Club.
Museum open: *Groups by arrangement only. Contact John Greig, Hon Curator.*
Tel: *020 8669 1501*
Webpage: *www.croydononline.org/hs/cnhss/index.asp*
Address: *96A Brighton Road, South Croydon CR2 6AD*

Museum without Walls
Posters and panels fixed to selected tram stops in Croydon giving information on some of the history and archaeological finds nearby.

Sites of interest

Croham Hurst, South Croydon TQ 338 632
Bronze Age barrow.

Croydon Palace, Old Palace Road, Croydon, Surrey CR0 1AX
Former residence of the Archbishops of Canterbury. Of particular interest are the Norman undercroft, 15th century Great Hall and the Tudor Long Gallery. Now a school, but open at times during the school holidays (tel: 020 8680 0467).

Farthing Down, Coulsdon TQ 300 588
Celtic field system and Saxon burial mounds.

Whitgift Almshouses, George Street, Croydon
Open to the public on one Saturday each year. Further information from Croydon Library Heritage Service (see entry under Croydon Clocktower above).

KINGSTON UPON THAMES

Museums

Kingston Local History Room
Significant collection of archives from 1208 to the present. Also a wide range of secondary research material including local books, directories, newspapers, maps, photographs, recorded reminiscences and census returns. Also available; Kingston University Centre for Local Studies database of Victorian sources.
Facilities: *Toilets, parking, local books and postcards for sale. The facility is on the first floor, accessible by stairs. There is no lift and disabled people are asked to telephone in advance for assistance.*
Local History Room open: Monday, Thursday and Friday, 10:00–17:00. Tuesday 10:00–19:00. Closed Wednesday and weekends.
Tel: *020 8547 6738*
Webpage: *www.kingston.gov.uk/museum*
Address: *Room 46, North Kingston Centre, Richmond Road, Kingston upon Thames KT2 5PE*
How to get there: *Between Fernhill Primary School and Tiffin Girls School. Train – 15–20 minutes walk from Kingston Railway Station. Bus – 65.*
Admission: *Free*

Kingston Museum
Kingston's recently refurbished museum has two permanent galleries telling the story of Kingston: Ancient Origins and Town of Kings, which include models, reconstructions and interactive exhibits, as well as original artefacts ranging from prehistory to the 20th century. The Eadweard Muybridge gallery describes the life and work of this internationally renowned pioneer photographer. The museum also holds a fine collection of Martinware art pottery. Temporary exhibition of art, crafts, photography and local history, including national touring exhibitions, are held in the first-floor art gallery.
Facilities: *Gift shop, access and toilets for disabled people and there is a lift to the first-floor art gallery. Friends Group.*
Museum open: *Daily 10:00–17:00 except Wednesday and Sunday.*
Tel: *020 8546 5386*
Webpage: *www.kingston.gov.uk/museum*
Address: *Kingston Museum, Wheatfield Way, Kingston upon Thames KT1 2PS*
How to get there: *In between Kingston Library and the Kingfisher Leisure Centre; 5 minutes walk from Kingston Railway Station; Cattle Market Bus Station adjoins site. Car parking in the vicinity.*
Admission: *Free*

Sites of interest

All Saints' Parish Church, Market Place
Grade I listed 14th/15th century church with Victorian alterations. Seven Saxon kings are reputed to have been crowned at an earlier church on the site.

Coronation Stone, outside Guildhall, south of the Market Place
Traditionally thought to be the stone upon which seven Saxon kings were crowned.

Kingston Market House, Market Place
The former Guildhall, built in 1840. The ground floor is open to the public during Tourist Office opening hours.

Lovekyn Chantry Chapel, London Road
Oldest free-standing chantry chapel in the UK. Built in 1309 by Edward Lovekyn and dedicated to St Mary Magdelene. Owned by Kingston

Grammer School since 1561. Access by appointment only during term time (020 8546 5875).

LAMBETH

Museum

Museum of Garden History

Replica 17th century garden. Exhibits on all aspects of gardening history.
Address: *Lambeth Palace Road, Lambeth, London SE1 7LB*
How to get there: *Located next to Lambeth Palace.*
Museum open: *Monday–Friday 10:30–16:00, Saturday closed, Sunday 10:30–17:30*
Admission: *Free*

Site of interest

Lambeth Palace, corner of Lambeth Road and Lambeth Palace Road

Town house of the Archbishop of Canterbury and the only medieval town house in London still used for its original purpose. The manor of Lambeth was acquired from Rochester Cathedral in 1197 and a house was probably built here immediately afterwards. Earliest extant part is early 13th century crypt of the chapel. Visits by prior arrangement only but Morton's Gatehouse of brick (c1490) and west sides of some other buildings can be seen from the road.
Tel: *020 7898 1200*

MERTON

Museums

Wandle Industrial Museum

The exhibition concentrates on the Wandle's snuff, tobacco and textile industries. The area is of unique importance with the world's first public railway, and the centre of the Arts and Crafts movement with Liberty's and William Morris.
Museum open: *every Wednesday 13:00–16:00. First Sunday of each month 14:00–17:00*
Tel: *020 8648 0127*
Webpage: *www.wandle.org*
Address: *The Vestry Hall Annexe, London Road, Mitcham, Surrey CR4 3UD*
Admission: *Small charge*

Wimbledon Society Museum of Local History

This award-winning museum shows local history in Wimbledon from the Stone Age to the present day, in words, pictures and objects. Established in 1916, the museum contains an archive of over 2,500 photographs, maps, manuscripts, ephemera, press cuttings and artefacts.
Facilities: *Books, maps and information leaflets about local history are on sale at the museum shop. Wheelchair access is not possible.*
Museum open: *Saturday and Sunday 14:30–17:00. Open by appointment at other times.*
Tel: *0210 8296 9914*
Address: *22 Ridgway, Wimbledon, London SW19 4QN*
How to get there: *Bus 93 and 200 stop close by. Limited car parking in nearby side streets.*
Admission: *Free*

Wimbledon Windmill Museum

The story of windmills and windmilling told in pictures, models and the machinery and tools of the trade. The museum is housed in a grade II* listed windmill built in 1817.
Facilities: *Café adjoining the windmill and free car parking. Teachers' notes on history, science and technology available. Wheelchair access is limited.*
Museum open: *Weekends 14:00–17:00 and Bank Holidays 11:00–17:00 April–October.*
Tel: *020 8947 2825*
Webpage: *www.wimbledonwindmillmuseum.org.uk*
Address: *Windmill Road, Wimbledon Common*
How to get there: *Windmill Road is off Parkside (A219). The 93 bus route runs along Parkside linking Wimbledon and Putney Stations. On-site parking for 300 cars.*
Admission: *Charge*

Sites of interest

Merton Abbey Mills, Watermill Way, London SW19 2RD

The Wheelhouse was a part of the 18th century fabric printing mill on this site; the working undershot water wheel was installed during the 19th century to drive the fabric rinsing spools used during the finishing of the printing process. Today craftsmen and women demonstrate their skills during opening hours.
Open: *Saturday, Sunday and Bank Holidays 10:00–17:00*
Admission: *Free*

Morden Hall Park, Morden Hall Road, Morden, Surrey SM4 5JD

Now a National Trust property, this former deer park has an extensive network of waterways, ancient hay meadows, an impressive avenue of trees and an interesting collection of old estate buildings. The workshops now house local craft workers, whose work is on show.
Open: *All year during daylight hours. Car park by the cafe/shop and garden centre closes at 18:00.*
Webpage: *www.nationaltrust.org.uk/main/placestovisit/index.html*
How to get there: *Underground – Morden. Tramlink – Morden Road. Bus – frequent from surrounding areas. Off A24, and A297 S of Wimbledon, N of Sutton.*
Admission: *Free*

Southside House, 3–4 Woodhayes Road, Wimbledon, London SW19 4RJ
Pennington family home of William and Mary's time. Still lived in and little changed by the descendants through the years. On display are paintings and memorabilia of the Royal Court and artistic, political and social circles.
Open: *For guided hourly tours: Tuesday, Thursday, Saturday and Bank Holidays at 14:00, 15:00 and 16:00 from 1 January to 21 June. Tours last approximately 1 hour 30 mins. Group visits by arrangement with the Administrator, any day except Sunday.*
Tel: *020 8946 7643*
Admission: *£5 (£3 under 21 concessions)*

The River Wandle
Runs through the Borough. Buy the Map and Illustrated Guide to follow the signposted Wandle Trail and discover the site of Merton Priory (conducted visits to the Chapter House by prior arrangement, telephone 020 8543 6656); Merton Abbey Mills, a craft market and visitor centre, with theatre, shops, restaurant, café and riverside pub; Morden Hall Park, a National Trust property with shop, tea room, restaurant, garden centre, craft workshops, city farm and the snuff mill environmental centre; as well as other mill sites and former country estates along the banks of the river.

RICHMOND-UPON-THAMES

Museum

Museum of Richmond
Old Town Hall, Whittaker Avenue, Richmond TW9 1TP
Facilities: *Wheelchair access.*
Museum open: *Closed Monday (excluding Bank Holidays).*
Tel: *020 8332 1141*
How to get there: *Bus nearby. Train – 10 minutes walk.*
Admission: *Charge*

Sites of interest

Ham House, Ham Street, Richmond, TW10 7RS (National Trust)
Built in the 1670s, the house has survived virtually unchanged and retains furnishings from the period.
Open: *Easter–October. Garden open all year. Closed Thursday/Friday.*
Tel: *020 8940 1950*

Hampton Court Palace, Hampton Court, KT8 9AU
Henry VIII's magnificent palace beside the Thames. Open all year.

Marble Hill House, Richmond Road, Twickenham TW1 2NL
Elegant villa beside the Thames built in 1724–29 for Henrietta Howard, mistress of George II. Today houses an important collection of paintings and furniture. English Heritage.

SOUTHWARK

Museums

Cuming Museum
Listed by the *Independent on Sunday* as one of the fifty best museums, it is home to the rich and unusual Cuming collection and the museum of Southwark's history. Includes finds from excavations of Roman, medieval and post-medieval sites in the Southwark area including the Guy's House Roman boat, Kennington Palace, St Mary Overie's Priory and delftware kilns; also objects relating to Shakespeare's and Dickens' Southwark.
Facilities: *Education programme delivering both science and history sessions; changing exhibition programme; hands-on exhibits; holiday activities; gift shop. No wheelchair access and no public toilets.*
Museum open: *Tuesday–Saturday 10:00–17:00*
Tel: *020 7701 1342*
Webpage: *www.southwark.gov.uk*
Address: *155-157 Walworth Road, London SE17 1RS*
How to get there: *Train – 5 minute walk from Elephant & Castle rail and tube stations. Buses – 12, 35, 40, 68, 171, P5, 343, 468. No car parking in vicinity.*
Admission: *Free*

The Rose
A light and sound presentation on this major archaeological site which uses a combination of old and new technologies to bring the story of The Rose theatre to life.
Museum open: *10:00–17:00 (11:00–18:00 in summer) every day except Christmas Day and Boxing Day.*
Tel: *020 7593 0026*
Address: *56 Park Street, London S1 9AR*
How to get there*: Train – 10 minute walk from Mansion House and Cannon Street tube and London Bridge rail and tube stations. Buses – 149, 34 and P11.*
Admission: *£4, senior citizens and students £3, children £2, family £10*

Sites of interest

Old operating theatre and herb garret, 9a St Thomas Street, SE1 9RY
Built for St Thomas' Hospital in the roof space of its chapel in 1821.
Open*: Every day 10:30–16:45 (closed 15 December to 5 January).*
Admission: *£3.25, senior citizens and students £2.25, children £1.60*

Southwark Cathedral, London Bridge, SE1 9DA
Church of the priory of St Mary of Southwark later known as St Mary

Overy. 13th century east end and transepts with fragments of a 12th century eastern chapel on the north transept. From corridor along the north side fragments of the late 12th century chapter house and late 17th/early 18th century delftware kiln can be seen.
Open: *10:00–18:00 (11:00–17:00 Sunday)*

Winchester Palace
Site of town house of Bishop of Winchester. The bishopric first acquired the site in the 1140s and parts of the Great Hall built c1220 are visible with early 14th century inserted service doors and rose window in the west wall; viewable from Clink Street (near west end of Southwark Cathedral) at any time.

SUTTON

Museums

Carshalton Water Tower
Early 18th century water tower with unique delft-tiled bathroom.
Facilities: Gift shop; toilets; special events; Friends Group. The Hermitage, an18th century garden feature, is also occasionally open.
Museum open: *Sunday and Bank Holiday Mondays 14:30–17:00, Easter to the end of September*
Tel: *020 8647 0984 (Friends' Secretary)*
Address: *Carshalton Water Tower, West Street, Carshalton SM5 1NR*
How to get there: *Train – 5 minutes walk from Carshalton station. Bus – stops nearby in Pound Street. No car parking in immediate vicinity, nearest is in Honeywood Walk.*
Admission: *Adults 75p, children 25p*

Honeywood Heritage Centre
The history of the Borough throughout the centuries, including Tudor, Victorian and Edwardian life in the area.
Facilities: *Displays, temporary exhibitions; slide show in the restored billiard room; gift shop; tea room; toilets; special events days; Friends Group.*
Museum open: *Wednesday–Friday 11:00–17:00, Saturday and Sunday 10:00–17:00, Bank Holiday Mondays 11:00–17:00*
Tel: *020 8770 4297*
Address: *Honeywood Heritage Centre, Honeywood Walk, Carshalton SM5 3NX*
How to get there: *Train – 5 minutes walk from Carshalton station. Bus – stops nearby in Pound Street and High Street. Car parking in Honeywood Walk or High Street car park.*
Admission: *Adults £1.20, children 60p*

Little Holland House
The former home of artist, designer, and craftsman Frank Dickinson (1887–1961). The house was designed, built and entirely furnished by Dickinson, inspired by the ideals of John Ruskin and William Morris. The Grade II* interior contains Dickinson's paintings, hand-made furniture, furnishings, metalwork and interior decoration, in an eclectic mix of Arts and Crafts and Art Nouveau style.
Museum open: *Occasional Sunday and Bank Holiday Mondays 13:30–17:30*
Tel: *020 8770 4781*
Address: *Little Holland House, 40 Beeches Avenue, Carshalton SM5 3LW*
How to get there: *Train – 3 minutes walk from Carshalton Beeches station. Bus – stops nearby in Beeches Avenue. No car parking in immediate vicinity.*
Admission: *Free*

Whitehall
Outstanding timber-framed Tudor house with later additions set in beautiful gardens. There is a case dedicated to finds from the Nonsuch Palace excavations.
Facilities: *Displays; temporary exhibitions, gift shop, tea room; toilets; special events days; children's summer workshops; Friends Group.*
Museum open: *Wednesday to Sunday and Bank Holiday Mondays 14:00–17:00, Saturday, 10:00–17:00*
Tel: *020 8643 1236*
Address: *1 Malden Road, Cheam Village, SM3 8QD*
How to get there: *Train – 10 minutes walk from Cheam station. Bus – stops nearby in Broadway and Malden Road. Car parking behind Cheam Library opposite.*
Admission: *Adults £1.20, children 60p*

Sites of interest

Carew Manor, Church Road, Beddington
Sutton's only Grade I listed building, with late medieval hammer-beamed hall roof and cellars which have medieval, Tudor and 18th century features. Also 18th century brick dovecote nearby.
Occasional guided tours (tel: 020 8770 4781 for details).

Carshalton House (St Philomena's School), Pound Street, Carshalton
Early 18th century house with 19th century and later additions.
Occasional open days and guided tours (tel: 020 8770 4781 for details).

The Grotto, Carshalton Park TQ 284 641 and The Orangery, The Square, Carshalton
Two 18th century garden features related to the now demolished Carshalton Park House.

WANDSWORTH

Museum

Wandsworth Museum
Exciting interactive displays tell the story of Wandsworth from prehistoric times to the present day. Discover how Battersea, Balham,

Putney, Roehampton, Tooting, Earlsfield, Wandsworth and Southfields grew from a scatter of rural and riverside villages into a bustling London suburb. Items on display include a fossil skull of a woolly rhinoceros and a fossil tooth of a woolly mammoth, both dating to c20,000 BC. Also on show are artefacts from the collection of the Wandsworth Historical Society, dating from prehistoric to Tudor times, found locally during archaeological excavations.
There is a programme of temporary exhibitions, evening lectures, holiday activities and other events.
Facilities: *The Museum is fully accessible with a lift to all floors, disabled toilet and hearing loop; gift shop selling local publications, maps, cards and souvenirs; photographic reproduction service.*
Museum open: *Tuesday to Saturday 10:00–17:00; Sunday 14:00–17:00; closed Monday and Bank Holidays.*
Tel: *020 8871 7074*
Webpage: *www.wandsworth.gov.uk/museum*
Address: *The Courthouse, 11 Garratt Lane, London SW18 4AQ*
How to get there: *Train (BR) Wandsworth Town – 10 minutes. Underground East Putney – 15/20 minutes. Bus: 28, 37, 39, 44, 77A, 156, 170, 220, 337. Car – shoppers' car parks nearby.*
Admission: *Free*

Youngs Brewery Museum and Visitor Centre
Museum open: *By appointment*
Tel: *020 8875 7100*
Address: *The Ram Brewery, Wandsworth High Street, London SW18 4JD*

Sites of interest

All Saints' Church, High Street, Wandsworth
The present tower was erected in 1630. The church was largely rebuilt in 1779 but still retains the three galleries added between 1597 and 1647. John Griffiths, vicar of Wandsworth, was hung, drawn and quartered on 8 July 1539 for denying the supremacy of Henry VIII over the Church in England. The church contains many fine monuments.

Fireproof House memorial, Putney Heath
Built by David Hartley in the 1770s and incorporating his invention of sandwiching thin sheets of iron or copper between double walls and floors. To prove its effectiveness a fire was lit in a ground floor room in front of an audience which included King George III and Queen Charlotte; spectators stood in the room above in perfect safety. It was demolished in 1934 but is commemorated by an obelisk near Tibbets Corner.

Quaker Meeting House, High Street, Wandsworth
The first Meeting House was built on this site in 1673. The land was passed to Quakers as a gift by Joan Stringer who is commemorated by a plaque in the burial ground behind the building. The present building dates from 1778 and contains original panelling and stone flags.

St Mary's Church, Battersea
The present church was completed in November 1777 and was built on the site of a Saxon church that originally stood on an island of hard gravel surrounded by reedy marshland, close to one of the most important Thames crossings. The white marble font and the frame of the East window, together with its painted glass and tracery of 1631 survive from the old church.

Surrey Iron Railway
Sleepers from the original railway can be seen, set into the wall of the Ram Brewery, Ram Street, Wandsworth (see Youngs Brewery Museum above).

Windmill, Windmill Road, Wandsworth Common
The remains of a small windpump, erected in the 1830s to pump water back from the newly-built railway cutting to a nearby pond known as the Black Sea, in order to prevent flooding of the railway line. In use until 1870 when the pond was filled in. The windpump remains but its sails no longer exist.

All information contained within the gazetteer correct at time of going to press.

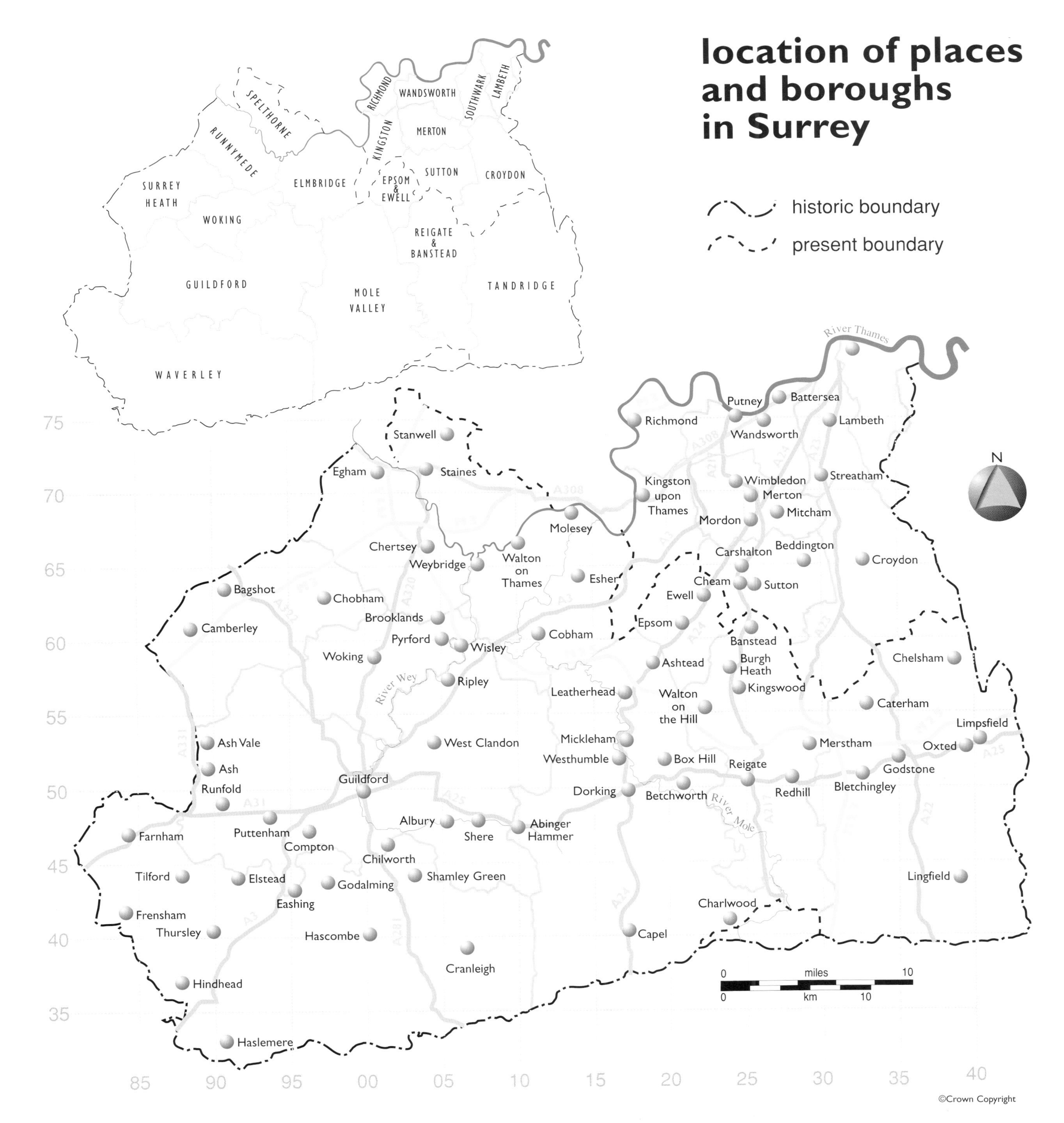
location of places and boroughs in Surrey
historic boundary
present boundary
SPELTHORNE
RUNNYMEDE
SURREY HEATH
WOKING
ELMBRIDGE
RICHMOND
WANDSWORTH
SOUTHWARK
LAMBETH
KINGSTON
MERTON
EPSOM & EWELL
SUTTON
CROYDON
REIGATE & BANSTEAD
GUILDFORD
MOLE VALLEY
TANDRIDGE
WAVERLEY
River Thames
Stanwell
Staines
Egham
Richmond
Putney
Battersea
Wandsworth
Lambeth
Kingston upon Thames
Wimbledon
Merton
Streatham
Mordon
Mitcham
Molesey
Chertsey
Weybridge
Walton on Thames
Esher
Carshalton
Beddington
Croydon
Cheam
Sutton
Ewell
Bagshot
Chobham
Brooklands
Epsom
Banstead
Camberley
Pyrford
Wisley
Cobham
Woking
Ashtead
Burgh Heath
Chelsham
Ripley
River Wey
Leatherhead
Kingswood
Walton on the Hill
Caterham
Limpsfield
Ash Vale
West Clandon
Mickleham
Merstham
Oxted
Westhumble
Box Hill
Reigate
Ash
Godstone
Runfold
Guildford
Dorking
Betchworth
Redhill
Bletchingley
River Mole
Albury
Shere
Abinger Hammer
Farnham
Puttenham
Compton
Chilworth
Tilford
Elstead
Godalming
Shamley Green
Eashing
Lingfield
Charlwood
Frensham
Thursley
Hascombe
Capel
Cranleigh
Hindhead
Haslemere
N
miles
km
0
10
©Crown Copyright

getting involved

If you would like to take your interest further you might consider joining one of the many local archaeological and/or historical societies in the county, but in particular you should join the **Surrey Archaeological Society**, one of the oldest county societies in the country.

It was established in 1854 'for the investigation of subjects connected with the history and antiquities of the County of Surrey'. Despite subsequent changes in administrative boundaries, the Society's objectives remain substantially the same, and the present area of interest includes the historic county up to the Thames.

The headquarters are at Castle Arch, Guildford, where the Society's Library, which includes a large and diverse collection of research material, is also housed. Excavations and fieldwork are organised by the Society, the most recent major excavation being that of the Romano-British temple at Wanborough, near Guildford. The Society, through its various representatives around the county, is constantly vigilant on behalf of the conservation of old buildings and archaeological sites of known importance. There is a large and enthusiastic Surrey Industrial History Group and other active local and specialist groups of the Society.

Publication is an essential part of archaeological and local history investigations, and the Society publishes regularly and distributes free to members the *Surrey Archaeological Collections*, a journal of reports, articles and notes on a wide range of subjects. In addition, special volumes and research reports are published from time to time. A list of Society publications can be obtained from the address below or from the web site.

Symposia, lecture courses and visits are organised and well-supported and the Society in a joint venture with Guildford Museum has set up a Young Archaeologists' Club for children from 8–16 years old. Society members keep in touch through the regular publication (nine issues a year) of the *Bulletin*.

Membership is open to individuals or groups interested in the work of the Society.

Surrey Archaeological Society
Castle Arch
Guildford
Surrey GU1 3SX
Tel/Fax: 01483 532454
e-mail: surreyarch@compuserve.com
Webpage: www.surreyarchaeology.org.uk

If you are interested in your family's history or that of your area you might consider visiting the **Surrey History Centre** at Woking. The Surrey History Service collects and preserves archives and printed material relating to all aspects of the history of Surrey, and makes them available for reference.

You can discover your family history, trace the history of your house, street or town, learn about famous Surrey people and landmarks, or research a school or university project. You can deposit or donate archive material for safekeeping. You can also contact the Service for advice on caring for your own records.

The archive collections date from the 12th century to the present day and the local studies collections cover all aspects of the history, geography and life of Surrey.

There are also copies of: census returns for Surrey, 1841–1891; microfilm copies of Surrey wills; International Genealogical Index for the British Isles; National Probate Calendars, 1858–1943.

Surrey History Centre
130 Goldsworth Road
Woking
Surrey GU21 6ND
Tel: 01483 594594
Fax: 01483 594595
e-mail: shs@surreycc.gov.uk
Webpage: shs.surreycc.gov.uk

Opening hours:

Monday	Closed	Thursday	9:30 – 19.30
Tuesday	9:30 – 17:00	Friday	9:30 – 17.00
Wednesday	9:30 – 17:00	Saturday	9:30 – 16:00

The centre is closed on Sundays and Bank Holiday weekends (including Saturdays).

How to get there:
By train and bus — 15 minutes' walk from Woking's railway and bus stations. Local bus services 24, 34, 38, 44 and 48 pass the Surrey History Centre. Car parking at the History Centre (access from Kingsway). There is reserved parking for visitors with disabilities at the centre but spaces should be booked in advance.

Surrey History Service is provided by Surrey County Council.

There are a number of museums listed in the Gazetteer that also offer research facilities and advice on local studies. Surrey County Council also maintains a list of archaeological sites in Surrey, known as the Sites & Monuments Record (SMR). This can be consulted by prior appointment (020 8541 9083).

acknowledgements

Hidden Depths is the result of a co-operative effort between Surrey Archaeological Society and Surrey County Council and is based on an original idea by David Graham, with the thematic approach being suggested by David Bird. It could not have been produced without the help of a number of people, but especially: David Bird, Jon Cotton, Glenys Crocker, Mike Dawson, Audrey Graham, David Graham, Audrey Monk, Gerry Moss and Pat Reynolds. Giles Pattison was responsible for the design and layout and Rob Poulton for much of the professional input into the project. The gazetteer was compiled by David and Audrey Graham with the assistance of the Society's local representatives and with additional information supplied by staff of the individual museums. The Society and County Council are grateful to all those whose hard work made the book possible.

picture acknowledgements

Illustrations are identified in the list below by page number and ordered in sequence from left to right across the page, regardless of vertical order, except where the upper of two in the same horizontal position is given first. We are very grateful to the organisations and people responsible for providing illustrations, and granting permission for reproduction. Illustrations included in the list below as SCAU are the copyright of the Surrey County Archaeological Unit (all artwork by Giles Pattison, photographs by various staff members), which is part of Surrey County Council. Modern map bases and outlines are all reproduced from Ordnance Survey mapping on behalf of The Controller of Her Majesty's Stationery Office © Crown Copyright. Licence Number MC 100014198, but the additional artwork is the copyright of SCAU: these maps are omitted from the list below. GM stands for Guildford Museum, MOLAS for Museum of London Archaeology Service, and SAS for Surrey Archaeological Society.

1 SCAU. **2** Stuart Needham. **4-7** SCAU. **5** Museum of London. **9** J Butler & A Male in *How Do We Know Dinosaurs Existed*, by permission of Hodder & Stoughton Ltd. **10** B Franczak in *Dinosaur* by permission of Pan Macmillan. **11** Roger Hunt. **12** Bourne Hall Museum. **13** SCAU. **15** SCAU. **16** SCAU. **17** SCAU. **18** Both SCAU. **19** © Copyright The British Museum. **21** Both Butser Ancient Farm. **22** SCAU. **23** SCAU. **24** SCAU. **25** Both SCAU. **26** SCAU. **27** All SAS. **28** SCAU. **29** SCAU. **30** Simon James & The Royal Archaeological Institute. **31** SCAU. **32** Richard Warmington. **33** Richard Harris/Weald & Downland Open Air Museum. **34** SCAU. **35** SCAU; John Russell. **36** Surrey County Council. **37** Harley 3749 f15v by permission of The British Library; © Copyright The British Museum. **39** SCAU; Roger Hunt. **40** Guildford Borough Council; Reproduced courtesy of Haslemere Museum. **41** Chris Shepheard; Brenda Lewis. **43** GM. **44** GM. **45** SCAU; MOLAS. **46** Both SCAU. **47** Both SCAU. **48** SCAU/Surrey County Council; SCAU. **49** SCAU; David Graham. **50** SCAU, after D Williams, after J Barrett & R Bradley; SCAU. **51** Museum of London; © Copyright The British Museum. **54** David Williams. **55** SCAU. **56** SCAU. **57** David Bird; Add Mss 42130 f181 by permission of The British Library. **58** SCAU. **59** Harley 3749 4v-4* by permission of The British Library; Public Records Office. **60** SCAU, after J Blair; Chris Shepheard. **61** Chris Shepheard. **62** Add Mss 42130 f170 by permission of The British Library. **63** SCAU; Faunal Remains Unit, Southampton University. **64** Crown Copyright. Historic Royal Palaces. Reproduced by permission of Historic Royal Palaces under licence from the Controller of Her Majesty's Stationery Office. **66** Chris Shepheard. **67** A fete at Bermondsey, c1570 by Joris Hoefnagel (1541 - 1600) Hatfield House, Hertfordshire, UK/Bridgeman Art Library. **68** Both SCAU. **69** SCAU. **70** English Heritage Photographic Library. **71** SCAU; English Heritage Photographic Library. **72** English Heritage Photographic Library; SCAU. **73** SCAU. **74** All SCAU. **75** © Copyright The British Museum; SCAU; SCAU; © Copyright The British Museum; The Museum of London. **76** The Museum of London/ Alan Sorrell. **77** Both SCAU. **78** Ashmolean Museum, Oxford. **79** SCAU, after D Williams; David Williams.; GM. **80** SCAU; MOLAS; SCAU. **81** Bryan Harmer; Bryan Harmer; Surrey Heath Archaeological and Heritage Trust. **82** SAS; GM. **83** Michaela Stewart; SCAU; SCAU. **84** Chertsey Museum, Runnymede Borough Council; SAS. **85** Roger Hunt; Nigel Barker. **86** © Copyright The British Museum; SAS; SAS. **87** © Crown Copyright. NMR; SCAU; SCAU. **88** SAS. **89** Roger Hunt. **90** Roger Hunt. **91** Museum of London. **92** Museum of London. **93** Museum of London. **94** Surrey County Council; Museum of London. **95** Museum of London; Oliver Trust. **96** David and Denise Longley. **97** SCAU; SCAU; GM. **98** © Copyright The British Museum. **99** Tim Strickland; MOLAS. **100** P Jones. **102** Bryan Harmer; SCAU, after D Williams, after J Barfoot & D Price-Williams. **103** GM. **104** SCAU; Michaela Stewart; SCAU, after A Lowther. **106** David Williams. **107** SCAU. **108** SAS. **109** SCAU. **110** Both reproduced by permission of Surrey History Service. **111** SCAU. **112** Roger Gill. **113** SCAU. **114** Brooklands Museum. **115** Chris Shepheard. **116** Museum of London; SAS. **117** Chris Shepheard; GM. **118** SAS; David Williams; GM. **119** Museum of London; Phil Dean/Stuart Needham; © Copyright The British Museum. **120** SCAU; Stuart Needham; Stuart Needham. **121** SCAU. **122** SCAU; David Bird. **123** Museum of London. **124** SAS/ SCAU. **125** Malcolm Lyne; Museum of London. **126** SCAU; MOLAS; MOLAS. **127** SCAU; SCAU, after D Williams; SCAU. **128** Michaela Stewart; SCAU; SCAU. **129** David Bird; SCAU; SCAU. **130** Chris Shepheard. **131** Kingston Museum & Heritage Service; MOLAS. **132** Both MOLAS. **133** GM. **134** SCAU. **135** Glenys Crocker. **136** Roger Hunt. **137** SCAU; Reproduced courtesy of Haslemere Museum; Reproduced courtesy of Haslemere Museum. **138** SCAU; Reproduced by permission of Surrey History Service. **139** SCAU; SCAU; Chris Shepheard. **140** Chris Shepheard. **141** Philip Harris; Philip Harris; David Graham. **142** Reproduced by kind permission of Croydon Museum & Heritage Service. **143** Both SCAU. **145** SAS. **146** SCAU. **147** E M Davies/C Hasler. **148** SCAU. **149** Both SCAU. **150** Surrey Advertiser; SAS. **151** David Williams. **152** Both SCAU. **Back cover** Christine Carrelo (author's portrait).

places

A

B

C

D

E

F

G

H

K

L

M

N

O

P

index

A

B

C

D

E

F

G

H

I

J

K

L

M

N